Villon and Other Plays

Villon and Other Plays

Murray Mednick

PADUA
PLAYWRIGHTS
PRODUCTION

Padua Playwrights Press, Los Angeles

Produced by Sideshow Media LLC, New York, NY

Editorial director: Dan Tucker
Cover design: Brian McWilliams
Interior template: CoDe. New York Inc., Jenny 8 del Corte Hirschfeld and Mischa
Leiner
Supervising Padua editor: Guy Zimmerman

Guy Zimmerman
Padua Playwrights Productions
840 Micheltorena Street
Los Angeles CA 90026

Printed in the United States of America

Distributed in the United States and Canada by Theatre Communications Group,
520 Eighth Avenue, 24th Floor, New York, NY 10018-4156
ISBN: 978-0-9907256-0-2

Contents

Advice on Reading Murray Mednick's Plays

by Anthony Byrnes

I want to tell you—don't worry, the actors will take care of you. (But there won't be actors).

I want to tell you to let the words wash over you (but you have to read them).

I want to reference Los Angeles theater and tell you how unique Murray Mednick is as a poet and playwright in Los Angeles (but you probably aren't from Los Angeles).

I want to tell you to read all four plays at once and listen to their themes and poetry resonate (but that's impossible).

I want to tell you it's all about repetition, accumulation (but you can only appreciate repetition, like youth, after you've experienced it).

I want to tell you not to worry about the plot. It's about the words, the rhythms (there, I can offer that. . .).

I want to tell you these are plays of contemplation.

*

Sitting down to read a play is always a strange experience. On the one hand, there's a freedom, an intimacy. Freedom to imagine the world of the play, to cast it in your imagination, design it as the scenes unfold, direct it as your mind sees fit. Intimacy because it's just you and the playwright's words. It's direct, personal. A communion between your imagination and the playwright's.

But I've always found it a bit lonely, foreign. These are, after all, plays: meant to be heard, meant to be played. They are blueprints for the actors to realize, suggestions of rich, densely layered worlds that have yet to be lived in. For me, there's always something missing, an untapped potential energy.

Actors.

As I sat down to devour the four plays in this collection, I was shocked to discover that the actors were there with me—imaginatively, at least. And not just any actors, Murray Mednick's actors. You see, Murray's plays attract strangely talented actors. In Los Angeles, where I've had the pleasure of seeing his plays for nearly two decades (and where they've been produced for more than three), there is no lack of talent, but Murray's plays call forth a different breed. They're more complicated, quirkier, darker than what comes to mind when you think "L.A. actor." They are people who have lived, people with needs, people with scars. Like Murray's characters, they have stories to tell because they're still working it all out, trying to make sense of it all, struggling to balance different systems of belief. As his title character in *Adele,* an actress herself, says "The play takes care of you, if you're prepared, if the language is good, if you obey the rules."

I was relieved to have these imagined but familiar actors with me as I tried to bring these plays to life in my mind. They served, as they do in production, to ground the world, to bring an honest intensity to Murray's questions, to fill the silences that are as crucial to his poetry as the words.

Even if this is your first experience with Murray's words, it's easy to see what brings actors back production after production. It's the rhythms, the wonderfully tortured characters, the dialogue that begs an actor to tease out the nuance in the lyrical poetry. When you go to see a Murray Mednick play in Los Angeles, there's a sense that you are entering back into the next chapter of a decades long process. There's something familiar to not only the faces but to the rhythms and the themes—creating, for the faithful audience member, a shorthand that helps you return to these worlds you've never visited. It's the magic of ritual—repetition.

It's not that you know what to expect from a Murray Mednick play. That's always a surprise. The four plays in this collection hint at the breadth of the creative exploration at work—ranging from the "historical play"—*Villon*—to the contemporary, minimalist worlds of *Borderline*, *Destruction of the Fourth World* and *Adele*; from the formal experimentation and meta-theatrical antics of *Villon* to the dark quotidian realism of *Borderline*. At times these theatrical worlds are so disparate, stylistically and thematically, that they seem to defy a single collection or even a single playwright.

As you read more closely there are details that keep popping up. Suddenly, the plays begin to speak to one another. You begin creating a web of connections and parallels. In *Borderline*, there's the insult that Spotzie, the erstwhile Rabbi who lives in his car, is haunted by: "'You're one of those little Jews,' my second wife—a Gentile by the way—said, 'who got on the trains.'" Adele is haunted by the question of whether she would have resisted. And as if to answer them both, David, the older brother in *Destruction of the Fourth World*, owns Spotzie's insult and Adele's fear, "We lost already. We lost forever. We got on the trains." You recognize a playwright who's grappling with a rich Jewish heritage but in unpredictable and exciting ways. At one moment he's trying to recover the lost Jewish treasure of his youthful memories, in another Coyote, the mystical Lakota, confronts the audience with, "What does this have to do with the fate of the Jews, they wonder. The Jews are us, says I, Coyote, calmly, in Lakota—we are all Arabs. Well, it's all right if you don't think so. Me and my Hopi friends are not Arabs and you are all shit and not too bright. How's that? No, insults don't seem to work well, either."

The contemporary American theater is rife with "issue plays"—playwrights tackling an idea with an allegorical bent. "Here's a problem and here's my thinking about it. Period."—you can almost hear the playwright's process. While these plays have a nifty compressed structure and clear message, they tend to be unsatisfying and rarely stand up to repeated reading (much less viewing). The world of Murray Mednick isn't nearly that ordered, nearly that compact. Instead of packaged ideas, Murray wrestles with ideas, tosses them around, contemplates them.

It's easy to imagine another playwright's take on the reclusive, troubled teenager, Bernie, in *Destruction of the Fourth World*. We would get a simpler answer to his father Caleb's worry, "What if he comes out of there with a gun or a knife?" He likely would. . . and there would be a tragic, implied Columbine or Sandy Hook ending. If tidy endings are your thing, you are going to bristle at Murray's endings. That kind of hollow, if structurally taut, conclusion isn't part of Murray's world. Why Bernie stays in his room and exactly what's going to happen when he comes out remains a more troubling mystery. Murray's plays don't end so much as they announce "to be continued." And they will, he will. (One need look no farther than his octet *The Gary Plays* to see how deeply and broadly Murray will meditate on an idea.)

While it demands more time, and certainly more attention, I'd suggest you read across Mednick's plays rather than through them. Allow yourself to let one play inform the other. Follow the fears as they manifest across different characters. Listen to ideas evolve and the past be reinvented while the future remains uncertain. Hear the same language and same rhythms reappear in different plays and different character's mouths. Permit the plays to bleed into one another.

What you will discover is that these are plays of contemplation.

You will discover a poet, a mind that is restless and more concerned with process than goal. You will recognize an artist who is contemplating language, religion, fear, writing, the role of the artist. . . the human condition. You will appreciate the value of a body of work over a single play. You will discover why so many playwrights have found inspiration in his work. You will recognize why Murray Mednick is such a complicated and indispensable figure for Los Angeles theater, for the American theater.

Borderline

For my sister, Blanche
(1948–2010)

Characters

CARL — *Sixty, a ceramicist, teaches in the California State College system. Married to FRANCES. Father of MYRA, an adopted girl from China.*

CRAIG — *Sixty. Teacher and writer, also father of a Chinese adopted girl, VICKI, and an acquaintance of CARL'S. Married to CINDY.*

CINDY — *Fifty-five. CRAIG'S wife of many years. Mother of VICKI.*

FRANCES — *Fifty. Taiwanese-American ophthalmologist married to CARL, and mother of MYRA.*

SPOTZIE — *Sixty-five. Jewish-American ex-hipster who lives in his car. Friend of CRAIG'S.*

MYRA — *Fifteen. Chinese, overweight and troubled, adopted daughter of CARL and FRANCES.*

VICKI — *Fourteen. CRAIG and CINDY'S adopted Chinese daughter.*

GISELLE — *Forty-five. CARL'S girlfriend during his last months.*

SCENE — *Minimal. Props or furniture are probably not needed. Simple set with one or two projection screens to be used for several of the monologues, as indicated.*

1. *(CARL enters to find CRAIG. Pause.)*

Carl   You may think things are copacetic, but I am here to tell
        you, they are not. They are not copacetic. You have got a
        problem.

Craig   What's my problem?

Carl   You know what "borderline" is? You know what a
        "borderline personality" is?

Craig   No.

Carl   Listen. We're sitting at the Chinese restaurant, and the
        women are all there, all the wives and moms, and they're
        talking about their men. They forget I'm there. They
        don't see me. That's how alert they are. Because they are
        preoccupied with themselves and their problems, and
        they think I'm a harmless idiot.

Craig   What problems?

Carl   Us. You and me. We are the problems.

Craig   Oh. My wife Cindy, too? Cindy was involved?

Carl   Cindy, and the rest of them too, all the moms.

Craig   I can't believe that.

Carl   I'm telling you, I was there. They are complaining, and
        dishing it out, and they have a lot to complain about, and
        especially my wife, Frances, who is talking to your wife.

Craig   Cindy?

Carl   Cindy and Frances. You don't believe me?

Craig   She doesn't do that kind of thing.

Carl   Then she is two different people, my friend. "I've had it
        with him," Cindy says, meaning you, "I can't stand it

anymore," she says, "I've had it, I'm not going to put up with it anymore, he's not a father, he's a drug addict, and he never makes a dime." She means you, she's talking about you.

Craig	Cindy is saying that about me?
Carl	Your wife, Cindy. (*Pause*)
Craig	I'm not a drug addict.
Carl	She thinks you are. Because you take painkillers.
Craig	Painkillers? You mean for my back?
Carl	Yes. And so on.
Craig	And so on?
Carl	And you drink. You and me, we both drink. We're alcoholics. I drink wine at night. I don't know what you drink.
Craig	Vodka.
Carl	I drink wine. I drink red wine in my studio. I'm a ceramicist. I have a little wine and I work, with my clay, with my kiln, with my dog. That's why I'm an alcoholic. According to Frances. And not only that, she thinks I'm too nice. Too nice to everybody, because I have no substance, I'm too needy, and I'm a drunk who drinks wine. I suck up to people, according to Frances. So, I'm too nice. (*Pause*) I'm too nice. I've been teaching in the University of California system for thirty-five years and I'm too nice.
Craig	Cindy, too? Cindy is talking about me to people?
Carl	Yes. Sorry. Me, I've had showings of my pots and my sculpture all over the country, all over the United States. It means nothing to her.

Craig	Why?
Carl	Why what?
Craig	Why was she putting me down to the other moms?
Carl	Why, because you're too shy to be a father. And you wear the wrong clothes. And you're fat. And so on.
Craig	I'm fat?
Carl	And you drink and you're a drug addict, mainly.
Craig	And I wear the wrong clothes?
Carl	You don't dress right. You don't dress like a dad.
Craig	She said that in front of people?
Carl	I'm just telling you what I heard, Craig. Me, I had smallpox when I was a kid, so I have pockmarks. It's ugly. The women went on and on, on and on, complaining, and they are trouble, so I am here to tell you. I am here to tell you.
Craig	Okay. I hear you.
Carl	I am here to tell you.
Craig	Okay.
Carl	So. You know what "borderline" is, you know what a "borderline personality" is?
Craig	No.
Carl	I'll tell you what it is. And I'll give you a book, okay? I'll give you a book and you'll give it back. (*Pause*) A "borderline" is somebody who thinks there's something wrong with you because there's something wrong with her. But it's not her, really, it's you. And she'll turn that screw. Like you never water the lawn and so the lawn is dying. Or you never say good night and your sex life is

dying. And you never do the dishes. And you never wash the dog. That's just a few examples. That's three or four examples. It doesn't matter what it is. It could be anything. Talk about sex. In fact, me and Frances, we never had a sex life. Frances was revolted by the whole sex thing. She didn't like it at all. So why do you think I was out there drinking wine and playing with my clay and hanging out with my dog, before crawling into a cold bed? This was while we were sleeping together, or pretending to be sleeping together. (*Pause*) Certain women. They can function all right. They seem perfectly normal. Only inside, they're not happy. Things haven't worked out. Something's wrong. The wrong is in the guy. Like I told you. This is called "borderline personality." That's what they call it. (*Pause*)

Craig   Okay, Carl, thanks.

Carl   So I'll bring you the book. And maybe we can organize a playdate with the kids. Just you and me and the kids. And I would tread carefully, if I were you. Keep your eyes open. She's got something going on with you, I don't know what. Some kind of big resentment. Keep your ears open. You might hear something.

Craig   Oh. I'm a little shaken up at the moment.

Carl   Sure, you're scared.

Craig   But I'll try.

Carl   It's not her fault, it's yours. Borderline, it's her own fault, her own problem, but the guy's the blame, something like that. Usually, it's like one thing, something stupid, like drinking.

Craig	I think I get it.
Carl	So I don't know, exactly, but it's like a specific mechanism, where they go after another person, usually a husband, or a wife. I'll give you the book. And I'd get a lawyer if I were you, a good one.
Craig	I don't want to get a lawyer.
Carl	Get a lawyer. I'm telling you, Craig. I am—I'm getting the toughest lawyer in town. (*Exits*)

2. (CINDY *enters to join* CRAIG)

Craig	Hi, honey.
Cindy	Hi.
Craig	How was the class?
Cindy	What class?
Craig	I mean the meeting.
Cindy	Which meeting?
Craig	About Vicki's dance class.
Cindy	Oh.
Craig	So how was it?
Cindy	I don't know how it was. I'll tell you what it was.
Craig	Okay.
Cindy	If you want to hear about it.
Craig	I do.
Cindy	Isn't the news on?
Craig	I guess it is.
Cindy	You don't want to miss that.
Craig	No, I could miss it.

Cindy	Really?
Craig	Yeah.
Cindy	We talked about the economy and about how the women are supporting the economy.
Craig	I see.
Cindy	No, you don't. Go watch the news. Have a drink and watch the news.
Craig	How are the women supporting the economy?
Cindy	By working and making the money. And on top of that, raising the kids.
Craig	I still have hopes for making some money.
Cindy	Sure you do, Craig. Hopes and dreams.
Craig	And our daughter?
Cindy	What about her?
Craig	She's doing her homework?
Cindy	She better be.
Craig	I'll go help her.
Cindy	No, thanks. I'll help her. Vicki is working hard. You only confuse her.
Craig	No, I don't.
Cindy	You're too lenient.
Craig	I try to give her a chance.
Cindy	You're too lazy. Vicki's doing fine now. She's studying. You go sit down with your drink, Craig, and watch TV.
Craig	I'm not too lazy. I just want to help.
Cindy	Never mind. She doesn't need you now. Go watch your news.

3. (CARL *and* CRAIG)

Carl   I'm not going to give her an inch. I promise you. She may think she can kill me, but I won't let her. I love my daughter. Like you, I love my daughter, but I will not be destroyed by this lunatic woman. So I'm telling you. I'm telling you now. I'm taking my dog and I'm out of there.

Craig   What do you think I should do?

Carl   I mean, you got to make up your own mind. (*Pause*) Okay, I'll tell you: Don't lay down. Fight back.

Craig   There's no attack from her yet.

Carl   There is one coming, I'm telling you. It's coming. Cindy is not rational, she is a nutcase. The attack is coming. I'm telling you. Get a lawyer. Get one now.

4. (CRAIG *and* SPOTZIE)

Craig   So then I was scared. I was tiptoeing around. I started feeling self-conscious by my fat gut, my little tire. I had to cover my stomach to have sex, though we didn't have any, really. Sex, I mean. She'd tell me, "Put on a shirt, Craig." So I put on a shirt. Then it was embarrassing, you know, and there was like nothing romantic left to go on. That was a while ago. I think sex was like once a year, if at all. So now I go around thinking, "She's going to leave me, she's going to throw me out, she's going to have me arrested," and so on.

Spotzie   Why should she have you arrested? You didn't do anything wrong.

Craig	But I felt like I might have.
Spotzie	Nothing wrong. Nothing illegal.
Craig	I felt like I was wrong. Inherently wrong. And she picked up on that. The more insecure I got, the more powerful she got. I had no business taking drugs for my shoulder, or my back, when there were all these holistic solutions around, according to her. She stopped talking to me or looking at me, and all I was allowed to do was walk the dog. When we came home, me and the dog, she said hello to the dog and ignored me. One day I threw the dog out the door on his ass. My daughter cried. I started watching for signs. Coming catastrophes. Watching Cindy's face, her eyes. The more I worried about it, the worse it became. I kept prefiguring the outcome. It's the strangest thing, like walking in emotional glue. And then, of course, it actually happened. "Leave now," she said. I remember lingering in the garage thinking how much I liked having a garage and then hating the thought of being exposed—me and the car, exposed to the hostile city, the nasty L.A. night. Thinking of Carl's warning coming true, like it was a film noir, only he wasn't much for the movies, himself. He liked his pottery and his wine. Chianti was his thing. And he was up for a good fight with his wife, Frances. Frances could be the way she was, a crazy person, but she wasn't getting off scot-free, as far as he was concerned. She would pay. He wasn't going to go anywhere until she got a court order to make him go. He said to me to tell Cindy to go.

"Tell her to fuck off," he said. "You don't go. Don't leave your home. That gives them an edge." So Cindy and the kid, they moved to a hotel. But I wasn't going to leave my daughter there. They'd been in a hotel for weeks. You go or I go, she said, referring to the house. I didn't realize I had rights. And there I was, days later, in the garage loading up the car, heartbroken, leaving my family and my home. (*Silence*)

Spotzie This used to be a civil community.

Craig Since when?

Spotzie Before proposition thirteen, when we said fuck you to education. So now we live among thieves and killers and ignorant barbarians.

5. (CARL *and* CRAIG. FRANCES OFF.)

Carl So, I'm trying to have a so-called evening at home. Myra is with me. It's one of my days with her. Myra is watching TV and munching on popcorn. And then there's this voice coming at us from the trees above the roof. It's Frances:

Frances (*Off*) *You prick. You think you can defeat me? You are nothing! You are less than nothing! You hear me, asshole?*

Carl So the trees are shaking and my wife is up in the tree, because I have walled off the household in Culver City. The only approach is from above. So she's up there in the tree. I don't know what kind of fucking tree it is, but I realize I am in deep trouble because it's not just legal, it's not just routine, it's a real problem with a real hysteric. You've heard of that?

Craig Come on, Carl, I know what a hysteric is.

Carl So Frances is up in the tree, shouting down at us. I quietly go into the living room, to quiet Myra, to reassure her of my commitment and my protection, but it was no use. Frances just kept on yelling down at me from up in the trees.

Craig So what did you do?

Carl I called the police, finally.

6. (CINDY *on screen.*)

Cindy *I'm tired of talking about this all the time, Craig, but you are a drug addict and you can't keep a job. It's not acceptable. There are homeopathic cures for every ailment. You don't need these Western drugs. I've been telling you for years now and I'm sick of it. I never use that horrible medical stuff. You don't see me ever using that crap and our daughter will never use it, either. You need to see a chiropractor for your shoulder and a psychiatrist for your mind, or you might try talking to a minister. And AA is an option, too. If you go to AA, Craig, I promise you, I'll go to Al-anon. How would you like that? I think that's fair. I think that's totally fair. I'll take some responsibility. I'll go to Al-anon. But you have to do it, Craig. Go to AA. There has to be some real effort on your part, Craig, REAL EFFORT.*

7. (CARL and CRAIG)

Carl   Then we go to court. I've got the masterpiece of all lawyers, a woman who will not lose. She was tougher than me and she hooked me up with a shrink who was even tougher than her. I said I got no DUI's. I got no problems with the school. I never once stepped out of line. Naturally, the custody problem comes up. I said, this woman is crazy, she doesn't have normal feelings for men or women or children.

Craig   Okay.

Carl   Don't say okay. I'm telling you and I'm warning you. Get off your spoiled little soft ass—it's you or her.

Craig   (*To audience*) I thought to myself, "get tough, Craig, get tough. You can do it. You're not a softie. You're not a creampuff. Just say NO. Just say NO. Hang in there, Craig." 'Course, nothing worked out that way.

8. (CRAIG and SPOTZIE)

Craig   Then she pulled the kid to a hotel and kicked me out of the house and took me to court and ruined my reputation, and so on. I tried in every way to save my marriage, my family. None of it worked. And I never read the book.

Spotzie   What book?

Craig   *Borderline.*

Spotzie   It had begun long ago, probably, long ago in her own life, maybe before she even knew you.

Craig	True. But I might have understood better, and held my ground better, if I had had some idea of what was going on. And I made sure I stayed tight with my daughter, no matter what. I stayed in touch. And I kept my job. Substituting the sixth grade. I don't know how I did that.
Spotzie	If people don't feel strong inside, they try to act superior. They have no other way. What that's got to do with marriage is beyond me, but it makes it very difficult, because one is always right and one is always wrong. Or unacceptable, or unworthy of the other, or fucked up in some way.
Craig	Is that "borderline?"
Spotzie	I don't know. I haven't read the book, either.
Craig	*Borderline.* Look it up.
Spotzie	No.
Craig	Look it up.
Spotzie	Okay. I'll look it up.
Craig	Thanks. (*Pause*)
Spotzie	When my sister died, there seemed to be something there, like in the sunlight. The sun was just coming up. She looked at the sun. Something looked, in her last breath, and she saw something.
Craig	What?
Spotzie	I don't know. Something in the light. (*Standing*) I've got a date.
Craig	A date?
Spotzie	You're surprised? (*Pause*) Something around the body. Something in the light. Like a flavor, or an essence.

Craig	Around the body?
Spotzie	Yes. Anyway, I have things to do, roles to play, and people to see. My date is waiting. Maybe I'll run into you soon.
Craig	Have a good time.
Spotzie	Thanks, Craig. (*Exits*)

9. (VICKI *and* CRAIG)

Vicki	Dad?
Craig	Yeah?
Vicki	They're putting oil all over the flowers!
Craig	What?
Vicki	Oil is covering the earth.
Craig	Oh, you mean in the waters of the Gulf?
Vicki	Yeah. Where is all that stuff coming from?
Craig	The earth is like a layer cake and there's oil in the cake, so they put a fork in there and the oil squirts out and all the frosting on the cake turns to muck.
Vicki	That's what I'm talking about.
Craig	I know what you're talking about.
Vicki	Why?
Craig	Why?
Vicki	Why?
Craig	Because people are people and companies are companies and they have to do what they do to survive, which is to find the oil, so that's what happens.
Vicki	That's why I don't believe in life anymore.

Craig	You don't believe in life anymore?
Vicki	No.
Craig	That's absurd.
Vicki	Why?
Craig	You're only a kid.
Vicki	It's out of control.
Craig	As far as we can see.
Vicki	What does that mean?
Craig	Maybe there's another vision of life on earth where it's not out of control.
Vicki	Like what?
Craig	Like it has to be that way. A splotch of brown appears on the waters of the Gulf, and somewhere else, a goddess sighs.
Vicki	That's crazy, Dad.
Craig	Maybe Spotzie's right, maybe something survives, something invisible.
Vicki	Is this true for everyone?
Craig	I don't know. Suffering is necessary, maybe. Sorrow. I don't know.

10. (CINDY and CRAIG)

Cindy	I have something to tell you, Craig.
Craig	What is it?
Cindy	It's very sad.
Craig	What happened?
Cindy	You remember my friend, Frances Wang?
Craig	Yes. Of course. Your friend, Frances.

Cindy	She killed herself.
Craig	She killed herself?
Cindy	They found her in the street.
Craig	In the street?
Cindy	They found her in the street.
Craig	In the street?
Cindy	That's what I said, Craig.
Craig	Why in the street?
Cindy	I don't know. I think she took some drugs and ran outside into the street and got hit by something or run over by something.
Craig	Something?
Cindy	She got hit by something. She had a lousy life. She didn't like her life.
Craig	Her husband, Carl?
Cindy	Carl?
Craig	Where is he now?
Cindy	I don't know. She left a note.
Craig	Did she leave a note?
Cindy	I just said she left a note.
Craig	What was in the note?
Cindy	What did you expect? She's been unhappy for years. They had a horrible divorce. You must have known that? It was very hard. Carl was unrelenting. He wouldn't let up, he wouldn't give in. She'd been unhappy for years. And then she'd get a call from Myra, "Daddy's been drinking."
Craig	"Daddy's been drinking."
Cindy	Yes.

Craig	I don't get it.
Cindy	What?
Craig	What business is it of hers?
Cindy	She asked Myra to tell on him.
Craig	Who did?
Cindy	Frances. Asked Myra. The kid's a mess.
Craig	Of course she's a mess. How could she not be a mess? "Daddy's been drinking." Frances asked her to spy on her own father.
Cindy	So she took her own life, Frances.
Craig	Why do you act like it's Carl's fault?
Cindy	Because it was.
Craig	He was protecting himself.
Cindy	What's a person to do, after all?
Craig	You weren't listening to me.
Cindy	Do you know?
Craig	You're asking me?
Cindy	You act like you know.
Craig	I don't know.
Cindy	She's dead, actually.
Craig	When did this happen?
Cindy	Maybe a week ago.
Craig	Thanks for telling me, Cindy.
Cindy	Yeah, sure.
Craig	I appreciate it.
Cindy	Sure.
Craig	Where is Carl?
Cindy	I don't know.

11. (CRAIG *and* SPOTZIE)

Craig	Hey, Spotzie.
Spotzie	Greetings.
Craig	This person we knew, she committed suicide.
Spotzie	Who is this?
Craig	You remember, when we were breaking up, me and Cindy, there was a woman I told you about, who my wife was friendly with, you remember her?
Spotzie	Yes.
Craig	Frances Wang? Carl's wife?
Spotzie	I think so. The Borderline person?
Craig	Yes.
Spotzie	I remember talking about her with you.
Craig	Yes. She was from Taiwan. She was an optometrist, a very good one, proud of her ability. Made a lot of money. Her name was Frances—and my wife, Cindy, they both had the same complaints. Like they were really unhappy with their situations, their married lives ... They were telling each other, how their husbands were drunks, and took drugs, and lied, and how they, the women, did the best jobs and made all the money, you remember that?
Spotzie	Yes, I think I do. Frances, from Taiwan.
Craig	Right. Frances. So we couldn't be good fathers, me and Carl. That would be me and her husband, Carl. "It's unacceptable," she'd said, "for things to go on like that."
Spotzie	Unacceptable?

Craig	Yes. That was a word she used. And she was the angry one, Frances, the most bitter, the most fierce. And she and Cindy supported each other in this view of their men, including me. They complained to each other. They'd go to this Chinese restaurant, or a coffee shop, the women, after the kids' dance class, and they'd eat and they'd talk about their husbands and one of them was my wife, Cindy, of course, talking about me. It was after class, a dance class for the kids, and then they'd all talk. And Carl would listen in from a table nearby. I find it strange now. I find it eerie. Because the woman killed herself.
Spotzie	Of course.
Craig	Remember? How they helped each other with the story. So they could have a story. They helped each other with the story and then she kills herself.
Spotzie	And the story was how bad it was with you guys.
Craig	Yes. How they'd had it with the men. Because their men were drunks and drug addicts and moochers and they had to get rid of them. And I was one of them. I was one of them. I didn't have a clue. Though they didn't know me or talk to me much and they all looked at me funny. The women did. I thought I was just being paranoid. (*Silence*) I didn't think my wife would talk about me like that, in public. How she could be so outraged, how she could be so fed up. And this guy comes over one day, Carl, Frances' Carl, he was one of the fathers, and his kid was a friend of my kid's, and he comes to my office and he's got this look on his face. Like, "Guess what Pal,

we're in this together, we got a couple of troubled wives, and trouble is on its way, trouble is on its way, and you're in for it too, Pal, not just me." I had no idea. I had no clue. He was sitting at one of the tables, listening to them, and I guess they forgot him sitting there, because it all came out at the table. How the two of us are these dysfunctional fuck-ups and something had to be done. Something radical. They were coming up with these radical solutions. So Carl comes over to my office, with that look of triumph on his face, "like I told you, motherfucker."

Spotzie   Why triumph?

Craig   Yeah, it was like, "Don't forget how I told you about all this, Craig. You didn't believe me, did you? And now the shit has hit the fan, Pal. You have got some trouble coming your way. It's gonna come out of Cindy's mouth, with her lies and her lawyers and all kinds of bullshit. It's on its way."

Spotzie   Frances. The optometrist.

Craig   Right, the wife of Carl, like I said. Because he was going to fight her, he wasn't going to give an inch, he was going to make her pay, while I was still having trouble believing all this was actually happening. You know, that you could break up these families out of a kind of madness. I'd be in my office and she'd come over, you know, Frances, and she'd start talking about Carl with Cindy. She was ranting and raving about Carl to Cindy. And then Cindy started ranting about me. And so on. You're in trouble, big trouble, he says. And there's a certain irony there, and a certain satisfaction, and a certain glee. Because he's not alone—he's got me now for companionship. We are both the victims, he says, of these borderline personalities.

Spotzie   People mean all kinds of things. Some women have a hatred for men. Cindy may not have known what she was doing. It's not necessarily Borderline.

Craig   No, this was Borderline. We talked about it at the time. He tried to warn me, because I didn't seem to believe him. I didn't think Cindy would do some of that shit she said and did. And lie about me like that. But it all turned out to be true, as you know, Frances couldn't control Carl's life and her daughter's life and now she's committed suicide. (*Silence*) I'm sorry. I mean, Frances definitely meant to do harm, and Carl didn't let her get away with it, and she ends up taking some pills and running out into the street. I didn't like her much, but I'm sorry for her—

Spotzie   Where's Carl now?

Craig   —I think she did do it. Cindy. Put me down, after a dance practice with the kids. With all the women there, and the kids, and the whole nine yards. About what a shit I was. And I didn't believe it. Not until she started lecturing and hectoring me about it herself. How I was a drunk and drug addict and it was entirely unacceptable. Frances was mean, like I said, and she had a big influence on what my wife, Cindy, proceeded to do. Carl kept trying to warn me, you know, Carl did, and I wouldn't believe him. But Cindy started in, eventually. She started laying it on me hard, every single night. Cindy.

12. (CINDY *and* CRAIG—*in the past*)

Cindy   It's the culture, Craig. It's a culture of hookers and
half-naked girls in advertisements. You can't let girls
wear those types of clothes. Those are clothes that
prostitutes wear. You should see the glamour pictures
our daughter takes. She photographs herself in various
poses. It's shows no self-esteem. I'm not blaming you, but
I don't want you buying Vicki any more clothes—tight-
fitting, revealing clothes. I know you don't look at the
clothes, but you should look at the clothes, see what she
wants to wear. I won't put up with it. I'm going to throw
them away. She picks up the worst of the culture that
shows such little self-esteem, trying to get attention by
looking attractive to boys. Is that what you want? Well,
I won't stand for it. I'm throwing them away, so if I were
you, I would look in the bag, look at the clothes. It's your
money anyway. You want to spend your money on those
cheesy clothes? Go ahead, but I'll throw them away. I'm
not saying it's all your fault, but you better start paying
more attention.

Craig   Carl? Have you seen Carl?

Cindy   No, why?

Craig   He wants to have a playdate for Myra with Vicki.

Cindy   No way.

Craig   Why not?

Cindy   Why not? Because of Carl.

Craig   Carl?

Cindy	He drinks and I don't trust him.
Craig	What do you think he'll do?
Cindy	I've heard things, believe me.
Craig	What things?
Cindy	Things. That's all. Just things.
Craig	I don't believe them.
Cindy	I wouldn't put it past him, according to Frances.
Craig	That's bullshit, Cindy. Carl would never do anything like that, not in a million years.
Cindy	That's not what I heard.
Craig	What, are you talking to the dead now? Frances is a dead person. You didn't hear that anywhere but in your own head.
Cindy	Don't you dare talk to me like I'm a crazy person! I don't appreciate it and I won't put up with it! Do you hear me?

13. (CRAIG *is speaking with* GISELLE.)

Giselle	So? Craig? You know Carl, what's his name, very nice guy, German, pockmarked? I heard you knew him.
Craig	Carl?
Giselle	Carl.
Craig	Yeah. I do know him.
Giselle	He died.
Craig	He died?
Giselle	Yeah, he had a blood clot in his brain. I think I told you, his wife, you knew her, she died in the street. Frances. She was a suicide.

Craig	Frances. Yes.
Giselle	So a week after, he's not feeling good, he goes to the hospital, his head hurts. Turns out he's got a clot in his brain and he goes right into a coma.
Craig	That's terrible.
Giselle	I thought so.
Craig	Thanks for telling me.
Giselle	Poor guy. He had a hard life, you know.
Craig	I did know. He was an orphan in the Midwest somewhere.
Giselle	True, he was an orphan. In Omaha. And then, later on, his daughters disowned him.
Craig	He had daughters?
Giselle	Yeah, he had daughters somewhere. Not the Chinese one, not the new one, Myra, whom he loved. There was one in New England, and one in the Northwest, I think, and they had some problems over the mother's money.
Craig	I'm sorry. I didn't know any of that.
Giselle	He didn't talk much about it. I don't think they got along.
Craig	I'm sorry.
Giselle	So that's it for Carl.
Craig	Thanks.
Giselle	No problem. He's out of it now. Poor kid, though. His kid, Myra. I don't know what's going to happen to her.
Craig	Where is she?
Giselle	I'm not sure. Carl had a girlfriend at the end, you know, who loved him. He had me. He had some happiness before the end, some good times, which I'm very glad of.

Craig	Me, too. I'm glad, too. Thank you.
Giselle	Don't thank me. I'm just glad he had some good times happen to him before the end. He was very fine with ceramics, you know.
Craig	Yes, I did know. He was one of the best in the world.

14. (CRAIG, SPOTZIE, CARL *and* CINDY.)

Craig	He died, Carl. He got a blood clot in his head, a week after they found Frances dead in the street, and he died. I saw him once before that, before he started getting those headaches.
Spotzie	And?
Craig	This is how it went (SPOTZIE *steps aside and* CARL *enters to re-enact the scene.*)
Craig	So, Carl.
Carl	Craig.
Craig	How are you?
Carl	I don't feel so good.
Craig	Same headaches?
Carl	Yeah. Don't let them put me in a hospital.
Craig	I'll try, Carl.
Carl	I hate hospitals. I can't stand them. I don't want to die in a hospital.
Craig	I'll try.
Carl	Try.
Craig	I said, I'll try.
Carl	Okay. Thanks.
Craig	How's your kid?

Carl	Myra? She's fat. Fat as a house.
Craig	Some people eat. Some people watch television.
Carl	She eats while she watches.
Craig	What do you do?
Carl	What can I do?
Craig	You have a girlfriend?
Carl	Yes. I do. It's very nice. Giselle. Someone who actually likes you and enjoys your company. And you?
Craig	No. I'm too old and too stressed.
Carl	What does that mean?
Craig	Sex is for baby-making. I'd be a grandpa. And I get too nervous on dates. I can't go out on a date.
Carl	Too bad. I highly recommend it. Maybe later, when you're really too old.
Craig	Maybe.
Carl	How's Vicki?
Craig	She's doing okay. It's an adjustment. She spends most of her time now with her mother.
Carl	I'd fight that if I were you. You have rights.
Craig	I know that, Carl. I'm doing the best I can.
Carl	I'm sure you are. (*Pause*) You know, Frances committed suicide?
Craig	Yes, I heard about it. From Cindy.
Carl	I figured, but I wanted to tell you myself. Knocked herself off. You could see it coming.
Craig	She was hard to deal with.
Carl	She couldn't stand losing. She couldn't stand not having custody. She couldn't stand that I had a new girlfriend and a new life.

Craig	Weird how she did it, though. Running out into the street. . .
Carl	A madwoman.
Craig	You must feel sorry for her?
Carl	I do, but it's hard. She was bad news for me, Craig. Now I have a real life, finally, and I appreciate it. I protected it from being destroyed by that miserable maniac. If it weren't for these stupid headaches, I'd be fine. And you?
Craig	I live alone now, as you can see. In lovely Santa Monica.
Carl	I warned you. I tried to warn you.
Craig	I know you did. Borderline and drugs and alcohol.
Carl	Exactly.
Craig	Are you an alcoholic, Carl?
Carl	Oh, fuck that shit. I drank my glass of wine at night and did no harm. My girlfriend now—Giselle—doesn't even mention it. I did all the court routines and that's that. No DUI's. Bracelet on my ankle. Answer is no, I'm not an alcoholic, whatever that is. It was all borderline bullshit. Answer to that is bullshit. The answer is no. Fucking bitch. And you?
Craig	Me? I'm in therapy at the moment.
Carl	That's another one. A con. A long con. A lifetime con. Frances had a shrink, too. It was like paying an indemnity, a tax. It should be illegal.
Craig	I'm afraid of women and I live alone.
Carl	Oh, come on. Who says?
Craig	My friend, Spotzie.
Carl	How does he know?

Craig	He's smart. He lives in his car.
Carl	He can't be that smart if he lives in his car.
Craig	He used to be a rabbi.
Carl	So what?
Craig	Nothing.
Carl	What's so smart about that?
Craig	He lives life to a minimum.
Carl	Not me, I want to live it to the max.
Craig	He tries his best.
Carl	Good for him.
Craig	I'm sorry about Frances.
Carl	She never let up. She was never happy about anything. I'd help out with the dance, with the various buffets, with this and that, I got along, people appreciated it, but she thought I was a wuss, too much of a handyman. She called me "Carl, the handyman." She loathed sex and she loathed me and when she got a lawyer I got the toughest one I could find, the toughest one in the city. She didn't expect that. She thought I'd lay down. But I'm an artist. I'm an artist. I showed my ceramics all over the country. I'm worth something. We fought her on everything. Right along the line, the custody, the house, the money. No DUI's on my record, no felonies, nothing. I held a regular job in the California university system for thirty-three years and she was not going to bring me down. She did not win, I can tell you that.
Craig	Did you go to the funeral?

Carl	No. There was no service. They cremated her and put her in a box. No ceremony, nothing.
Craig	Where is the box?
Carl	It's with Myra. Don't you think that's odd?
Craig	And Myra?
Carl	She's miserable about the whole thing. I'm hoping she gets over it. We go to counseling. I try to give her a feeling of family. But she eats a lot. She eats and she watches the TV.
Craig	School?
Carl	She hardly goes anymore. And Vicki?
Craig	She's fine. She seems to have adjusted, like I told you. She likes to shop. Spends most of her time with Cindy. A couple days a week with me.
Carl	Take the gloves off, Craig. Sue the bitch and take the kid and some money and put an end to it.
Craig	My daughter likes it that we all try to get along.
Carl	Yeah, yeah, I'm sure Cindy likes it, too.
Craig	She does.
Carl	Sure, she's in complete control. You're no threat. Find a woman, Craig. Get laid once in a while.
Craig	I've forgotten how to do that.
Carl	Cindy just brainwashed you, Craig. Now you don't think you're worth anything.
Craig	I'm too old. I'm out of the game. They don't even see me no more. And I used to be good-looking.
Carl	Not true. Lonely women are all over the place.
Craig	Where?

Carl	Are you kidding? They're all over.
Craig	I'm not interested in old ladies.
Carl	Forties, Craig, forties and fifties, I'm telling you, you can't go wrong. But you got to be available, you can't be hiding out, and I think Cindy's still got her hooks into you.
Craig	No, I can't hardly talk to her anymore.
Carl	But you do, and you have to, because of Vicki.
Craig	Right. I do have to do that.
Carl	But you can't live like that. You got to have people to talk to you. Vicki won't talk. She's a teenager. It's companionship, companionship is the thing. Someone to talk to.
Craig	No.
Carl	Why?
Craig	Like I told you, it's too stressful. I can't go out on dates.
Carl	What's her name's a teenager.
Craig	Vicki.
Carl	Vicki, of course. Teenagers, they don't talk to their parents. They talk to their friends. So who do you talk to?
Craig	I watch TV. Movies, mostly.
Carl	Get out, Craig, and meet some people. I'm living my life. I'm the happiest now I've ever been in my life.
Craig	Well, good for you, Carl. I'm happy for you. And I appreciate it.
Carl	What?
Craig	You taking the time to check up on me.
Carl	You're a friend, for chrissakes. That wasn't nothing. I didn't do nothing. Drink?

Craig	No, thanks.
Carl	Abstinent, are you?
Craig	Not really.
Carl	You can't be one or the other, that's why I quit the program.
Craig	You're correct on that. That's why I quit, too.
Carl	People quit.
Craig	There's all kinds, actually. It's one of the better programs in America, AA.
Carl	I agree with you there, though that may surprise you.
Craig	It doesn't.
Carl	Whole country should join, like the Peace Corps. Gotta go.
Craig	Thanks for coming over.
Carl	Well, if I meet someone I'll let you know.
Craig	What?
Carl	You know, fix you up.
Craig	Maybe you could wait on that.
Carl	Why?
Craig	Can't handle it right now.
Carl	Can't date? Can't conduct a conversation?
Craig	No.
Carl	Well, then, whatever.
Craig	Thanks, anyway.
Carl	Trouble with this country. Just want to blow up mountaintops for coal and the devil take the hindmost. Frack down and ruin the water. No community at all. No sense of worth. They have no Christian sense of responsibility, just a bunch of no-accounts want to drive their car over to Denny's, eat a cheap meal. (*Exits. SPOTZIE steps back on stage.*)

Spotzie	So that was Carl.
Craig	That was Carl. Died a week later. Brain aneurysm.
Spotzie	You sit with him?
Craig	I didn't know about it until this woman told me afterward. I didn't know her, but she seemed to know me.
Spotzie	Could have been his new girlfriend.
Craig	Yes, Giselle. He knew her at the college. (*Pause*) Then Cindy told me. (*Enter* CINDY, SPOTZIE *steps aside.*)
Cindy	He was in a coma. He had a blood clot in his brain. A week after they found Frances, he collapsed.
Craig	He's in a coma now?
Cindy	No. He's dead. As we speak.
Craig	And the kid? Myra?
Cindy	She's with a relative of his. They found her, Frances, on the street, laid out in the street. Three days later, Carl went into a coma. She was wound up like a pretzel, arms and legs in the wrong positions, eyes vacant, mouth hung open on the last gasp. (*Exits.* SPOTZIE *steps back on.*)
Spotzie	So you got a double suicide here and a murder.
Craig	What's that?
Spotzie	Something wrong with your ears? I say you got a double suicide here and a murder. (*Long silence*) Say something.
Craig	Yeah, I see what you mean, she got him in the end.
Spotzie	She got him.
Craig	Yeah, Frances couldn't kill him any other way. Carl wasn't going to buy into any of it. So she takes some pills one night and goes out into the street.

Spotzie	Right.
Craig	So how is that a double suicide?
Spotzie	They knew each other. They were married.
Craig	I don't get it.
Spotzie	I don't either. I'm guessing.
Craig	What?
Spotzie	You can't know these things. But I'm thinking she knew how to kill him. (*Silence*) He knew how to be killed.
Craig	Thanks a lot, Spotz. That's just crazy psychologizing.
Spotzie	Sorry. It's my intuition.
Craig	Now what do I do?
Spotzie	I don't know.
Craig	Should I see a therapist?
Spotzie	See a therapist.
Craig	Carl did. The long con, he calls it. He didn't believe in it, but he did it.
Spotzie	He was buying time. His lawyer made him do it. Maybe he learned something, but I doubt it.
Craig	Spotzie.
Spotzie	What?
Craig	I've come to the end and there's no way out.
Spotzie	Did you hear that line on television, or what?
Craig	I'm an old man and I'm alone now most of the time.
Spotzie	Me, too.
Craig	Why do you doubt the therapy?
Spotzie	Buddha, maybe he understood something. Mohammed, maybe. Jesus Christ. The Baal Shem. Therapists, I don't know.
Craig	Why not?

Spotzie   No verticality. I was committed for a time, if you remember, in my youth. I was a nineteen-year-old maniacal junkie. Finally, I introduced myself to Bellevue Hospital, in New York. I had suicidal impulses. One of the things I couldn't get over was the Holocaust. Not that you ever get over it. But I kept asking myself, "Would I have gotten on the trains? Would I have fought and killed? Would I?" Nobody knows what they'll do until it happens. I don't know to this day what I would have done. So this still bothers me. Would I have walked into the gas chamber and sung the *Shema* with my last breath? "You're one of those little Jews," my second wife—a Gentile by the way—said, "who got on the trains." That one hurt. So I don't blame you, feeling bad about the suicide. Think of all the suffering caused by mental illness and the little anyone can do about it.

Craig   What did you mean about the verticality?

Spotzie   When I was a kid, in the summer, in the woods. There was a path before you got to the Kanter house. You walked up there through the woods and there was a *shul* hidden away up there. My uncle used to go there, carrying his *tallis* in his little bag. I never went myself. I thought it was a secret place. There were chicken farms and chicken shit all over, I remember that, thinking you can believe in chicken shit and God at the same time. Maybe without chicken shit there is no God. You can't miss the chicken shit. And then the moment comes, the last breath comes. I'm thinking of my sister, Sharon. We don't know for sure. But she said, "No." No to chemo.

No to therapy. No to morphine. One morning she turned her face to the sun and breathed her last. What all this has to do with verticality, I don't know. Something. Come on, we'll have an honorary schnapps. (*Pause. They drink.*) In the old days, you know, someone in your situation, they'd go to a matchmaker.

Craig Carl offered to fix me up. His ex-wife commits suicide and he gets a new girlfriend and offers to fix me up. Maybe I should call her or e-mail her.

Spotzie Who?

Craig His girlfriend.

Spotzie What for?

Craig I don't know. Pay my respects.

Spotzie Your daughter?

Craig My daughter?

Spotzie So you buy her things?

Craig Right.

Spotzie You're bribing her for attention?

Craig I don't think so.

Spotzie Think it over.

Craig Why do you live in your car?

Spotzie I can afford it. It's a Volkswagen. I'm a musician. Take a look. It's not so bad. We'll have another schnapps. *L'chaim.* To Life. To my sister, Sharon.

Craig Your sister.

Spotzie And to Lazer, who was the father of her father.

Craig To Lazer.

Spotzie She turned her face to the sunrise and said, "I'm out of here." A good death. It was light. Like the turning of a leaf.

15. (GISELLE and CRAIG)

Giselle	What do you want? We had the memorial already. I invited you. I e-mailed you.
Craig	I never got it. Actually, I got it too late.
Giselle	Oh. That's strange.
Craig	We didn't know each other that well, me and Carl. We only knew each other through our kids.
Giselle	And your wives.
Craig	Right.
Giselle	I worked with him over at the college. He was a good man, you know. He put up with a lot from that woman, mainly because of his adopted Chinese kid, Myra, he did the best he could with his situation, married to this Asian borderline psychotic. What happened with you?
Craig	She left and took the kid.
Giselle	You have custody?
Craig	Part-time.
Giselle	Too bad. She's Chinese, too, right?
Craig	My daughter is, yes. Not my wife. How did you get together with Carl?
Giselle	Everybody liked Carl, pockmarks and eagerness to please and all. He'd help out at these adoption functions and she'd say to him in the car, "Why'd you do that, Carl? You don't have to volunteer for everything, you don't have to do so much. Why do you do that?" Like it was an insult to her or something. (*Pause*) Anyway, what did you ask?
Craig	How did you and Carl get together?

Giselle	He saw where the wind was blowing and he didn't waste any time. He got that house in Culver City and we started seeing each other. I'm glad he got some happiness in his life. Myra, when she was over, would just sit there, depressed, looking at the TV. That bothered him, along with the monitor Frances had the judge put on his ankle, about alcohol. But he and Myra, they got along all right.
Craig	Where is she now?
Giselle	I don't know. She's with some foster parents somewhere. I doubt she's doing real well. What I don't understand is how he quick got this stroke in his brain and went into a coma and died. Just like that, when he was getting his life together. She was some piece of work, that woman. Okay?
Craig	Thank you.

16. (CRAIG *and* SPOTZIE *on stage together, while* FRANCES *and* CARL *speak on the screens.*)

Frances	(*On screen*) *What is this happiness shit anyway? What is there to be happy about? I'm normal. I'm sane. Without any frippery or trumpery. I live in the real world. Not like Carl, who drinks and dreams. I work hard, I make money, I take care of my kid. I do my best, for her and for me, the best I can, even though I hate this dark house with it's crazy dog and the homeless on the street and Carl in the back playing with his pots and drinking wine while the radio blares out obnoxiously to the neighbors.*
Craig	He died, Spotzie, he died still in his coma, a week after she killed herself.

Spotzie	You told me. (*Pause*) Mental illness. Dirtbags on the street and people in prisons and their minds are not right. There's little sympathy for those. I'm right on the edge myself, in my car. Seems like life is thin as an illusion, blown about by invisible currents. Raise a family, and so on. Everything looks okay. Only it's not for us. There is hope, but not for us.
Craig	You lost me there, Spotz.
Spotzie	Sorry. I don't know. Maybe the strong-minded. I was quoting Kafka. There was no hope for people like Frances. Maybe that's what the Buddha meant. No need to come back. He got sane. He got refined.
Frances	(*On screen*) *I did well in school. I worked hard. I went into ophthalmology because the eye is a wondrous thing. Very complicated. You wouldn't think such a complicated mechanism could evolve on the earth. You know, we turn to shit in the end, which is not a bad thing necessarily. What I mean is, you have this complicated mechanism that creates vision, seeing, and then acts as fertilizer. It's recycled, you could say. Imagine, vision is caused on the earth and then returns to the earth. It's just hard to see the point of it all unless the idea is to turn to shit in the end. So things grow on the earth. Maybe it's the earth seeing and sensing itself through us? That's an idea. I mean, I don't usually talk like this, usually I'm more circumspect and careful, but it's the earth, isn't it, sending out feelers and senses like sight and sound so it can have a kind of awareness? The earth's*

awareness. I think that's an amazing thought, a little far out for me, but if that's what we are, you know, little bits of awareness for the earth's brain, you know, okay, it's okay with me, but I don't give a shit really, I'm not crazy about it, being a little bit of shit for the earth. I am not a good servant, you could say. You could say that. There's no sin in dying intentionally, to get off the map, as it were, quit the job, you know. My friend's ex-husband's sister, Craig's sister, no, his friend Spotzie's sister Sharon, she denied the chemo because it did nothing but make her sick. She wanted some good days before she died. So I started thinking about it myself, the meaning of it all, and that's all I could come up with, not having any good days, and I won't be missed, this little bit of seeing not much of a light going out. Sharon went to a Chinese restaurant and tried to enjoy the food when she decided. I remember the day. A nice spring day and she could hardly think straight, but she had that thought. I'm not even worth that much, as much as Sharon, I mean, in terms of awareness. At least she was interested in the subject, while I stuck with the mechanics of eyeballs and lenses. I want to have good days, she said, and I agreed totally with her. And then I thought, well, Jesus, she has good days. Do I? Do I have any good days? And the answer is No, a definitive No. I'm destroyed basically, on the inside. You can say mean and rotten if you want. Good for the flowers. Good for the soil. I remember Montana, a Buddhist friend of ours, asked

*us to come and see her when she was dead. So Carl
and I went over there—we were still together then—
she was in the basement of the hospital laid out on a
metal table, twisted up like a pretzel and dead as a
door nail. She wanted us to see that, what it all comes
to, Buddhist that she was. A twisted corpse, died
in agony, looked like to us. I thought, Oh shit this
is a fucking drag, and Carl did his emotionally
overwrought thing, and I sighed and told him what a
shithole it was we were all living in and he said, Don't
think like that, Frances, and I said Fuck you I'll think
what I want, this place is a shithole and we end up like
shit. And he goes on with his pots and I go on fixing
eyeballs, like corpses are not falling into morgues,
sickened and bewildered by it all as they die. I wasn't
going to no hospital to die, and I wasn't buying any of
the bullshit that it meant anything but money in
somebody's pocket. Keep me out of those places, dear
God, wherever you are, death traps and wires and evil
bugs. But death is not so bad, you're not feeling anything
then, your worth, or worthlessness, then, to the earth or
your family or your country or any other fucking thing.
You're fertilizer now, which is at least useful.*

Carl *(On screen) I had made a new life for myself. I wasn't
going to let Frances ruin my life. I grew a beard and a
moustache to cover my pockmarks and I looked good
and felt good. I had a new girlfriend. Giselle. I had my
classes and I was making good pots. Myra was settling*

*down. She had her nasty comments and then she
dropped them. She had her bullets she had to shoot,
especially at her mother, but at me, too. I just took
it calmly and went on with my life. Then the bitch
took her pills and walked out into the city to die.
I wasn't going to let it get to me, but I started getting
headaches. I knew she did it for revenge. I knew she
was jealous and miserable and had failed. It drove
her nuts that I went out and made a new life, a happy
life. She had no idea how strong I was, as a teacher
and an independent man, and it rankled her to have to
live with that. She'd come over and climb up a tree and
scream things at me. She'd pound on my door. She'd
leave messages on my phone. Finally, she killed herself.
I thought I didn't feel anything at all. It was like there
was another person in me doing the feeling, another
Carl, while I went on with my daily responsibilities,
and that other Carl, the one with the feelings, snuck up
into my head, right there in the center at the top of my
head. The Indians say there's a hole there where the
soul escapes from the body. Finally, I had an MRI and
they said it was a clot, a blood clot in my brain. I think
it was the hidden stress, the other Carl, under a lot of
pressure and trying to get out. I fell asleep, into a
coma, and then after a while, he got out, and the rest of
me is gone back to the empty space that I always knew
was there, the space in the pots, not empty, full of air,
air and water and dust and the ghosts of the defeated.*

*She had got to me, and won. (Screens dim out. SPOTZIE
and CRAIG remain on stage.)*

17.

Spotzie   So, Craig, they got on the trains and sang the *Shema*
and kept on singing. Their spirits were high until the
end. They were the heroes. They never denied their
faith. Either they thought life was so full of meaning
that it all mattered to the end, or they thought it was so
meaningless that it didn't matter at all—either way,
both groups turned out to have the same fate. Burnt to
ashes.

Craig   This woman, Frances, she decided on her own, and then
she decided—ashes. Nothing spiritual involved, a
voluntary exit.

Spotzie   Is that a question?

Craig   Yes, Rabbi.

Spotzie   I have no answer. The earth is a spinning ball. Maybe
only a few organisms get to know anything before they
recede back into the planet. The more you look, the more
strange it gets. Don't call me Rabbi.

Craig   I blame her for trashing me to Cindy and killing Carl off
and ruining her daughter's life. On the other hand, why
not blame myself for all the passivity and blindness?

Spotzie   These people on the trains, some of them, they also
volunteered. Passive, blind. They martyred themselves,
I suppose.

Craig   I would have preferred to fight. Disease and old age come
along anyway. I'm sure Frances thought of that.

Spotzie	And the following generations?
Craig	The same.
Spotzie	No. They need to live honorably and have a good time. Breed. Remember.
Craig	I don't know if I would've fought either. I don't know what I would have done.
Spotzie	Nobody knows.
Craig	Died fighting. Shot or hanged or gassed.
Spotzie	You will never know.
Craig	What can I do, Spotz?
Spotzie	I've been thinking. Maybe go and see her, the daughter. Myra.
Craig	Good idea. I think I'll do that. I'll go see Myra.

18. (MYRA *and* CRAIG)

Craig	Hello.
Myra	Hello.
Craig	You remember me?
Myra	No.
Craig	I was Vicki's Dad. I mean, I am Vicki's dad.
Myra	You're not sure?
Craig	I'm sure. *I am.*
Myra	Her real Dad is in the wild mountains of China.
Craig	You don't know anything about it.
Myra	No.
Craig	The wild mountains of China?
Myra	Wild mountains.

Craig	We don't know anything about her birth parents.
	(*Silence*)
Myra	Vicki. Is she all right?
Craig	Yes. She's fine. And you?
Myra	I dream a lot.
Craig	Are you going to school?
Myra	Sometimes. I live with white people and I dream.
Craig	What do you dream about?
Myra	Oh, come on.
Craig	What?
Myra	Fuck off. (*Silence*) China.
Craig	You want to go back?
Myra	Not really. I don't know a word of Chinese. There are too many people there and a lot of mental illness.
Craig	Mental illness?
Myra	Yeah, you know, guys with hammers and knives and shit, and floods of people, drowning.
Craig	I see.
Myra	Are you pretending that you understand me?
Craig	No, I don't think so.
Myra	People do that. They act like they know what I'm talking about.
Craig	Do you?
Myra	Of course, but I don't think you do. I'm a writer, like you. I write down my dreams. You want to hear one?
Craig	Sure.
Myra	"And so it began, in the winter of 1945, a procession of burning women in the carriages of the Innocents, women in white, all dead, on fire, driven from Moscow and St.

Petersburg, carriages without drivers, carriages on fire, by the thousands, the hundreds of thousands, driven out of the cities, women on fire, carriages, on fire, driven from the cities to the sounds of bells and whistles, beautiful blondes, teenagers, their dresses on fire, in carriages on fire, burning, the horses of the carriages burning, as they were driven from the cities, sparks and flames shooting from the carriages, cannons, drums, whistles from hell, as the beautiful young women arrived on fire to the wilderness." (*Silence*)

Craig	Very good, Myra.
Myra	Thanks.
Craig	That was Russia, at the end of World War Two.
Myra	I know that.
Craig	What else was there?
Myra	Where?
Craig	In the wilderness?
Myra	It was China, I think. There were dragons and drums and firecrackers, acrobats and musicians.
Craig	In the wilderness?
Myra	Yes. And there was all manner of luscious foods. Real Chinese food, dim sum, cakes and whole pigs roasted in the ground. No chicken chow mein. My real father was there. He sat like a large, pudgy, smiling Buddha, a brass statue with glittering black eyes. You could hear laughter coming from the forest, or an underground cave.
Craig	I knew your father. Carl.

Myra	I know you did. We had playdates with Vicki. He wasn't my real father, of course. He was my stepfather and he was white, with marks on his face. He died, you know, from a mix-up in his brain. Blood was supposed to go someplace and instead it made a lake in his head. He never said a word after that. My real father was a fat Chinaman, in China.
Craig	And the women in white?
Myra	They became dolls, you know. You can buy them in Chinatown. They're quite nice. They have real hair.
Craig	You remember your mother?
Myra	What's that got to do with anything?
Craig	Nothing. Sorry.
Myra	She wasn't my real mother, either. She was Taiwanese-American. She adopted me.
Craig	Where is your real mother now?
Myra	She's in China, living a nice life, in an apartment.
Craig	How do you know?
Myra	I saw it on TV. It's what I do. I watch. And you?
Craig	What?
Myra	What are you doing?
Craig	Good question. I'm getting old, basically.
Myra	That's just an excuse. I think you're a spy of some kind. Yeah, I used to spy on Carl. I'd tell my mother if he was drinking wine. He had a secret stash in the cupboard above the fridge. At five o'clock. Five o'clock he'd go in there and gulp down a glass. He'd just ignore the thing on his ankle. I'd stay in the living room watching the TV. He'd come in, pretending he was normal and all, but his eyes were soft. I said, "Hi, Dad."

Then I told my mother. She'd come around outside and climb a tree and scream at him, because he wouldn't let her into the house. Finally she killed herself. He was so worried about it that his blood stopped working. So.

19. (*SPOTZIE and CRAIG*)

Spotzie   You talked to the daughter?

Craig   I did. When I left her place—it was this tiny New England town, with a church and a village green, and plane and maple trees—it all seemed odd, so I sat down on a bench and I decided I wasn't going to worry about getting home to Southern California, but sit there in the sun and be glad I was alive.

Spotzie   So you stopped worrying?

Craig   Yeah, for a minute. The sun was warm and absurd. People dying all over and a fat, crazy, over-intelligent Chinese teenager watching this little old man—me— through the curtains of the living room on the ground floor of a white clapboard house across from the green. I thought this was awfully mature because of these weird ideas I have about the Chinese, you know, that they're all smart and well adjusted. She was awfully smart and not adjusted and trusted no one.

Spotzie   Can you blame her?

Craig   No. And she was definitely nuts. And nasty.

Spotzie   What's an old guy like you doing, prowling around New England and getting lost, looking for a Chinese girl who can do very well without him?

Craig   Exactly.

Spotzie	It's because we had someone to blame for our failures, Frances the Borderline. Otherwise, all would be well. But you were living in a trance. I knew the life, too. In the old days. Smoke a joint in the morning, and so on. Then I realized there was a living God.
Craig	Oh for crying out loud, Spotzie.
Spotzie	Yeah, I'm high, high as a kite. All I have to do is breathe these days, and I'm high.
Craig	She's a terrific writer, Spotz, this kid.

20. (*On screen.*)

Frances	*For what are people, really? Worms with teeth and hair and pretension? I can hardly speak about it. Beneath contempt. Easily coerced. Dying within minutes, hours, days, years. Dying, like worms, like I say, so inevitably, they have no chance but to dream, dream that they are lions and titans and so on, whatever. Money talks, the worm talks. You have to make such an effort to be positive, or at least neutral. Not to take a negative stance, put yourself down, put the race down, put the earth down and its whole trip of flying through space like a marble. I knew people who tried, they tried as best they could, to have a good attitude and a good approach, and deny themselves, and efface their faces, and they, too, paid the exorbitant price of living. Which is pain and suffering. No point to it at all. And I am one of them, wandering in and out of the bathroom, talking to myself, hoping for the best,*

wishing for love from my child that will never come.
And what do I mean by love? Just love, like something
in the air, like electricity or light, or wind, something
coming through that gives a person reason to live. As
an organism or something in the ocean, but fuck all
that, I don't believe any of it, and I am not some
crustacean wandering on the bottom, I am a woman,
black-haired and Asian, come to the end of her fantasy.
I feel like an animated crumb jumping to life like an
electronic toy, like, like, like, so here I am, a twisted
corpse on your fucking street, fuck you. Bye. Put on
your glasses. (Dim out screen.)

21. (*Live*)

Craig   So here I am. I live alone. I'm an aging little fat man
who lives alone in a building full of old people. Women
don't look at me, or they look at me and then look
away, and they expect me to forget things and make
stupid mistakes. Like buying a first-class ticket to Paris
and then forgetting to get on the plane. I have trouble
coming home from the store because there is a little rise
before my building and my hips hurt when I climb it.
I thought it was my back, but it's my hips. Slowly I am
falling out of the whole biological system of life on
earth. It's strange, like an owl watching life pass by
from an invisible tree—a pair of eyes, otherwise
invisible, mute. But you still have to buy things and go
to the bathroom. Maintain. Frances must have seen

that, and got tired of it all, plus the disappointment with Carl and the lack of love anywhere. You see excitement and vitality but no love in the young. Frances was no longer young but she wasn't an old coot either, like me, declining out of the system. I do what I have to, I pay my bills, I maintain, I go to a meeting once and a while. I don't have to work. Frances worked but she was getting no satisfaction because her asshole of a husband aggravated her weakness, which was pride, I guess. It's strange. Herschel Spotzie's right. Spotzie's got the right idea. He's got his bathrooms in certain malls, his bed in the back seat of his car, his disability, and he tries with all his might to do no harm.

The End

The Destruction of the Fourth World

Characters

BERNARD (BERNIE)	*A thirteen-year-old*
DAVID	*His brother, thirty-one*
ROSE (ROSIE)	*Their grandmother, seventy-five*
CHRYSTAL	*David's wife, thirty*
CALEB	*The boys' father, Rose's son. Fifty-six.*
&	
COYOTE	*(Visible only as projections on the walls, or reflected in windows or mirrors)*
SCENE	*No sets or props are really necessary, except for the projections, and* ONE RED TIRE IRON.

Bernie and Caleb

(Lights up on BERNIE *and* CALEB*)*

Bernie	How do I pray?
Caleb	I don't know. Why pray?
Bernie	I can't control the ox.
Caleb	What ox?
Bernie	The one in my head.
Caleb	Why control the ox?
Bernie	He leads me to stray.
Caleb	Stray from?
Bernie	My own mind.
Caleb	Your own mind.
Bernie	You know about that?
Caleb	What?
Bernie	Straying and praying?
Caleb	I'm not sure that I do, no.
Bernie	Okay, thanks.
Caleb	I don't know. *(Pause)*
Bernie	Then why sit before me, thinking about it, leaning forward seriously like you care?
Caleb	It's my duty.
Bernie	Looking concerned and intelligent.
Caleb	You're a good kid, Bernie.
Bernie	Say something, Dad.
Caleb	I just said something.
Bernie	About prayer.
Caleb	I don't know anything about it.

Bernie	Come on, Dad.
Caleb	You figure it out.

(*PAUSE, AS THEY CHANGE POSITIONS—
minimally, but definitely and formally—in relation
to one another.*)

Caleb	You could look it up.
Bernie	That's what I'll do.
Caleb	Make it hard.
Bernie	I will.
Caleb	Make it hard on yourself. Maybe you'll find something. It's all there somewhere.
Bernie	In the books.
Caleb	In the books.
Bernie	The text. The teachings. The Laws.
Caleb	It's all there, if you search.
Bernie	That's what I'll do then.
Caleb	Because I don't know myself. I don't know the first thing.
Bernie	That's okay.
Caleb	About prayer or God. Or what, or who. You're supposed to pray to.
Bernie	Or how.
Caleb	Right. I don't have a clue. It's in Hebrew. But I know one thing. You don't do it for yourself. You don't ask for yourself.
Bernie	Or the songs?

Caleb	You sing it for others, Caleb. You sing the song for others. So they'll have rain.
Bernie	Crops.
Caleb	So they'll have good fortune. In their lives. Not only you, not yourself.
Bernie	It's for them.
Caleb	For them, not you.

(*PAUSE—THEY CHANGE POSITIONS.*)

Caleb	Bernie. Let me ask you something.
Bernie	Ask.
Caleb	You steal clothes?
Bernie	Me? I don't go out much. It's not me.
Caleb	Who is it, then?
Bernie	I can't say.
Caleb	Who steals clothes?
Bernie	I can't say, but she likes style, she likes new things.
Caleb	I know who it is.
Bernie	You knew all along.
Caleb	She's into style.
Bernie	Grandma Rosie. She forgets.
Caleb	Definitely, but it's not her.
Bernie	She gets mixed up.
Caleb	I won't mention any names.
Bernie	Chrystal?
Caleb	Your mother did it, too, before she died.
Bernie	She did?
Caleb	Not often. Once in a while.

Bernie	Where is my mother now?
Caleb	She's in the ocean.
Bernie	No, her body was in the ocean. They say there is a long line.
Caleb	Who says?
Bernie	The Hopi.
Caleb	The long line of what?
Bernie	The long line of the Dead. (*Pause*)
Caleb	Like between your mother and your grandmother?
Bernie	No. Of course not. It's a line that begins at the beginning. Grandma is still living and mama is dead. But the living one forgets everything. Not a very long line there, Dad. (*Pause*)
Caleb	She had to win, your mother. She had to be above me at all times.
Bernie	I know.
Caleb	And your Grandma is losing her memory.
Bernie	I know.
Caleb	A withering away of the branches.

(*PAUSE—THEY CHANGE POSITIONS.*)

Caleb	You buy cookies? You buy cookies?
Bernie	Yes.
Caleb	You buy cookies for the class?
Bernie	No.
Caleb	She blames me. Your grandmother.
Bernie	For Maysie.
Caleb	Who is Maysie?

Bernie	Not for the class.
Caleb	No more cookies.
Bernie	Not for the class. Just Maysie.
Caleb	No more cookies for anybody.
Bernie	Why can't you be nice?
Caleb	I am nice.
Bernie	You're not being nice.
Caleb	I'm nice to you.
Bernie	Just be nice.
Caleb	You don't have to bribe your friend with cookies.
Bernie	I'm proud.
Caleb	You don't have to be proud.
Bernie	I'll be proud.
Caleb	I don't care if you're a little proud.
Bernie	Okay, I'll be a little proud.
Caleb	But no more cookies. Let her buy you cookies.
Bernie	Can you be nice?
Caleb	Only once.
Bernie	Can I give her the cookies then?
Caleb	This once.
Bernie	Okay.
Caleb	That's all.
Bernie	Okay.
Caleb	Just this once.
Bernie	Okay.
Caleb	You'll bring them to school? The cookies? You'll bring them to school?
Bernie	Maybe I will.
Caleb	That's the only way, Bernie.

Bernie	What?
Caleb	School.
Bernie	Okay, Dad. (*Pause*) I saw her, Dad.
Caleb	Who? Maysie?
Bernie	No. My mother.
Caleb	No, you didn't.
Bernie	I saw her in a window. She was a reflection in a window.
Caleb	It's impossible.
Bernie	I'm telling you.
Caleb	What was she wearing?
Bernie	Something from the fifties or sixties.
Caleb	You're imagining things.
Bernie	You can see things from the spirit world in a reflection.
Caleb	Who told you that?
Bernie	The person's not there but their image is in the window.
Caleb	Who told you that?
Bernie	I can't say. (*Aside*) Coyote.
Caleb	Okay, Bernie.
Bernie	Okay.
Caleb	Do your homework.
Bernie	I'm doing my homework.
Caleb	That's all I can say, do your homework.
Bernie	I'm doing my homework.
Caleb	Let me see it when you're done, please.

(*PAUSE—THEY CHANGE POSITIONS.*)

Caleb	Don't hide from Dad.
Bernie	I'm not.

Caleb	Don't hide things from me.
Bernie	I won't.
Caleb	Or try to lie.
Bernie	I'm not.
Caleb	Because I'll know.
Bernie	Yeah, yeah, of course. Coyote is under the bed.
Caleb	Who is?
Bernie	Coyote. He's under the bed.
Caleb	He's under the bed.
Bernie	Right, Dad. He's under the bed and on the ceiling.
Caleb	I said don't bother to lie.
Bernie	I'm not lying. You don't have to look.
Caleb	I'm not looking. It's absurd.
Bernie	You can't see him.
Caleb	I'm talking about cookies, candy and clothes. Cookies, candy and clothes.
Bernie	Okay, Dad.
Caleb	Because I hear about that shit from your grandmother. *(Pause)*
Bernie	Were you afraid of my mother?
Caleb	Your mother is dead.
Bernie	You're afraid of my mother?
Caleb	Did you hear what I said?
Bernie	You should stand up to her.
Caleb	Who told you that?
Bernie	She told me.
Caleb	Maybe you didn't hear me? Your mother killed herself.
Bernie	You should stand up, and then I'll be proud.

Caleb	She didn't want to hear about the murder of the Jews. And I don't, either.
Bernie	I'm a Jew.
Caleb	That's right. By birth.
Bernie	What do you mean?
Caleb	Otherwise you're a complete American, like me.
Bernie	I'm not hanging around for that. I don't want to be an American. I'd rather be an Indian.
Caleb	Forget it, Bernie.
Bernie	My grandmother said I was from the Middle East.
Caleb	You're not.
Bernie	By origin.
Caleb	Your grandmother?
Bernie	Yes.
Caleb	Forget about it. And don't say you went to school if you didn't go. You lied to Grandma and you lied to me.
Bernie	I'm sorry.

(*PAUSE—THEY CHANGE POSITIONS.*)

Caleb	One more thing. Why did you complain?
Bernie	I didn't complain.
Caleb	Your grandmother calls me to tell me you complain.
Bernie	She called you? Grandma Rosie?
Caleb	Yes. So why did you complain?
Bernie	I didn't complain. About what?
Caleb	You go somewhere? And you know you're not allowed.

Bernie	I'm not allowed?
Caleb	To buy junk.
Bernie	I don't buy junk.
Caleb	I don't like the building.
Bernie	It's an ordinary building.
Caleb	No. It's depressing.
Bernie	All buildings are depressing.
Caleb	No, it's that particular building.
Bernie	What's wrong with it?
Caleb	It's a mall. And she can't control you there.
Bernie	I don't buy junk.
Caleb	What do you buy?
Bernie	I buy equipment.
Caleb	What kind of equipment?
Bernie	Electronics.
Caleb	Electronics?
Bernie	Electronics.
Caleb	She doesn't know anything about electronics.
Bernie	I know she doesn't.
Caleb	So you take advantage.
Bernie	I take advantage?
Caleb	You take advantage and then you complain.
Bernie	How did I complain?
Caleb	She won't let you buy things.
Bernie	It's my money.
Caleb	It's money she gave you.
Bernie	She gives me the money and she forgets where it is.
Caleb	I know.

Bernie	I try to buy something and she won't let me.
Caleb	It's her prerogative.
Bernie	It's my money.
Caleb	She's trying not to spoil you.
Bernie	Electronic equipment?
Caleb	Because she knows you have no mother.
Bernie	She can't remember from one minute to the next.
Caleb	So she thinks she's your mother?
Bernie	Yeah, Dad. And she isn't. She's my grandmother.
Caleb	Okay, Bernie.
Bernie	So I can buy what I want.
Caleb	I didn't say so.
Bernie	I can buy whatever I want.
Caleb	If you go to school. Only then.
Bernie	I'm done.
Caleb	What do you mean?
Bernie	I'm not going to buy anything anymore. I'm done.

(*PAUSE—THEY CHANGE POSITIONS.*)

Bernie	Please don't leave the door closed.
Caleb	I don't like the door open.
Bernie	Leave it open.
Caleb	She wouldn't like it.
Bernie	Who wouldn't like it?
Caleb	Your mother. She never liked it with the door open.
Bernie	My mother's in the spirit world now, Dad.
Caleb	Your mother is dead, may she rest in peace, but she never liked the door open.

Bernie	Why?
Caleb	Because the whole outside world could walk in.
Bernie	Was she right?
Caleb	Of course, she was right.
Bernie	Well, that's all good then.
Caleb	What is?
Bernie	You can leave the door open.
Caleb	And I still see her, I see her everywhere.
Bernie	What was it she didn't like?
Caleb	She didn't like the door open.
Bernie	No, besides that.
Caleb	Anybody could walk right in.
Bernie	Besides that, Dad.
Caleb	She didn't like complaining.
Bernie	You don't either, Dad.
Caleb	I know.
Bernie	Can you leave it open?
Caleb	The door?
Bernie	Yeah.
Caleb	Why? Are you expecting company?
Bernie	Yes.
Caleb	Who are you expecting?
Bernie	I'm expecting a friend.
Caleb	They can knock. Your friend can knock on the door.
Bernie	Okay.
Caleb	Your friend could knock on the door and then you can open it.
Bernie	Great.

Caleb	You can leave your own door open.
Bernie	Okay, thanks.
Caleb	You can leave the door to your own room open.
Bernie	I got it.
Caleb	There. I think that's a fair arrangement.
Bernie	Thanks a lot, Dad.
Caleb	The house door is closed, and your door is open. I think that's fair.
Bernie	Thanks.

(*THEY CHANGE POSITIONS.*)

Bernie	Dad?
Caleb	What?
Bernie	Grandma thinks she's in Brazil.
Caleb	I know she does.
Bernie	What are you going to do?
Caleb	What can I do?
Bernie	Maybe she should have an operation.
Caleb	They don't have that kind of operation, Bernie.
Bernie	It's very primitive there.
Caleb	That's right. Things are very primitive in Brazil.
Bernie	She thinks weird things about the building.
Caleb	This building?
Bernie	Yes.
Caleb	It's just a building.
Bernie	I know.
Caleb	So don't complain.
Bernie	I didn't.

Caleb	Don't complain about your grandmother.
Bernie	I didn't.
Caleb	Then don't.
Bernie	It's you that complains.
Caleb	Me?
Bernie	You complain all the time because she picks on you.
Caleb	I do?
Bernie	Because you're chicken.
Caleb	I'm not chicken.
Bernie	Otherwise I'd be proud.
Caleb	You should be proud.
Bernie	I'm not.
Caleb	It's because she's nuts.
Bernie	So are you.
Caleb	No, it's because she has to.
Bernie	What?
Caleb	She has to.
Bernie	What?
Caleb	She has to be above me.
Bernie	Then you should fight.
Caleb	Fight?
Bernie	No matter what. Fight back, Dad.
Caleb	I can't fight. The woman's nuts.
Bernie	Then why not fight?
Caleb	She's my mother. I can't win.
Bernie	Why can't you win?
Caleb	You don't understand.
Bernie	And she can't remember.

Caleb	Well, you never know.
Bernie	Dad? I'll keep my door closed.
Caleb	You can't keep your door closed.
Bernie	I thought that's what you wanted.
Caleb	No, that was the front door. The front door should be closed.
Bernie	I want to keep my own door closed, unless I come out.
Caleb	Why?
Bernie	I need to keep my door closed, Dad, like you said.
Caleb	What did I say?
Bernie	So the whole world doesn't come in.
Caleb	I don't remember saying that.
Bernie	The outside world.
Caleb	What about it?
Bernie	I don't want it coming into my room.

David and Caleb

Caleb	He says he saw his mother—your mother—in a window.
David	In a window?
Caleb	In the mall.
David	He was hallucinating.
Caleb	When he told me, I could see her clearly.
David	Well, you would, Dad.
Caleb	I don't know about women, David.
David	I have my problems, too, Dad.
Caleb	Without any pestering from her.
David	Which is not what my mother thought.
Caleb	Without any hysterical oppression.

David	Are you talking about Grandma?
Caleb	Without the bullshit.
David	Or are you talking about my mother?
Caleb	Definitely bullshit.
David	Dad?
Caleb	She was a secular woman with a lot of morals.
David	My mother? Sarah?
Caleb	Yes, and so am I. I'm secular. And so is everybody else, except for Rosie. Including you.
David	Rosie is a survivor.
Caleb	When she remembers anything.
David	So, what's Bernie doing with a *bar mitzvah* coming up?
Caleb	He's not doing it. He doesn't do his Hebrew homework.
David	He's into Indians.
Caleb	What's the Indians got to do with him?
David	According to him, everything else is lies.
Caleb	This his mother would approve.
David	Maybe that's why he's not doing his homework.
Caleb	She hated the survivors.
David	But that wasn't right. It wasn't their fault.
Caleb	The special pleading. The righteousness.
David	So she didn't get along with Rosie.
Caleb	No. The special pleading. Where you can't forgive and you can't forget.
David	I don't know if that's right.
Caleb	True, you don't know and I don't know.
David	I wasn't raised to be a religious… uh…
Caleb	No, you're a secular person, like we all are.

David	Still, I'm not sure. The future and the past, they mean equally nothing.
Caleb	Is that right?
David	As far as I'm concerned.
Caleb	And the present?
David	This is it.
Caleb	Tell Rosie that.
David	I don't think so.

(*PAUSE—THEY CHANGE POSITIONS.*)

Caleb	Where were we?
David	When?
Caleb	Before.
David	We were right here.
Caleb	No. I mean, what were we talking about?
David	How my mother hated the attitude of the survivors.
Caleb	Yes, and she was a Marxist, too. On top of everything else.
David	So why did she kill herself?
Caleb	I don't know why.
David	She had a lot of integrity. I remember that. (*Pause*)
Caleb	So a person can't go around stealing clothes and shit.
David	Who does that?
Caleb	I don't know, whoever.
David	Who does that?
Caleb	Whoever does it.
David	Not me.
Caleb	That's how husbands kill their wives.

David	It happens.
Caleb	You don't want to hear that voice.
David	No.
Caleb	That voice that thinks it owns you.
David	I know it. (*Pause*)
Caleb	What's your wife's name?
David	You don't know her name?
Caleb	I know her name. I just forgot for a second.
David	See a doctor, Dad.
Caleb	I just forgot. (*Silence*) Is it Chrystal?
David	Yes. It's Chrystal. My mother's name was Sarah.
Caleb	Right. Chrystal. And Sarah.
David	Your wife's name was Sarah. Now deceased.
Caleb	Of course. I know that. I just forgot.
David	How could you forget?
Caleb	What kind of name is Chrystal?
David	That's her name.
Caleb	Stupid name.
David	That's her name.
Caleb	What's up with Chrystal?
David	Nothing's up with Chrystal.
Caleb	She like her father-in-law?
David	Not really.
Caleb	What's she like?
David	She's like a girl, she's like a female.
Caleb	Meat-time in the universe.
David	What?
Caleb	I was just thinking.
David	Aloud?

Caleb	I was thinking aloud.
David	I don't know, Dad. Thinking aloud?
Caleb	So where is she now?
David	Who?
Caleb	Chrystal.
David	Why, Dad?
Caleb	We're nothing without our families.
David	She'll be home soon.
Caleb	We're abnormal. (*Aside*) I liked to sneak into her from behind.
David	What?
Caleb	It's disgraceful. I was thinking aloud. It's so cowardly and disgraceful.
David	No, that's you thinking, Dad.
Caleb	In magazines it all looks normal.
David	It's the photo, the glossy.
Caleb	Right, no scum in the photo. No stupid jism.
Caleb	The dreaded reproductive act.
David	Pretty bodies writhing like larvae.
Caleb	Hey, not bad, Dave.
David	Like larvae. Only they look nice.
Caleb	To us, Son, to us they look nice.
David	It looks nice in the magazines.
Caleb	They know how to do it, Son. They know how to make it nice and glossy.

(*PAUSE—THEY CHANGE POSITIONS.*)

David	Did you go to see Grandma?
Caleb	I'll go tomorrow.

David	Tomorrow is good.
Caleb	I'm afraid she won't recognize me.
David	It can happen, Dad.
Caleb	You went today?
David	Yes.
Caleb	What happened?

(*ROSIE is revealed upstage, sitting in a chair, facing away.*)

David	When I came in, her back was to me. She was sitting there, holding her head pensively in one hand. Just sitting there, sadly. I watched her for a second and then I went around and stood in front of her. (*Crosses to ROSIE*) She looked up at me. I said, Hi, Grandma.
Rosie	Hello.
David	I'm your grandson, David.
Rosie	Of course, you are. I'm sorry.
David	(*Aside, To CALEB*) I felt hurt that she hadn't recognized me.
Rosie	Do you have a girlfriend?
David	I'm married, Grandma.
Rosie	I heard she dresses nice.
David	Who told you?
Rosie	A little birdie told me.
David	Her name is Chrystal.
Rosie	Of course, it is.
David	Dad is going to come again tomorrow.
Rosie	Oh, good. (*Pause*)

David	How are you doing?
Rosie	Doing?
David	Yes.
Rosie	I'm very busy with issues.
David	Issues?
Rosie	The Germans. You know, many of them settled here after the war. War criminals. Murderers. They found refuge.
David	Where is that, Grandma?
Rosie	Where?
David	Where.
Rosie	Brazil, Argentina. Other places in America. They created problems for the working class, of course, especially here in Rio.
David	I see.
Rosie	My whole family vanished. I'm the only survivor.
David	I know.
Rosie	Sometimes I feel like jumping out the window, like that Chinese fellow.
David	Who is the Chinese fellow?
Rosie	But I think I have another family here in America.
David	You do.
Rosie	So I don't want to hurt them by committing suicide.
David	That's good, Grandma.
Rosie	I don't know if that's good or not.
David	I think it's good.
Rosie	Well, that's good.
David	My Dad will be here tomorrow. Caleb.
Rosie	Oh, yes. I know someone named Caleb. It's a biblical name, isn't it?

David	I believe so, yes.
Rosie	I went to Berlin, to the Jewish Museum, after many years of denial. And I came out shriven and released. We had survived, after all, in spirit, like the oxygen in the air and the water and in us. Could you follow that, Boy?
David	I think so.
Rosie	Well, I'm glad you came to see me. It was good talking to you.
David	I love you, Grandma.
Rosie	Take care.
David	You, too. (*Crossing back to* CALEB) She said she had some work to do, which I knew was a lie.

Bernie and Caleb and David

Caleb	So, listen up. We'll have to come up with a plan.
David	A plot?
Caleb	A plan.
David	Why?
Caleb	To keep an eye on my mother.
David	Why? She's not going anywhere.
Caleb	Your brother and me and maybe your wife, Chrystal.
David	Rosie's not going anywhere.
Bernie	I don't think so.
David	She's already there.
Bernie	In Rio.
Caleb	How old are you?
David	I'm thirty-one.
Caleb	Not you, Bernie.
Bernie	I'm thirteen.

Caleb	That's old enough.
Bernie	I'll stay in my room, if you don't mind.
Caleb	I do mind.
David	You can't do that.
Bernie	Shut up, David.
David	You can't do that.
Bernie	I'll stay in touch. I'll talk on the phone, I'll e-mail every day. I'll text.
David	That's not the same.
Bernie	Not the same as what?
David	Don't play those tricks on me.
Bernie	What tricks?
David	Questions on top of questions. Stop right there.
Bernie	I'm done.
Caleb	No going back, now. We're committed.
David	From where? Where'd we go?
Bernie	We didn't go anywhere.
Caleb	From the principle.
David	What's the principle?
Caleb	It's the principle of humiliation.
David	Which is?
Caleb	Thou shalt not be brought to tears by your son.
David	When?
Bernie	Dad?
Caleb	While you're washing the dishes.
Bernie	That's not what we were talking about.
David	We weren't talking about that.
Caleb	While you're disciplining your child.

Bernie	I don't have a child.
Caleb	Brought to tears in your ladies apron.
David	It's true, I wash the dishes. (*Aside. To* BERNIE) He needs to see a doctor.
Bernie	You need to see a doctor, Dad.
Caleb	Get your gun and we'll shoot the motherfuckers.
Bernie	Who?
David	The women?
Caleb	No, the swells on their thoroughbreds in their fine boots.
Bernie	Dad, we weren't talking about that.
David	He's got a point there, though.
Bernie	You're watching a movie, Dad. You're in a movie.
Caleb	So what?
Bernie	And you are too, David.
Caleb	Okay, you know what I mean. Relax. We blow the fuckers off their horses. Excuse me. (*Exits*)
David	What was that?
Bernie	We're sitting here talking and he goes to the movies.
David	What is that?
Bernie	I don't know what that is.
David	I think it's brain malfunction.
Bernie	Too many movies. And why do you go along with it?
David	It's fun. Give the guy a break why don't you?
Bernie	Get him to a doctor.
David	No, you do it.
Bernie	No. You do it.

Caleb

(I'm not in plastics. I'm a chemistry and biology teacher. But you have thousands of these creatures, they want to have money, so they manufacture a hundred million plastic machines that will never disintegrate for eternity. In other words, they'll be here with God at the end of time. That's pretty much all I know about God. When the Messiah comes, which is the King of Israel, the plastic will be here with him. That's all I know about the Messiah. But do I really care? About plastics? About God? About the Messiah? Do you? When we can go to an alternative reality, as my boys say, as my mother does? To Rio de Janeiro? Or as my wife did, into the ocean, even if my son says he sees her once in a while? I don't know. I'm only asking. What do you think, if you ever think? Obviously, I need help. I'm sorry, I didn't mean to insult you. That was the last thing I wanted to do. They'll never get me to a doctor. Not a chance. I don't believe in doctors. On the other hand, my mother said she'd never set foot on German soil, and then she went to the Jewish museum, in Berlin. So, you never know. Oh, here's Bernie.)

Bernie and Caleb

Bernie	Dad?
Caleb	I was talking to myself.
Bernie	You do that.
Caleb	I know I do. I'm aware of it.

Bernie	That doesn't make it okay.
Caleb	What's so wrong with that?
Bernie	Only crazy people do it.
Caleb	That's your opinion.
Bernie	You should pray.
Caleb	Why?
Bernie	It's a better alternative.
Caleb	I don't know how to pray.
Bernie	Look it up in the Sages.
Caleb	No, you look it up. You're supposed to be the Bar Mitzvah Boy.
Bernie	I'm not. I quit.
Caleb	Manhood is on its way.
Bernie	I'm postponing manhood.
Caleb	Until?
Bernie	Until the Messiah comes, as you say.
Caleb	I never said that.
Bernie	Anyway, it's postponed.
Caleb	That's for sure.
Bernie	I know one thing. You be sincere. You put your heart into it.
Caleb	But it's not for yourself.
Bernie	Right. That's what the Indians say.
Caleb	It's true. I agree with them.
Bernie	You always say that.
Caleb	I still say that.
Bernie	Pray for the Messiah to burn away the plastic.
Caleb	I don't know how.
Bernie	And pray for your mother.

Caleb	I don't know how.
Bernie	And pray for your wife.
Caleb	I don't know how.
Bernie	Who lost herself into the currents of the ocean.
Caleb	God bless her.
Bernie	Say Lord have mercy.
Caleb	Lord have mercy.
Bernie	Otherwise there's no hope.
Caleb	There's no hope. Lord have mercy on my wife, my dear wife.
Bernie	She's in the spirit world.
Caleb	Maybe she's in the spirit world. I think she was eaten by the fishes.
Bernie	She's in Brazil, Dad, with Grandma.
Caleb	Is that a joke?
Bernie	I'm sorry. I didn't mean to make a joke.
Caleb	Maybe she is in Brazil, for all I know.
Bernie	Was she mean to you?
Caleb	What do you think?
Bernie	I think she was.
Caleb	I brought it on myself.
Bernie	How did you do that?
Caleb	That's what she would say. She'd say, Oh? How do you do that?
Bernie	What did she mean?
Caleb	She meant Jerk, she meant, you're a jerk.
Bernie	Why a jerk?
Caleb	Because I'd make these statements of over-certainty.
Bernie	I never heard that word before.

Caleb	It's when you say something that's overly sure of yourself.
Bernie	Oh, yeah, you tend to do that.
Caleb	Yeah, like I brought it on myself with my pride. Like I just figured out what parenting is. Or, I got that about Aristotle. I thought so at the time. Finally. He was an observer, Aristotle.
Bernie	Maybe you did get it.
Caleb	Yeah, a one word analysis. She'd say, Oh, really, how did you do that?
Bernie	No reason to break up a family.
Caleb	I agree with you. But who could live with false bravado? (*Pause*) You seen her lately?
Bernie	I only saw her once at the mall. One time.
Caleb	At the mall?
Bernie	In the window at the mall, like I told you. I don't go anywhere now.
Caleb	We miss her, God knows, with all her positive opinions.

Bernie and David

Bernie	Dad is having problems. He stands there, he forgets why he's standing there.
Bernie	Take him to a doctor.
David	What's a doctor going to do?
Bernie	Maybe they have drugs.
David	For sure they have drugs.
Bernie	So take him.
David	He won't go.

Bernie	You have to make him go.
David	You do it.
Bernie	You have to trick him into it.
David	First you have to leave your room.
Bernie	I'm not leaving my room.
David	Okay. Forget it.
Bernie	Why did Mom kill herself?
David	I don't know. Why are you changing the subject?
Bernie	I'm saying, maybe it was Dad?
David	Don't say that.
Bernie	I said it already.
David	No, I think it was the murder of the Jews.
Bernie	It's a fatal error in the brain. The earth's brain. Not some little German idiot's brain.
David	Can we stay on the same subject?
Bernie	This is the only subject.
David	She couldn't stand it. She thought the world was a death machine.
Bernie	Well, that makes sense to me. Rosie stays alive because she won't be defeated. She wants to win.
David	We lost already. We lost forever. We got on the trains. One-third of the genes. (*Pause*) People as smart as you, Bernie. Thousands. Why don't you go out lately? Why?
Bernie	It's shitty out there. Everybody is pretending. I don't want to see their faces.
David	You have to go to school. (*Pause*) Every day.
Bernie	I don't think so. I have everything I need right here. (*Pause*) It's funny about the disease.

David	What disease?
Bernie	That Grandma has and Daddy's getting. Forgetfulness. I have an idea. Grandma, she still has the feelings connection. But she loses the mental connection.
David	The context.
Bernie	It has nothing to do with all the bullshit that's been written or read. The paradigms and synapses and MRIs.
David	You're a prodigy.
Bernie	She loses association and context.
David	A genius. (*Pause*)
Bernie	Fire.
David	Fire?
Bernie	She's lost fire. Fire in the sense of combustion, oxygenation.
David	I take it back, Bernie. You're nuts.

Caleb and Rosie

Caleb	I've been meaning to tell you, Mom. I've been having my own problems.
Rosie	Issues?
Caleb	Issues. Memory issues. I seem to lose my train of thought sometimes.
Rosie	Trains. Evil.
Caleb	I forget the names of things.
Rosie	Do you read Hebrew?
Caleb	No.
Rosie	Anyway.
Caleb	It's quite frightening.

Rosie	I know it is. I think it's poison. Poison got into the earth somehow. Poison chemicals and gases. I was telling someone about it.
Caleb	Bernie. Bernard.
Rosie	Yes, they'll have to burn it off, cleanse the earth.
Caleb	My other son—
Rosie	Of course he is. That would be David.
Caleb	No, Bernie.
Rosie	Of course, Bernie.
Caleb	There's a big difference in age between them, so it confuses people.
Rosie	I know I could be confused.
Caleb	I'm confused myself sometimes.
Rosie	Is he the Bar Mitzvah Boy?
Caleb	Yes, Bernard.
Rosie	Good for Bernard. Make sure he studies.
Caleb	I will. I mean, there's some resistance there.
Rosie	Resistance?
Caleb	Never mind.
Rosie	He's an angel and he should sing like one. He'll join the other angels. I saw them on the walls of the Jewish Museum. They couldn't defeat us because they're only animals, bugs and things.
Caleb	I don't think they want to hear about this anymore, Mom.
Rosie	Who doesn't?
Caleb	The Germans. Maybe you and me, too.
Rosie	I wouldn't let them in.
Caleb	Excuse me?
Rosie	I wouldn't let them in here.

Caleb	Okay.
Rosie	Without a ticket. (*Laughs*) And you watch out. Watch your step.
Caleb	I'll bring Bernard.
Rosie	Keep an eye out.
Caleb	I will.
Rosie	The fucking murdering idiots. Who cares what they think?
Caleb	I'm just wondering, does he take you to the mall?
Rosie	Who?
Caleb	Bernie, your grandson. He take you to the mall?
Rosie	It sounds like it.
Caleb	Do you forget to pay?
Rosie	For what?
Caleb	For items, like clothes, you forget to pay?
Rosie	I must, mustn't I? How humiliating! But it goes to show you, doesn't it, nobody is playing with their own money in the first place, that's why all this stuff at the mall is so odd, don't you think?
Caleb	All right, Mom.
Rosie	It's like monopoly money!

Bernie

(I had a dream. I was riding a little scooter. The scooter was about the size of my hand. Tiny. You made it go by pressing a button that was attached with a wire. I had to put it down somewhere to go on foot. I think it was to shop in a handicrafts area. So I put the little

contraption down—that is, my scooter—on a shelf
somewhere, and when I looked for it again, I couldn't
find it! I panicked. I had lost my little scooter! Wherever
I looked for it was—a place of business owned by
beautiful young black women! Oh, how I loved them,
but they ignored me, or didn't see me, and I never found
my scooter. This tells you all you need to know about
me and the Author.)

Caleb, Bernie, David

Caleb	Here we are, me and both my sons.
Bernie	And the earth is shaking its booty.
David	The earth is shaking its booty?
Bernie	We're in a tremor?
David	We're in an earthquake?
Bernie	Are we going to fall into a hole?
Caleb	I don't think so. It's shake, rattle and roll.
David	That wasn't funny.
Bernie	The earth is shaking off the white bugs with clothes.
David	You scared me.
Bernie	Shaking out the bugs.
David	We're the bugs?
Bernie	We're the bugs.
Caleb	That's a good example.
David	Of?
Caleb	Annoying misstatements of half-truths.
David	That's you, Dad, in a nutshell.
Caleb	Don't say nutshell.
David	Nutshell.

Caleb	It's bad grammar.
Bernie	Nutshell?
David	No, shaking off the white bugs with clothes.
Bernie	He meant the earth shaking off the humans.
David	I know it.
Bernie	With hurricanes, earthquake and tornadoes.
David	Fire and flood.
Bernie	Drought and sinkholes.
David	Starvation.
Bernie	Cyclones. So get ready for the Fifth world.
Caleb	What does that mean, Bernie?
Bernie	Sorry. It has no meaning.
David	It's another typical example.
Caleb	Of what?
David	An over-statement. You got it from him.
Bernie	Sway and pray and bow and praise. It's the Jewish religion in a—
Caleb	Nutshell?
Bernie	Thanks, Dad.
David	Pray to what? The Sun? The Solar System? The Universe?
Caleb	Pray to the silence and the void.
David	That makes no sense at all.
Caleb	Help others, help others!
David	Even if a human being is a piece of shit?
Caleb	In America you're even less than that.
Bernie	You're a bag of chemical soup!
David	Oh that's good.
Bernie	Only because it makes you feel better.
Caleb	And you can pay off the debt you owe for your stupid existence.

David	Okay, how?
Caleb	If you go to meetings and donate soup and admit your failings, and help the homeless and the lonely and the mad, then you can save your souls.
Bernie	I can't do that, Dad.
Caleb	Why not?
Bernie	I don't have a soul.
David	I can't stand the stench.
Bernie	I don't like people.
David	I'm not interested.
Bernie	I have other things to do.
David	I'm trying to believe in something real.
Bernie	Actually, I don't believe in anything.
Caleb	You're not trying anything and you have no idea what's real.
Bernie	So what?
Caleb	So you should both shut up about trying and believing and real.
Bernie	I have a test tomorrow.
Caleb	How can you have a test if you don't go to school?
Bernie	I take it on the Internet.
David	You're turning into a recluse.
Bernie	Call it whatever you want.
David	You're turning into a recluse. I'll go and visit Rosie in Rio.
Bernie	There is no Rio.
Caleb	There is no Rosie.
David	Rosie is in Rio!

Bernie	Right down the street in Assisted Living is our Grandma Rosie, either in Rio or Buenos Aires.
Caleb	Maybe we should all go.
Bernie	It's too crowded.
David	It's too crowded?
Bernie	There's just all this biology running around trying to make more biology. I don't know if I can stand it.
David	That's a totally different subject.
Caleb	I agree with you there, Son.
David	That was a totally different subject!
Bernie	It's true.
David	It had nothing to do with Assisted Living.
Bernie	True, except maybe in Rio it does.
Caleb	I see what you mean, David.
David	That's good.
Caleb	Nothing to do with Assisted Living.
David	Even though an act of kindness brings you to tears.
Caleb	It's true. I cry.
David	And it's not even real, it's on television.
Caleb	Television?
David	You know, where you see sweet people helping each other.
Caleb	You never see that in life. Not in this country.
David	So we got that straight, Dad.
Bernie	That's why I'm not going to school or to the mall anymore.
David	You're not? Ever?
Bernie	No. Never.

David	Go and see your mother. She asked for you.
Caleb	She remembered my name?
David	"My oldest son."
Caleb	I'm her only son. And she's in Brazil. It's too far.
David	She's in Assisted Living.
Caleb	I don't want her not to know me. It hurts.
David	Actually, I don't know if I want to go anymore.
Caleb	So why ask me to go?
David	I don't know why.
Caleb	Talk to Chrystal.
David	What does Chrystal have to do with it?
Caleb	She'll tell you.
David	She'll tell me what?
Caleb	About your mother.
David	She'll tell me about my mother?
Caleb	Yes.
David	What?
Caleb	I don't know what. And ask her about the clothes.
David	The clothes?
Caleb	She wears nice clothes. Outfits.
David	What's the question there?
Caleb	I don't know what the question there is.
David	Oh. Where does she get the clothes?
Caleb	In the mall.
David	In the mall?
Caleb	In the mall.
David	Okay.
Caleb	She goes to the mall, she gets the clothes.

David	Okay.
Caleb	And maybe she pays for them. But it's Rosie who walks out with the clothes.
David	Rosie?
Caleb	Yes, she's a kleptomaniac.

David and Chrystal

David	Chrystal.
Chrystal	What?
David	You look great.
Chrystal	Thank you.
David	Chrystal.
Chrystal	What is it?
David	Nothing's wrong. He asked me to ask you.
Chrystal	Who did?
David	My father.
Chrystal	So, ask.
David	Who am I?
Chrystal	Don't start.
David	About my mother?
Chrystal	What about her?
David	I have no idea.
Chrystal	Yes, you do. She left.
David	Maybe she killed herself.
Chrystal	She did.
David	Why?
Chrystal	She was an idealist.
David	Did you ever talk?
Chrystal	Of course we talked. We did dishes. We did laundry.

David	What did she say? About the situation.
Chrystal	What situation?
David	Our situation. The human situation.
Chrystal	That it was based on murder and it was getting worse. Because there's a limited amount of water, and a limited amount of land, so people are gong to kill each other for it. Okay? (*Pause*) Stalin made a deal with Hitler and sold out the Jews.
David	So why was she mad at the Jews?
Chrystal	Because they were ashamed of themselves, because they felt disgraced, because they had an ancient, proud tradition. And they couldn't protect it. And no one helped them. But it happens all the time. People get it into their heads to slaughter their neighbors. But you knew all this already David, so it's annoying to have to explain it to you.
David	But it's not so simple.
Chrystal	No, it's not. That's why you better keep an eye on Bernie.
David	On Bernie?
Chrystal	Bernie.
David	Which brings me to another question.
Chrystal	What is it?
David	It's the strangest thing.
Chrystal	You want to eat?
David	Not right now. Maybe later. You look great.
Chrystal	You said that.
David	I don't know what he meant.
Chrystal	Who?
David	My father. Caleb.
Chrystal	About?

David	Women.
Chrystal	We bleed.
David	You bleed?
Chrystal	That's what he means. About women.
David	That's what he meant?
Chrystal	I think that's what he meant.
David	Who doesn't know that?
Chrystal	Well, what else could he mean?
David	He means dangerous.
Chrystal	Dangerous.
David	He means women are dangerous.
Chrystal	I don't think that's what he means.
David	That's what he means. That's why he's strange. He means dangerous.
Chrystal	I don't think so. Unpredictable.
David	Unpredictable.
Chrystal	No. Dangerous. It is what he means. You're right.
David	Dangerous.
Chrystal	For him. That's his experience. They've left him. They've left him alone in a dangerous situation, where the world is falling apart. They've gone mad, and they've killed themselves. And he's alone. Don't you see?
David	Yes, I do.

Bernie and Caleb

Caleb	What's up? So, what's up?
Bernie	What's up?
Caleb	Sky's up.
Bernie	You always say that.

Caleb	I'll stop.
Bernie	I'm doing homework now.
Caleb	What's the homework?
Bernie	Algebra. It's Algebra. X's and Y's. I like it.
Caleb	I liked it, too, when I was a kid.
Bernie	That's good.
Caleb	You miss your mother?
Bernie	Yes.
Caleb	So do I.
Bernie	I figured, or you wouldn't have asked.
Caleb	What do you miss?
Bernie	I miss her smell.
Caleb	Yeah. I miss her smell.
Bernie	You don't know where she is?
Caleb	Her bones are in the ocean. They'll be recycled. (*Enter David*) Yes. She'll be in the air eventually.
Bernie	She's in the Land of the Dead. (*Pause*) She left a note.
David	We know that.
Bernie	You want to hear it?
David	Again?
Bernie	You want to hear it again?
Caleb	Go ahead.
Bernie	I know it by heart. I'll recite.
Caleb	Recite.
Bernie	Here it goes: "I wanted to say something in my own behalf. After all, I have a right to speak, though I live between worlds, the world of the seen and the world of the unseen." (*Pause*) You wanted to comment, David?
David	No. Proceed.

Bernie	"The world of reflection in windows, of glances in mirrors, quick cuts in movies, and other magical illusions. Clearly, my views of life and the premises—
David	Principles.
Bernie	"Principles of living that I accepted when I was alive were not romantic. So it's impossible to have a tragic view. Things happen and no one is to blame."
David	Except you yourself. Sorry.
Bernie	"We are meant to breathe air and drink water. To eat well and be intelligent and not to go on murderous rampages. I saw the destruction of the Fourth World coming and decided to drown in the water."
David	Someone told her that.
Bernie	Coyote.
David	Who is Coyote?
Bernie	Never mind.
David	Where is he?
Bernie	He's here. (*Pause*) You can't see him.
David	He doesn't exist. Get it over with, Bernie.
Bernie	"I had believed in Reason and a just scientific re-orientation of the world. These principles turned out to be false, and those people selling them turned out to be self-serving idiots and clowns. This is a message for my sons: Believe in nothing and keep an eye out for Coyote, for that will be the beginning of the End. He is the signal you are to watch for. Your loving mother, Sarah." (*Silence. Exit CALEB*)
David	Now you did it, Bernie. (*Pause*)
Bernie	I have seen Coyote.

David	I haven't.
Bernie	You'll never see him with the eyes you have on.
David	I see with my own damn eyes.
Bernie	Sure you do.
David	The eyes of a grown-up.
Bernie	*Mazel tov.*
David	What happened with your *bar mitzvah?*
Bernie	What happened?
David	What happened, Bernard?
Bernie	Nothing happened, David.
David	Okay.
Bernie	Okay is right.
David	Okay.
Bernie	And nothing is going to happen.
David	Fine with me.
Bernie	Fucking thing is in Hebrew.
David	I know.
Bernie	It's a language I don't understand.
David	*Baruch atah.* It means blessed art thou.
Bernie	I know what it means.
David	That's Hebrew.
Bernie	I know what *Baruch atah* means.
David	That's all they do is praise.
Bernie	Who's that?
David	The Jews. They stand up, they bow, they praise God, they sit down, they murmur more praise.
Bernie	There are not enough Jews in the world.
David	Not funny.
Bernie	There are not enough, and I have a solution.
David	What's the solution?

Bernie	It's a one-state solution. The Jews and the Arabs in one state.
David	Talk to Dad.
Bernie	Why?
David	He's a Zionist member.
Bernie	What does he know? He doesn't know anything about it.
David	It's a radical solution you're suggesting.
Bernie	One state. And we'll be brothers with the Arabs.
David	I'm telling you, he won't go along with it.

Caleb and David

David	In the synagogue, they praise God. The rest of the time, they complain.
Caleb	It's singing. What's wrong with singing?
David	I don't like the praise, and I don't like the complaints.
Caleb	Who are you?
David	Good question.
Caleb	You like and you don't like.
David	Actually, I lied.
Caleb	Who doesn't lie?
David	Everybody lies. Why? There's a substance in the brain.
Caleb	There's a substance in the brain.
David	There's a substance in the brain, it has trouble.
Caleb	There's a substance in the brain, it has trouble.
David	It has trouble with reality. So it says things.
Caleb	It has trouble with reality. So it says things.
David	Stop repeating me.
Caleb	Through the mouth.
David	It's a sin, a substance in the brain that lies its ass off.

Caleb	Excuse me. What is this substance?
David	It's a kind of plaque.
Caleb	Plaque?
David	So you see hate, for example, instead of love.
Caleb	That was your mother. That's what she saw.
David	Is she loved now, Dad? Who loves Sarah now?
Caleb	Sarah is in another world, where love doesn't matter.
David	Which world is that?
Caleb	Brazil?
David	You never been to Brazil.
Caleb	I saw the movie. That's all I need to know. Every day she looks at the horizon and she thinks about her soul.
David	How do you know?
Caleb	I know because I know. She did that here in New York City.
David	She looked at the horizon and thought about her soul?
Caleb	Yes. She wonders: Do I have a soul, and where does it go?
David	Why the horizon?
Caleb	Because it's round, and because it meets the sky. So you get a sense of the infinite.

(*PAUSE—THEY CHANGE POSITIONS.*)

David	I can't believe in God if he's in such deep shit all the time.
Caleb	Well said.
David	He like can't do anything about anything.
Caleb	That's why I asked you.
David	About?

104

Caleb	Prayer.
David	Well, there's your answer.
Caleb	"Maybe you should better yourself and forget about God."
David	That's Rosie talking.
Caleb	"Maybe it's you, not God."
David	Me?
Caleb	Yeah.
David	What can I do? Can I make a new world? Can I reverse time? Can I bring back the dead?
Caleb	"So, pray. Pray for forty hours with no food or drink or rest." That's Rosie. "Prepare. Sit down. Suffer. Maybe you'll make something of yourself."
David	Benedictions from Grandma. May she find immortality.
Caleb	Amen.
David	There on the horizon, in Rio. In the world of Assisted Living. (*Pause*) So there's no *bar mitzvah* for Bernie?
Caleb	No. He won't come out of his room.
David	I don't blame him. And if he talks to my mother again, I want to hear about it.
Caleb	Why? You believe Bernie is channeling your mother?
David	No.
Caleb	Then what?
David	Whatever it is. I just want to hear about it.

Bernie and Caleb

Bernie	Dad?
Caleb	What?
Bernie	I think there should be a one-state solution.

Caleb	I don't think so, Bernie.
Bernie	So why don't they do it?
Caleb	They don't like each other. They hate each other. They kill each other.
Bernie	That's ridiculous. What are we alive for?
Caleb	You're asking me?
Bernie	What are we doing here?
Caleb	I don't know.
Bernie	It's ridiculous.
Caleb	What do you want from me?
Bernie	Do something. Say something. There should be one state for Arabs and Jews. Everybody equal.
Caleb	Don't tell me. Tell the world.
Bernie	I'll do it now. I'm writing. The idea is to go fast. I'm writing now. (*Thinks*)
Caleb	Are you done?
Bernie	No. (*Thinks*)
Caleb	Are you done?
Bernie	Give me a minute why don't you?
Caleb	Okay, you done?
Bernie	I'll say what I have. "There's different kinds of love. There's love of the family, which is one kind of love. Like when my grandmother went to the Jewish museum, she saw all the families, and she imagined all the arguments. And the love of one's people, which she also saw there, in herself. There's romantic love, like my love for my mother, Sarah, which has some fantasy in it, and biology."
Caleb	Are you finished?
Bernie	No. "And then there's a bigger love, Love in general, a kind of Universal love."

Caleb	That was good.
Bernie	Thank you.

(*PAUSE—THEY CHANGE POSITIONS.*)

Bernie	I'm feeling very suspicious of what you just said, Dad.
Caleb	So am I.
Bernie	Because it should also include the paramount question. I meant to say "permanent."
Caleb	Which is?
Bernie	What are we doing here?
Caleb	Praise God.
Bernie	And?
Caleb	Serve God.
Bernie	And?
Caleb	Obey God.
Bernie	And?
Caleb	That's enough. I'm tired.
Bernie	What is this God?
Caleb	He has no beginning and no end.
Bernie	And me? What kind of material?
Caleb	You or God?
Bernie	Both.
Caleb	I'd say both.
Bernie	Both what?
Caleb	Same kind of material. Some coarse, some fine. Some you can't see, some you can. Sunlight is made of particles.
Bernie	I had a beginning. I was a thought in someone's eye.
Caleb	You were an impulse in someone's body. Mine, probably.
Bernie	People have to eat.

Caleb	Correct.
Bernie	They eat fish. They ate all the fish. They eat animals. They ate all the animals.
Caleb	Good. You did good.
Bernie	What did I do?
Caleb	You did good. Good writing.
Bernie	Usually you have behavior. He drinks, he smokes, he hits, and so on.
Caleb	And?
Bernie	Here we have no behavior.
Caleb	Fine and good.
Bernie	No behavior.
Caleb	Okay, Son. Okay. No behavior.

Rosie and Caleb

Rosie	Hello, this is Rosie.
Caleb	Hello, Mom!
Rosie	Hello.
Caleb	Hello, hello.
Rosie	So what's up with you guys?
Caleb	Marriage and school and school and marriage. What else? And you?
Rosie	Me, I'm in Rio, I'm experiencing life for others.
Caleb	That's what you did here, am I wrong?
Rosie	Wrong.
Caleb	How am I wrong?
Rosie	There, I did my duty. Here I serve.
Caleb	What can I say?
Rosie	Don't say anything.

Caleb	You're all right?
Rosie	I'm perfect.
Caleb	Perfect?
Rosie	Certain things are the same, I'll have to admit. It's the same human body, it's just the same, only worse. That's why I left the states.
Caleb	Say again?
Rosie	Flesh and blood idiots. Teeth and tongues and toilets.
Caleb	You thought you could get away from that?
Rosie	No, only my own genes.
Caleb	You brought them with you. I have the same or different genes.
Rosie	I knew you like the back of my hand. I'm sick of the back of my hand.
Caleb	You're sick of me.
Rosie	I'm sick of you.
Caleb	I'll hang up now, if you don't mind.
Rosie	How can you blame me?
Caleb	I don't blame you.
Rosie	Even you don't like being you. Definitely, though not all the time.
Caleb	Nobody does anything all the time.
Rosie	There is no same state for long.
Caleb	That's what I mean.
Rosie	You can't do anything all the time.
Caleb	That's what I said.
Rosie	So what reminds you of?
Caleb	Of?
Rosie	Never mind.
Caleb	I know—a same state solution.

Rosie	That's ridiculous. That's absurd.
Caleb	One state for Arabs and Jews.
Rosie	Forget about it.
Caleb	It's Bernie's idea.
Rosie	Don't blame Bernie.
Caleb	Hang up, why don't you?
Rosie	One-state for Jews only.
Caleb	Hang up.
Rosie	The others can go ahead and die.
Caleb	I'll hang up now.
Rosie	No, I think I will.
Caleb	Go ahead. Go.
Rosie	Bye.
Caleb	I'll call you.
Rosie	Call. See if I care.

Chrystal and David

David	The other rule is, you don't say the name of G-d. You say G-d with a dash. Or you say, *Shem*. The name.
Chrystal	God has a name?
David	In Judaism, He has a Name.
Chrystal	This must only be for the Gentiles.
David	Excuse me?
Chrystal	His Name.
David	No, never mind.
Chrystal	I mean the dash.
David	You're not supposed to say the Name.
Chrystal	That's fine.
David	That's all I mean.

Chrystal	Fine and good.
David	And no interpretation.
Chrystal	No interpretation?
David	No interpretation.
Chrystal	It's because people have limitations.
David	It's beyond limitations.
Chrystal	What do you mean?
David	You should talk to my grandmother.
Chrystal	I have talked to your grandmother.
David	They're like incomplete beings, cells in a larger structure.
Chrystal	What is?
David	I take that back.
Chrystal	You can't take it back.
David	Why can't I take it back?
Chrystal	Because you already said it.
David	You mean it's written?
Chrystal	It's written down in the Book of Life.
David	Amazing, Chrystal.
Chrystal	It's like with predestination. People say that after it's already happened.
David	Maybe you should explain.
Chrystal	People say it had to happen after it already happened.
David	I don't know if I got that.
Chrystal	I talked to your mother, too.
David	When was this?
Chrystal	She used to sit in the mall while I shopped. She'd sit on the edge of the bench in her dark glasses, eyes half-closed.
David	She watched the creatures.
Chrystal	She watched and she despaired.

David	She knew what they were thinking. She could hear their greed.
Chrystal	She'd see a *kippa* and want to throw something.
David	"Don't be holy in front of me," she'd say.
Chrystal	"I know you," she'd say.
David	"You're in a state of self-righteousness."
Chrystal	On the other hand, she could smell an anti-Semite at a hundred yards.
David	You don't have to go far in a mall.
Chrystal	"I'm not interested in buying anything," she'd say. "It's all cheap shit."
David	Isn't that depression? Isn't that classical depression?
Chrystal	I think it is, actually.
David	I think it is. (*Pause*)
Chrystal	What is this larger structure you were talking about?
David	I believe it's life on earth.
Chrystal	"Either vermin or angels."
David	What angels?
Chrystal	Your mother would say.
David	What's the difference?
Chrystal	Angels take care, vermin eat and then they eat again.
David	It's all about reproduction, my mother said, and fertilizer.
Chrystal	Right. And all kids think they have a right to live.
David	My brother won't come out of his room.
Chrystal	He has to come out. He'll fuck up his life.
David	Get Grandma Rosie to come home.
Chrystal	No. You do it.
David	Okay, I'll do it.
Chrystal	Call her.
David	Okay.

Chrystal	On her cell.
David	I'll do it.
Chrystal	Do it now.
David	Okay, in a minute.

(*THEY CHANGE POSITIONS—A MOMENT LATER—THE CALL.*)

David	Hello, Grandma.
Rosie	Who is this?
David	You know me, Grandma.
Rosie	So say your name why don't you, what could it hurt?
David	It's David.
Rosie	I know why you called.
David	Tell me why I called.
Rosie	You called for your father, Caleb.
David	No, I didn't.
Rosie	How is your father?
David	You should call him.
Rosie	I'll call him.
David	Call him. (CHRYSTAL *gets on another phone.*)
Chrystal	Hello?
Rosie	Who's this?
Chrystal	This is Chrystal.
Rosie	What happened to the other one?
Chrystal	The other one?
Rosie	On the phone. He was a man, I believe.
Chrystal	That was David.
Rosie	David?
Chrystal	My husband. He's still on.

Rosie	You called for your husband?
Chrystal	I have to admit.
Rosie	Where is he? He's hanging by the phone?
Chrystal	He's hanging on the other phone.
Rosie	Say hello and tell him to take three steps back.
Chrystal	Hello and three steps back. (DAVID *takes three steps back*.) Okay, he did it.
Rosie	So what's the matter?
Chrystal	Bernie won't come out of his room.
Rosie	How do you know?
Chrystal	We look at his room. The door is closed. He won't come out.
Rosie	Oh.
Chrystal	This isn't the first time.
Rosie	Oh. He's not going to school?
Chrystal	And it won't be the last.
Rosie	I see.
Chrystal	You're not worried?
Rosie	Why should I worry?
Chrystal	It could be a sign of mental illness.
Rosie	Are you crazy?
Chrystal	Not me, him.
Rosie	The whole planet is nuts and you bring up Bernie?
Chrystal	You have a point.
Rosie	The earth is having a fit, a fever and a conniption. Guess why?
Chrystal	It's because of us humans.
Rosie	Congratulations.
Chrystal	That's why Bernie won't come out of his room.
Rosie	I don't blame him. Why should he?

Chrystal	And you won't come home.
Rosie	I'm in Rio. It's too far to travel.
Chrystal	You're not in Rio.
Rosie	Says who?
Chrystal	A bird told me.
Rosie	Fuck the bird.
Chrystal	Come on, Rosie.
Rosie	Why should I?
Chrystal	You're needed. We need you here.
Rosie	That's nice.
Chrystal	Seriously.
Rosie	Here, I'm working with the poor. They have some common sense. They know who their enemies are. By you, they believe anything and get it all mixed up with God. God forbid.
Chrystal	It's true. Here I'm attending to complete strangers.
Rosie	That's what I heard. They don't know which end is up.
Chrystal	I know, believe me. But I hear it's just as bad in Rio.
Rosie	Crazier than Brooklyn?
Chrystal	Yeah.
Rosie	I think so, too.
Chrystal	Well, there you go.
Rosie	I don't think so. I think I'll stay.
Chrystal	You might as well be here.
Rosie	No, thanks. I don't go anywhere and it's a bad situation. We're lucky we're not eating each other yet.
Chrystal	That's what I meant.
Rosie	No, it isn't.
Chrystal	There's earthquakes, tsunamis, torpedoes—I mean, tornadoes—fires and hurricanes.

Rosie	But don't explain too much.
Chrystal	I won't.
Rosie	The earth has bugs and we're the bugs.
Chrystal	I hear you.
Rosie	My own mother used to say.
Chrystal	I'll call again soon.
Rosie	Good.
David	I'll talk to her. Let me talk to her.
Chrystal	David wants to talk to you.
Rosie	Who?
Chrystal	David. Your grandson.
Rosie	So, talk.
David	Hi, Grandma.
Rosie	Hi Honey. I heard there's insanity going around.
David	You heard right.
Rosie	Kill them all and then kill yourself.
David	Excuse me?
Rosie	I said, kill them all and then kill yourself.
David	That's what I thought you said.
Rosie	It's the only solution. Myself, I couldn't stop shooting. People have yellow plaque on their brains. And fungi on their toes. And tumors in their lungs. I could go on and on.
Chrystal	Get off the phone, David.
David	But I have to get off now, Grandma.
Rosie	I got the picture.
Chrystal	I want to talk to her for a minute.
David	Here's Chrystal.
Rosie	Thank you, Chrystal.

Chrystal	You're welcome!
Rosie	Good-bye and good luck!
Chrystal	You too!
Rosie	It's a pleasure!
Chrystal	Me, too!
David	What did you want to say to her?
Chrystal	Just a minute.
David	Say it already!
Rosie	Who is yelling there?
Chrystal	Your Grandson, David.
Rosie	Tell him to shut up.
Chrystal	Shut up, David. Okay where was I?
Rosie	I'm in Rio and you're in Brooklyn. So far so good.
Chrystal	I've been meaning to ask you.
Rosie	Yes?
Chrystal	When you go to the mall, who takes you to the mall?
Rosie	The mall?
Chrystal	The mall.
Rosie	No one.
Chrystal	No one?
Rosie	No one takes me. Anymore.
Chrystal	Okay, if by any chance they do take you, remember.
Rosie	What?
Chrystal	You have to pay.
Rosie	No, I don't.
Chrystal	Why not?
Rosie	They are capitalist pigs and they owe us our very lives, that's why.
Chrystal	Okay, I'm sorry I brought it up.

Rosie	Put your son back on.
Chrystal	He's your grandson, Rose.
Rosie	Put him on.
Chrystal	He's my husband.
Rosie	So put him on already.
David	Hello.
Rosie	Listen, have a baby. You remember how to do that?
David	Sure, Grandma.
Rosie	Otherwise, keep your mouth shut.
David	Good-bye, Grandma.
Rosie	Good-bye.

David and Chrystal

David	You call that a conversation?
Chrystal	Yes, what do you call it?
David	There are no words.
Chrystal	I thought it was a wonderful conversation.
David	It was not rational.
Chrystal	Since when are you so rational? You're an anxiety neurotic.
David	What does that mean, exactly?
Chrystal	It means you're in a state of anxiety. Did you take your pill?
David	I'll take it now.
Chrystal	Good. You'll calm down and feel normal.
David	What about Rosie?
Chrystal	She's not gonna calm, I mean come.
David	Why not, I wonder?

Chrystal	Come on David, she's in Rio, it's too far.
David	The fanatical Marxist.
Chrystal	At least we know where the clothes are.
David	Where are they?
Chrystal	Where, I don't know.
David	You just said you know.
Chrystal	I mean in "Rio." How did they know it's this family?
David	My father's card.
Chrystal	Your father has a credit card?
David	That's all I can think of. My father has a card.
Chrystal	And for your information, David, I pay for my own clothes.
David	With your own card, I presume.
Chrystal	Correct. It wasn't me, David.
David	I'm not saying it was just you, obviously. I have a card.
Chrystal	You have a card?
David	Of course I have a card. And you have a card.
Chrystal	Think of this: No more money. No more goods. No more nothing.
David	That was a thought?
Chrystal	That was the beginning and ending of a thought. No more money, ending with no more nothing.
David	What's in the middle?
Chrystal	The middle is to make money on money—extreme capitalism.
David	I'm not even going to comment on that.
Chrystal	Okay.
David	That's what I do, obviously. I'm in the top one percent and so are you.

Chrystal	I'm so happy, I can't stand it.
David	Good.
Chrystal	Meanwhile, your brother Bernie has packed it in.
David	He's on the Internet. He doesn't have to go anywhere. The chickens come home to roost.
Chrystal	They have to go somewhere.
David	They're running around in his head.
Chrystal	I thought you were a nice guy, David.
David	I am.
Chrystal	What happened?
David	Everything's out of control.
Chrystal	Meaning?
David	People can't remember and can't think straight.
Chrystal	They never could.
David	It's gotten worse.
Chrystal	It's always been the same.
David	You have to have educated people in a democracy, not consumist idiots who can't spell.
Chrystal	That's not a word, consumist.
David	Consumer, okay?
Chrystal	It's true. People don't know much, but they never did.
David	Why not?
Chrystal	They're animals.
David	So we let them vote?
Chrystal	Idiots will take us to war and take our money, too.
David	Thank God we live in a democracy, Chrystal.
Chrystal	Where the idiots aren't taking us to war?
David	I can't argue with that, honey.
Chrystal	So this conversation is nearly over?
David	It is as far as I'm concerned.

Chrystal	Wait for a tornado, David.
David	What does that mean, wait for a tornado?
Chrystal	Wait for a tornado.
David	What does it mean?
Chrystal	To sweep you into the sky.
David	Sweep?
Chrystal	Vanish.
David	Okay, Chrystal.
Chrystal	Into the sky.
David	Thanks.
Chrystal	In the wind. A big wind. Over the rainbow.
David	What is going to be the answer to this situation?
Chrystal	I don't know. Who made the wind? Was it Job? I mean, God?
David	Nature made the wind.
Chrystal	Nature made the wind and we made the velocity.
David	I don't disagree with you.
Chrystal	You don't?
David	No.
Chrystal	The Hopi had it right.
David	The Hopi had it right.
Chrystal	So it doesn't matter—Rosie in Rio, Bernie in his room.

Caleb and Bernie

Caleb	So what are you doing in there all day and all night?
Bernie	I'm connected.
Caleb	To what are you connected?
Bernie	I got computer software variations, video games, TV, radio, plus an iPod and a cell phone. I can do everything

	from here that a person could do from anywhere else. There's no reason at all for me to leave this room except to burn down the neighborhood.
Caleb	Excuse me?
Bernie	Just a thought, Dad.
Caleb	That's the thing, you're thinking too much.
Bernie	I'm not thinking. I'm planning, I'm looking, I'm listening, I'm figuring it out.
Caleb	That's not thinking?
Bernie	Call it whatever you want.
Caleb	Maybe you should do some real thinking.
Bernie	You're contradicting yourself again, Dad. *Otra vez.*
Caleb	You can see that a normal human teenager doesn't stay in his room all the time. Only prisoners do that. On death row.
Bernie	That was good, Dad.
Caleb	You can't stay in your room all the time. That's final. You have to go to school. You have to go out and play. You have to help your Dad.
Bernie	I'll help my Dad from here. The rest you can forget about.
Caleb	How do you figure that?
Bernie	By phone and by e-mail and so on.
Caleb	I'll call the police.
Bernie	Go ahead. I'll stay in jail.
Caleb	I'll call an ambulance.
Bernie	I'll stay in the hospital.
Caleb	You can't stay in the hospital.
Bernie	Why not?
Caleb	Hospitals kill you. And there's nothing wrong with you.

Bernie	I see and hear Coyote, often.
Caleb	Except in the head.
Bernie	It's what they call a *mitzvah*, Dad. Only the sublimely gifted can see Coyote.
Caleb	You don't say?
Bernie	I just said.
Caleb	I'm your father.
Bernie	There's nothing wrong with that.
Caleb	That's not what I meant.
Bernie	What did you mean?
Caleb	You have to do what I tell you, and if you don't—
Bernie	What?
Caleb	I'll kick the shit out of you.
Bernie	Sure, you will.
Caleb	You heard me!
Bernie	You haven't raised your voice in anger in thirteen years. Now you'll start? I don't think so.
Caleb	You never know. But you better listen to me.
Bernie	Or?
Caleb	I'll kick the shit out of you and I'll take away your toys, that's what! I'm your father! (*Stands*)
Bernie	Where are you going?
Caleb	I'm not going.
Bernie	Then why are you standing near the door?
Caleb	I'll sit down again, because I'm not done.
Bernie	Sit down, why don't you?
Caleb	I have more to say here. I have a tire iron.
Bernie	You have a tire iron?
Caleb	I have a tire iron.
Bernie	Everybody has a tire iron. In their car.

Caleb	I keep it near me at all times. (*Reveals a red tire iron, the only actual prop in the play, and swings it like a club.*)
Bernie	Dad, can we take a break?
Caleb	Sure we can take a break.
Bernie	Go out and come back later.
Caleb	Okay, let's say I did that and now I'm back, we'll take a pause and start over. (*Pause*) Of course, it's all quite mysterious. She drowned, you know, your mother. Sarah. She drowned.
Bernie	I know.
Caleb	It's a good way to go. We'd talked about it often. You swim out into the ocean until you get tired and then you keep on swimming, and swimming, and then it's too far, you've gone too far and you can't make it back, and you're so tired, it's easy to let it go, so you let go.
Bernie	I used to dream about that.
Caleb	What was the dream?
Bernie	I can't remember exactly. Only, I couldn't save her, mainly.
Caleb	Let's take another break.
Bernie	Okay. (*Pause*) The tire iron, Dad?
Caleb	I'd just like to point out, I don't think it's a conscious intention, of course, it's more a subconscious intention, which is much more important and consequential. I'll tell you one thing that happened. I wanted to go armed. I mean, I wanted to arm myself. The idea began occurring in my mind—while dozing, or waking up in the morning, the sense of wanting to be armed, with a stick or a club, even a gun. I ended up using a tire iron.

I keep it near me at all times. I know that if I'm attacked, I'm going to use it, I'm going to beat my attacker to a bloody pulp. (*Pause*)

Bernie Should we pause?

Caleb This may have some relevance to your ideas about the Jewish State, but I'll tell you one thing: I will always be armed with this tire iron.

Bernie Thanks, Dad.

Caleb I'm leaving now. I can't stay in this one room so long. And you can't, either. (*Exits. Enter* COYOTE's *image, projected on a wall.*)

Bernie

Coyote leers at the audience. He is a Hopi Black
Arabian Jew.
You have turned everything to shit, he says,
And you blame it all on me!
The hell with you! (COYOTE *disappears from the wall.*)

Caleb and Rosie

Caleb Bernie won't come out of his room.

Rosie Who can blame him? America is ugly and mean.

Caleb Who's talking about America?

Rosie It's full of devils and I'm never coming back.

Caleb Devils? You believe in devils?

Rosie Of course I believe in devils and demons and God knows what.

Caleb Only America is ugly and mean?

Rosie	No. The whole world is ugly and mean.
Caleb	You believe in Coyotes?
Rosie	I don't believe in Coyotes. Coyotes are dogs. Dogs are dogs.
Caleb	Bernie has a friend who is a Coyote. (*Silence*) Okay. Did you hear what I said?
Rosie	When?
Caleb	A minute ago.
Rosie	What?
Caleb	Bernie won't come out of his room.
Rosie	Maybe he needs a break from people.
Caleb	That's what he says.
Rosie	Maybe it's true.
Caleb	What if he comes out of there with a gun or a knife?
Rosie	Why would he do that?
Caleb	I don't know. I told him I had a tire iron, which I do.
Rosie	That's good.
Caleb	I don't know if it's good.
Rosie	Then why are you asking? (*Caleb sighs*) What's the matter?
Caleb	Nothing. (*Silence*) I do have one. (*Silence*) When Sarah died I had a violent paranoid streak.
Rosie	I'm sorry to hear that, but it's entirely your own fault. (*Caleb sighs*) What's the matter now?
Caleb	Nothing, Mom.
Rosie	People have forgotten their ideals, their responsibilities to the working class.
Caleb	I agree with that.
Rosie	Good.
Caleb	People just want to buy things. Made in China, of course. By Chinese.

Rosie	You could send them to Harvard, whatever, the London School of Economics, but they're still Chinese.
Caleb	I don't know if I got that, Mom.
Rosie	What is it with this Coyote?
Caleb	He's a figure.
Rosie	I thought he was an animal.
Caleb	He's a legendary figure.
Rosie	Like Stalin, the Man of Steel.
Caleb	Not really.
Rosie	Me, I live in Rio, where the animals are animals and there are no men.
Caleb	He'll come out of there and open fire or start a fire.
Rosie	Stalin?
Caleb	No, Bernie. (*Sigh*)
Rosie	Where do the dogs come into this?
Caleb	Coyotes. He has a friend named Coyote.
Rosie	He talks to his friend, Coyote?
Caleb	So he says.
Rosie	That can't be all bad. Only divine intervention can help us now.
Caleb	He'll burn the place down, Mom.

(VOICE OF COYOTE: *A fire will go around the earth. The earth's crust will burn to a cinder.*)

| Rosie | And then what? What? What? What? |

(VOICE OF COYOTE: *The earth will burn. The atmosphere will evaporate. Nothing will live. Including Brazil, where the water is going fast and the trees are burning. And these assholes continue lying and leering while they burn down the forests.)*

Rosie	All right, I'll talk to him, whats-his-name.
Caleb	Bernie.
Rosie	I'll talk to him. And his friend, too.
Caleb	Coyote.
Rosie	I'll talk to him, too.
Caleb	You can't see him. He's invisible.
Rosie	Good. It's just as well.

Rosie and Bernie, and Caleb

Rosie	Only divine intervention can help us now.
Bernie	Should I pray?
Rosie	Pray.
Bernie	I don't know how to pray.
Rosie	Get down on your knees and get ready to die.
Bernie	Is that prayer, Rose?
Rosie	That's all I know. Don't call me Rose.
Bernie	That's not prayer.
Rosie	It's either that, or join the Party.
Bernie	The Communist Party?
Rosie	You heard me.
Bernie	All right. I'll do that.
Rosie	Go for a walk.
Bernie	A walk?
Rosie	I said go for a walk.
Bernie	No.
Rosie	No?

Bernie	I'll tell you what, Grandma.
Rosie	What?
Bernie	I see devils.
Rosie	Devils? Who told you that?
Bernie	They look like American people, but they're not.
Rosie	I understand.
Bernie	They're stupid and mean.
Rosie	That's not devilish. That's us.
Bernie	Well, they're trying to trick you, so they can go to the store. They want to buy stuff.
Rosie	Well, you seem friendly enough, and young.
Bernie	It's Bernie, Grandma.
Rosie	And I know you'll do everything you can to help the unfortunate, which is all of us. (*Enter* CALEB)
Bernie	You don't recognize me, Grandma, but I love you.
Rosie	Yes, I can feel that you do. Likewise, I'm sure.
Caleb	Hi.
Bernie	Here's my Dad.
Rosie	Yes, I feel like I know you as well and that you are a very good person. You probably take good care of the people around you.
Caleb	Thank you. This is Bernie, remember, the kid who stays in his room?
Rosie	Yes, and this must be his room. Bernie, I heard you stay in your room a lot.
Bernie	I do. All the time, actually.
Rosie	Why?
Bernie	I have everything I need here.
Caleb	Electronics. He has a lot of equipment in his room.

Rosie	What if he has to go to the bathroom?
Caleb	He has his own bathroom.
Rosie	Don't you need to go to school?
Bernie	No.
Rosie	You seem young. Don't you need friends your own age?
Caleb	He has contacts.
Rosie	Contacts?
Bernie	Certain forces of nature, as represented by the Hopi Prophecy, and a legendary figure named Coyote.
Rosie	The happy what?
Bernie	It's hard to explain.
Rosie	Of course it is. I had a visitor recently who had a lot of equipment.
Caleb	Cameras.
Rosie	She had come a long way to see me.
Bernie	All the way to Brazil. (*Laughs*)
Rosie	What's funny about that?
Bernie	I'm sorry.
Caleb	That was Mrs. Jonah, Mom, an old friend of yours.
Rosie	Yes, I recognized certain qualities in her.
Caleb	She's making a documentary, about survivors.
Rosie	Oh, yes, I am a survivor. I don't know if that was good or bad, and you don't either. Thank you both for coming.
Caleb	I'll take you home, Mom.
Rosie	You're very nice. I have a lot of work to do at the moment. Soon as I get there. To prepare.
Bernie	To prepare?

Rosie	You know, flyers, meetings, e-mails, the whole gamut. Organization is the key. Try to remember that.
Caleb	Let's go, Mom.
Rosie	Bye, bye.

Rosie

(Here in Rio. They don't look at you in the eye. They look at the sidewalk. They jiggle their money. They're thinking bad things about themselves or others. They want to have a good time. They like to watch television and go to a ballgame. They're interested in sex. That is, for fun, more than reproduction. They drive their cars into each other and enjoy the noise. They want to survive. They fear their own nonexistence. I wanted to explain about the Jewish Museum, how my mind was changed at that time, and I felt happy for the Jews, how we had not been slaughtered in vain, how History was alive in some way. It was seeing the pictures of the children, and the books, and the wisdom of the Fathers. I know there are those who don't believe me and don't want to hear about it. I know from my own experience. The Germans, they don't want to hear about it. Myself, I said I would never go to Germany. But then, in my old age, I saw with my own eyes how my mind could be changed. My own mind.)

Bernie and David

David	You were saying, what happened in the dream?

Bernie	I wasn't doing anything or saying anything. (*Silence*)
David	So, Bernie?
Bernie	They don't realize they're alive, they think they're going automatically to heaven. Is that right?
David	That's what you've been saying.
Bernie	I was only asking, is that true of them? What Coyote says?
David	I don't know. How would I know?
Bernie	You can't not know. You know, or you don't know.
David	Forget it.
Bernie	I'm not looking. (*He looks out over the audience.*)
David	Don't let them see you do that. Look at me.
Bernie	Okay.
David	Look at me.
Bernie	I'm looking at you. (*Pause*) I have a question.
David	Go ahead.
Bernie	What do you mean by heaven?
David	According to the Gentiles, it's where our Father lives.
Bernie	Dad?
David	No, Bernie, I think they mean, God.
Bernie	What about us?
David	Us?
Bernie	Do we go to heaven?
David	For us it's not so automatic.
Bernie	What do we have to do?
David	We have to be nice. On Yom Kippur we pay our dues. We apologize. We atone.
Bernie	I don't get it.
David	Me, neither.
Bernie	You're supposed to be a teacher.

David	I don't teach theology. I should, but I don't. I have lost faith.
Bernie	What is heaven? What does it mean? It's absurd. (*Pause*) And then you got these other ones making bombs to blow people up. They go to heaven, too?
David	I don't know, Bernie. You figure it out.
Bernie	That's what Dad said, too.
David	He doesn't know either. We have failed.
Bernie	He doesn't remember my name half the time.
David	I know.
Bernie	I'm his son. He calls me you.
David	He calls me Bernie. He might go to hell because he can't remember our names.
Bernie	That's not funny. This is serious.
David	Is that why you stay in your room?
Bernie	People are blowing themselves up with bombs.
David	You didn't answer me.
Bernie	What was the question?
David	Can you tell me what she said? Mom. Can you tell me what she said? Come on, Bernie. You told Dad you had a dream about Mom.
Bernie	I did.
David	Tell me what she said in the dream.
Bernie	She said the Indians had it right.
David	What did they have right?
Bernie	They had a lot of things right, David.
David	What did she say?
Bernie	"They didn't bury their dead, because they would contaminate the earth."
David	And?

Bernie	"They didn't burn their dead because they would contaminate the air."
David	Oh, so what did they do?
Bernie	"They put them on scaffolds in the sky so the vultures could eat them." I was dreaming. The dreamer doesn't say things. My main idea was we should have one country, Palestine. But I didn't speak it. She said, "They won't have water or air." One country with Arabs and Jews together. I thought: "What could be wrong?" She said, "Don't burn the oxygen out of the air." (*Silence*) Are you being nice because you might want me to come out of my room?
David	Who said anything about coming out of your room?
Bernie	No one.
David	Look this way. Good. I have to go now. I have a wife. Speaking of whom, she'll give you a call soon.
Bernie	Well and good.

Bernie and Chrystal

Bernie	Chrystal?
Chrystal	Yes, yes, yes?
Bernie	It's nice to speak with you.
Chrystal	Hello, Bernie.
Bernie	Hi, Aunt Chrystal.
Chrystal	Oh, that's nice. Hi.
Bernie	Hi.
Chrystal	Actually, I'm your sister-in-law.
Bernie	Exactly.

Chrystal	Nice talking to you.
Bernie	I know.
Chrystal	I was wondering.
Bernie	What?
Chrystal	You want to go to a ball game?
Bernie	Oh, God, no.
Chrystal	Why not?
Bernie	Too many people and too many cars. And the garbage is a foot deep.
Chrystal	How about a concert?
Bernie	What kind of concert?
Chrystal	Classical?
Bernie	No.
Chrystal	Rock 'n' roll?
Bernie	No.
Chrystal	Jazz?
Bernie	No.
Chrystal	Punk?
Bernie	No.
Chrystal	What kind of music do you like?
Bernie	The kind I can listen to in my room. Here, I have total freedom of choice.
Chrystal	It's also social. It's also about being with other people. Concerts. Events.
Bernie	I don't want to be with other people, obviously.
Chrystal	Don't you want to be with your Aunt Chrystal?
Bernie	You can visit me.
Chrystal	You can visit me, too.
Bernie	I said it first.

Chrystal	You could come to my school.
Bernie	I don't go to schools.
Chrystal	Why not?
Bernie	They're out of control. You know how it is with like a *dreidel*?
Chrystal	I'm not sure.
Bernie	Are you Jewish?
Chrystal	You know I'm Jewish.
Bernie	You're a convert.
Chrystal	True. The best kind of Jew is a convert.
Bernie	So you know what a *dreidel* is. You spin it and eventually it wobbles. The earth is spinning but not quite at the right rate, so there's a glitch in the rotation. Could you follow that?
Chrystal	I think so.
Bernie	The way you can tell that is in the schools. No one knows how to be because the spin is out of control. So there's no ideal and the hierarchy is out of whack. In these kinds of situations, the cosmic forces have to re-do the situation from scratch.
Chrystal	That's a fantastic theory.
Bernie	Well, you can believe it or not, it's up to you. Because all things are connected.
Chrystal	Of course they are.
Bernie	So, you see what I mean?
Chrystal	I think I do, yes.
Bernie	Why I stay away from the schools.
Chrystal	Where did you learn about this, if you don't mind my asking? (*Silence*) Don't tell me if you don't want to.

Bernie	From the Hopi.
Chrystal	Are they Indians?
Bernie	They're Native Americans.
Chrystal	That's what I meant. You have time for another question?
Bernie	What's the question?
Chrystal	What does this all have to do with fire?
Bernie	Who told you about fire?
Chrystal	Your brother, David.
Bernie	He doesn't know anything about it.
Chrystal	That's why I'm asking you.
Bernie	Fire is oxygen combining with other elements to create heat and light. And rust.
Chrystal	Is that why you want to burn things?
Bernie	Who said I wanted to burn things?
Chrystal	I don't know. Somehow I got that idea.
Bernie	There's all kinds of ideas sloshing around in people's heads.
Chrystal	Like what?
Bernie	Like the amount of oxygen is always the same.
Chrystal	Isn't it?
Bernie	No. The higher you go the less there is.
Chrystal	What are you doing all day long?
Bernie	I have everything I need, right here in my room. I study, I watch things, I talk to my friends. I play video games. I'm like any normal teenager.
Chrystal	Bernie, come out of your room and go to a real school.
Bernie	No.
Chrystal	If you're such a normal person, act like a normal person.
Bernie	Okay, I'm not normal.

Chrystal	Yes, you are.
Bernie	No, I'm not.
Chrystal	You have a window?
Bernie	A window?
Chrystal	In your room.
Bernie	Of course.
Chrystal	Good.
Bernie	What are we talking about now?
Chrystal	I don't know. You lost me, or I lost you.
Bernie	Come on over, we'll play something on my digital electrics.
Chrystal	What?
Bernie	You know, music or a speech or an opera.
Chrystal	Okay, Bernie.
Bernie	Anytime.
Chrystal	I will do that.
Bernie	Okay, I'll see ya.
Chrystal	So long.
Bernie	Thanks for calling, Aunt Chrystal.

Caleb and David

Caleb	The sins of the fathers.
David	What does that mean, the sins of the fathers?
Caleb	I'm not sure. It sounds right.
David	The sins of the fathers. Where is that written?
Caleb	I don't know. I never learned where things were written. Somewhere in the Bible. Your grandfather, he came to

America in 1905, he never learned a word of English. All his life he was illegal.

David So?

Caleb That must mean something. On the other side, Rosie was the only one to come over. She lost everybody. Not a single relative survived. (*Silence*) They are gone forever.

David Is that why Bernie wants to burn things down?

Caleb No. I don't know. Why don't you have a kid?

David I don't want to.

Caleb You won't procreate?

David No. Something is passed down, it has consequences for generations. You have these German kids now, I wouldn't be surprised if they had problems, like autism.

Caleb You could look it up on the Internet. (*Pause*) Excuse the expression, but your brother is an idiot.

David Yes, the genius Bernie who wants to burn things down. I'll say it again, the fuckin' idiot is a fucking idiot.

Caleb And you, you won't have children, and you walk around with a yarmulke, and you have no idea why you do or what it means.

David Okay. What does it mean?

Caleb It's so birds don't shit on your stupid head.

David Thanks, Dad.

Caleb Don't mention it.

(*PAUSE—CHANGE OF POSITION.*)

Caleb	It's like Rosie says. Half-assed so-called human beings shitting on their own world.
David	So what did you think was happening?
Caleb	I don't believe in anything. I believe in nothing.
David	You repeated yourself.
Caleb	I don't give a shit.
David	Neither do I. They're not rapturing US up.
Caleb	So what's the plot?
David	What's the plot?
Caleb	What's the plot?
David	You mean the theory?
Caleb	Yes.
David	The plot is that some Christian people are planning to ratchet up to the heavens, and I don't think they're taking us with them.
Caleb	Explain it to me again, how does this affect the State of Israel?
David	The State of Israel is told about in the Bible.
Caleb	This I know already.
David	Because of the war over there, the time has come for these people to be catching the train to heaven.
Caleb	Oh.
David	Well, it's not a train.
Caleb	What is it?
David	We've reached the limit, Dad, of my understanding.
Caleb	And this is why Bernie wants to burn things down?
David	I don't know why Bernie wants to burn things down, maybe his grandfather never learned English and chased

after women. Like you said. And this is why he won't come out of his room.

(*PAUSE—CHANGE OF POSITION.*)

David   Why, I really don't know, but he lost all his relatives on his grandmother's side by their being shot in the head and suffocated by gas and hung from the rafters and strangled and starved to death, and so on. The unspeakable. So, there's a possible reason. (*Silence*)

Caleb   Who goes first?

David   You mean, like Abbott and Costello?

Caleb   No, idiot.

David   You mean, Which crazy person goes to heaven first and where?

Caleb   Yes. Bingo.

David   Wait a minute.

Caleb   Why?

David   I have to catch my breath here.

(*PAUSE—CHANGE OF POSITION—A MOMENT LATER.*)

David   Well, you lost me there, Dad.

Caleb   I was only thinking. (*Pause*) The stealing could definitely be Rosie. Each day she goes more into Brazil. (*Silence*) Yes, you want to say something?

David   The sad thing is the connection between Chrystal and me.

Caleb	Who could blame her?
David	I don't blame her.
Caleb	She's not Jewish.
David	She is Jewish. She's more Jewish than I am. That's why people should stay together.
Caleb	I didn't get that.
David	That's why people should stay together.
Caleb	I still don't get it.
David	Because all that misunderstanding happens.
Caleb	Hopefully, you will stay together.
David	You and Mom didn't.
Caleb	No. She may have had a brain disorder. Sarah.
David	You don't know?
Caleb	We never found her. Maybe she got raptured.
David	I don't think so.
Caleb	Just a joke. Bad joke. Very bad joke.
David	I'm not laughing, Dad.
Caleb	I was a dedicated teacher, like you. Biology, chemistry. Then the respect went out the window and into the streets. I fell into a bad mood of various dimensions. For Sarah, it was a sign of the end of all things to come. (*Pause*) Shut the door, David.
David	Why?
Caleb	I don't know why I said that.
David	It's okay.
Caleb	Leave it open. You were here at the time. You heard the news.
David	It was hard to hear.

Caleb	Then I had to stand there feeling my teeth in my mouth, my feet aching on the floor and a lump of emotion in my chest I could do nothing about.
David	It's grief. We have no control over grief.
Caleb	Like Bernie, I was afraid to leave the house.
David	Maybe some people have control.
Caleb	No one has control.
David	Chrystal says I have no emotion.
Caleb	You have no emotion so you have plenty of control?
David	That's what she says. So I must be dead. I think I'm dead.
Caleb	You're not dead. She should get pregnant, that's all.
David	She can't get pregnant, Chrystal.
Caleb	Excuse me, but do you have intercourse?
David	None of your business, Dad.
Caleb	Excuse me for asking.
David	None of your fucking business.

Bernie and Rosie

Bernie	Grandma?
Rosie	What?
Bernie	I was trying to explain.
Rosie	What?
Bernie	This happens.
Rosie	This happens?
Bernie	Yes. (*Silence*)
Rosie	So, what happens?
Bernie	This.
Rosie	Bernie, don't talk to me if that's how you talk.

Bernie	A mega-volcano could erupt and destroy us all.
Rosie	Let it erupt.
Bernie	You're a misanthrope.
Rosie	What's that?
Bernie	You don't like people.
Rosie	Neither do you. What's to like?
Bernie	Seventy-five atomic bombs could go off.
Rosie	Why seventy-five?
Bernie	I don't know why. Do you care?
Rosie	No and yes.
Bernie	You can't say no and yes.
Rosie	Yes, I can. I'm in agreement with the Hopi, like you. I saw the end of mankind.
Bernie	In the camps?
Rosie	In the camps, and in your basic human stupidity. People don't understand anything, least of all each other. So it's a failure. The whole *megillah*. It's a failure.
Bernie	A few miles down, you come to hot magma.
Rosie	I know. That's what I said.
Bernie	Hot magma?
Rosie	Definitely.
Bernie	You're a smart grandmother, Grandma.
Rosie	Definitely. I was in a concentration camp when I was twelve. Angels were being prepared there for a life in heaven.
Bernie	Somehow I don't feel like I've explained myself successfully.
Rosie	That would be right, my boy, you haven't.

Chrystal and David

Chrystal   He plays with matches.

David   Who does?

Chrystal   Your little brother Bernie, for burning. He's out of his little "berning" mind.

David   He had the highest intelligence test score in his class.

Chrystal   What test?

David   I don't know what test. It was a smart test.

Chrystal   He's so smart, he won't come out of his room?

David   He's sensitive. Generations of rabbis came before him.

Chrystal   How do you know?

David   Intelligence is a wonderful thing.

Chrystal   Sure, if the brain is attached to the body.

David   Rabbis were in Poland since the fifteenth century. Rosie's family was into horses. It was the Ukraine in those days. They bought and sold horses near the town of Pinsk.

Chrystal   Where is that?

David   Ukraine, I think. They kept changing the borders.

Chrystal   Ultimately, we're all Jewish.

David   No, we're not. Tell me, what do you like so much about being Jewish?

Chrystal   It's simple, lots of rules, 24/7, remember who you are and what you're here for. You don't have to think too much.

David   What do you think about getting together?

Chrystal   How is that question related?

David   It's a commandment: Be fruitful and multiply.

Chrystal   I don't think so at the moment.

David	Maybe later?
Chrystal	I don't care if he never comes out.
David	Who is that?
Chrystal	Bernie. Bernard.
David	Did you hear what I said?
Chrystal	Especially not with matches or a lighter.
David	You didn't hear me.
Chrystal	I heard you. The answer is no.
David	Why?
Chrystal	Don't take it personally.
David	How can I not take it personally?
Chrystal	There are too many fucking people in the world already.
David	Kiss me, at least.
Chrystal	I'll kiss you, but that's as far as it goes.
David	Kiss me here.
Chrystal	All right. I'll kiss you there, too.
David	Thank you.
Chrystal	Don't thank me.
David	I take it back.
Chrystal	Don't take it back. Be quiet.

David

David	And then I submitted. She said "relax" and I relaxed. I felt the warmth of Mother Earth and the love of a woman. Things were all right for a couple of days after that. Then, to gratify her, I gave up all pork products, and after that, I separated milk from meat, and refused to eat the two together on the same plate, a kosher decision which made Chrystal happier still.

146

Caleb and Rosie

Rosie   You start with nothing and you end with nothing and nothing's in between.

Caleb   Motherhood?

Rosie   Maybe motherhood.

Caleb   Some people are just glad to be alive.

Rosie   Don't start.

Caleb   Breathing air.

Rosie   *Mazel tov.*

Caleb   Not six feet under.

Rosie   More power to them.

Caleb   Alive! Alive! Be happy!

Rosie   It's okay with me. *Zei gezunt.*

Caleb   Enjoy the moment!

Rosie   And now it's gone.

Caleb   It's so interesting.

Rosie   No, it isn't.

Caleb   The difference in attitude.

Rosie   It could just be an IQ test. You're my son, but I'm smarter than you. You got cheated on half the genes.

Caleb   I'm not that stupid.

Rosie   Let me ask you something.

Caleb   Ask.

Rosie   Why did you turn her to ashes?

Caleb   Who did I turn into ashes?

Rosie   Sorry. What's her name, your good wife, as you call her?

Caleb   Sarah. She was a good wife.

Rosie   It's against the Jewish religion.

Caleb   What is?

Rosie	To burn people.
Caleb	She wanted to be burned. She thought burning was good. In India, they're going up in smoke. But we never found her, actually.
Rosie	It's not a good idea, this burning.
Caleb	It's a totally different religion there.
Rosie	I don't care. I'm totally against it.
Caleb	We never found her, Mom, I just told you.
Rosie	Sarah?
Caleb	Yes. We never found her body. So there was nothing to burn.
Rosie	What do you do with the ashes?
Caleb	They're in a box, usually.
Rosie	And where do you put the box?
Caleb	The box is kept in a crypt.
Rosie	And where is the crypt?
Caleb	The crypt is in the cemetery.
Rosie	I've thought if over, I want a regular Jewish funeral.
Caleb	You've thought it over about cremation?
Rosie	Yes, but I'm against it. It doesn't seem right in this place.
Caleb	In the camps, of course, they had ashes.
Rosie	That's correct. Former human beings.
Caleb	I'm sorry I said that.
Rosie	Why? It's the truth. What do they do with the ashes here?
Caleb	Some people scatter their ashes.
Rosie	They scatter them?
Caleb	Yes. Over the water. Over the land.
Rosie	Over someone's head maybe.
Caleb	There's an idea.

Rosie	Life is strange and disappointing.
Caleb	People don't like to hear that.
Rosie	I don't like to hear it either.
Caleb	Nobody wants to hear about it.
Rosie	There are plenty of Jews here, believe it or not.
Caleb	Hard to believe.
Rosie	They were here before New York or Charleston.
Caleb	I don't think so.
Rosie	You could look it up. It's all written down.
Caleb	I will. I'll check it out, Mom.
Rosie	Do it before the earth burns up and the oceans boil, David.
Caleb	It's Caleb.
Rosie	Caleb.

Bernie and Caleb

Caleb	Bernie, why don't you come out of your room, finally, at last?
Bernie	I don't want to.
Caleb	Why not?
Bernie	I don't want to come out of my room.
Caleb	Come out of there this instant.
Bernie	No.
Caleb	Act like a normal person.
Bernie	I am a normal person. I did this already with Chrystal, Dad. We had a total conversation.
Caleb	So what? This is your father talking. Act like a thirteen-year-old.
Bernie	I *am* a thirteen-year-old. You didn't hear what I said.

Caleb	So come out of your room.
Bernie	No.
Caleb	Bernie, this is really hard for me.
Bernie	I'm sorry.
Caleb	I miss you.
Bernie	I miss you, too, Dad.
Caleb	Then come out and be with me once in a while. We'll go to a game, we'll go to the movies. We'll do things.
Bernie	Maybe later.
Caleb	When later?
Bernie	I don't know.
Caleb	You know what it's like for me?
Bernie	No.
Caleb	Do you want to know?
Bernie	No.
Caleb	It's lonely. I don't have anyone to talk to. I spend days and nights by myself.
Bernie	I'm sorry, Dad.
Caleb	I'm sick of myself. Aren't you?
Bernie	No. I have a lot to do. I talk to people all the time.
Caleb	I don't.
Bernie	You should, Dad.
Caleb	I should, but I don't. I have no one to talk to.
Bernie	David?
Caleb	He's a married man. He has no time for me.
Bernie	Your mother?
Caleb	That's a riddle, not a conversation. She thinks I'm David.
Bernie	Join a club, Dad, or go back to work.
Caleb	I suppose I could do that.

Bernie	Get married again.
Caleb	To who?
Bernie	Get out and meet someone.
Caleb	I don't know how to do that anymore. I think about the next thing with a woman and I lose interest.
Bernie	What next thing?
Caleb	The next thing to say, the next thing to do. The whole thing is a pain in the ass. On the other hand, I'm by myself too much. I'm afraid I'll start talking to myself.
Bernie	I'm sorry. It's not my fault. Don't start talking to yourself.
Caleb	I hear myself doing it.
Bernie	Call someone on the phone.
Caleb	Excuse me, but I don't understand. Do you?
Bernie	What?
Caleb	Call.
Bernie	Mainly, no. You took away my phone, remember?
Caleb	Yes, of course.
Bernie	So I only use the walkie-talkie. People. I don't like them and I'm afraid of them. I stick to videos.
Caleb	You watch TV?
Bernie	No.
Caleb	You don't watch TV?
Bernie	No.
Caleb	Because it's the last thing I want you to be doing in there.
Bernie	It's all lies, Dad. Lies and people selling you shit.
Caleb	That's what I'm saying.
Bernie	And bad acting. Like I can't stand another minute.
Caleb	So come on out of there and be with people.

Bernie	It's all over with people, Dad.
Caleb	Can't be, Son.
Bernie	Not like they have TVs in their heads, but something similar.
Caleb	I didn't follow that.
Bernie	Anyway, it's not that. It's the violence. But I make an exception for the relatives.
Caleb	Well, thank God for that.
Bernie	If they do the walkie-talkie thing, only.
Caleb	Why?
Bernie	Why?
Caleb	Why?
Bernie	Because of the Hopi.
Caleb	Leave the Hopi out of this.
Bernie	Because of the People.
Caleb	Why? Explain it to me, please.
Bernie	Because you don't know what they'll do next. You don't know and they don't know. So how can you trust them, how can you like them? Their only predictability is biological. They have to eat, sleep, shit, and reproduce. Otherwise, they'll kill each other at the drop of a hat—or if you bend over to tie your shoelaces, or if you lean against a building, or if you go for a walk with your dog—they'll kill you with a car bomb, should you be in the vicinity, so my advice to you is to stay out of the vicinity.
Caleb	So what can we do?
Bernie	Stay out of the vicinity. They'll kill you by air or by sea, you won't know when. And not only that, their minds are not attached to their tongues, their minds are

attached to their sex organs or to their intestines. That's where their minds are. So it's a mistake to talk to them. I only talk to my immediate family—like you, Dad—and I try to keep it to a minimum. They'll throw up on you, too.

Caleb   They?

Bernie   Yes. And I talk to Coyote. The people have no control over their functions, which makes them unpredictable, like I say, which makes them mad. So they want to destroy Earthmother. They just want to piss on her or pour poison into her veins. That's their attitude. Just ask anybody. Who comes first? Them. They come first. They come first over Earthmother.

Caleb   You're reading too much Hopi Indian material, Bernard.

Bernie   No, I'm not. I also speak with Coyote.

Caleb   Where is he?

Bernie   Right here. (*A glimpse of him somewhere—on a wall or in a mirror.*)

Caleb   That's why you talk like that. That's why you won't come out of your room.

Bernie   Look around you, Dad. Some of these people think they're going to heaven. They're rotting corpses and they think they're going to heaven. They're rotting while they're alive and they think they're going to heaven, and they throw their garbage into the street. They throw their garbage into the street and their shit they throw into the water, into the rain.

Caleb   Okay, that's enough.

Bernie   That's why I'm afraid of them and I don't like them. (*Silence*) You asked me, Dad.

Caleb	And you? You like yourself?
Bernie	I don't like me, either. I'm just like them and just like you. Full of shit and false ideas. So if I ever get out of here, I'll burn the place down.
Caleb	Stay here, then. Don't come out.
Bernie	I'm not ready right now to go out there and start burning it down.
Caleb	Good.
Bernie	Destroying the safe places and the armaments they all use.
Caleb	Okay. Good.
Bernie	Not just yet.
Caleb	I wish your mother was here.
Bernie	I don't.
Caleb	You don't?
Bernie	No, the earth is not the place for her these days.
Caleb	Your grandmother, then. Think of her.
Bernie	The days are numbered in Brazil, too, Dad.
Caleb	She's not really in Brazil.
Bernie	I know. But she is there, in her mind.
Caleb	Do me a favor, don't do anything until I talk to your grandmother.
Bernie	What does that have to do with anything?
Caleb	Just don't do anything until I talk to somebody.
Bernie	Talk to somebody, Dad.
Caleb	Please don't do anything weird.
Bernie	You too, Dad. Don't start talking to yourself. And Grandma can't remember anything.
Caleb	Bernard?
Bernie	What?

Caleb	What's that smell?
Bernie	It's the TV burning.
Caleb	Bernard!
Bernie	What?
Caleb	Just pull the plug! Pull the plug!
Bernie	Okay!
Caleb	Pull the plug! Pull the plug or I'll call the police!
Bernie	I pulled the plug! It's not burning!
Caleb	Put the fire out and pull the plug!
Bernie	I did!
Caleb	Or I'll call the fire department, the police, and an ambulance!
Bernie	I did, Dad!
Caleb	Is the fire out?
Bernie	It's out.
Caleb	Thank God. Now, give it to me, please. No more TV.

Rosie and Caleb

Caleb	Rosie. It's me. Caleb.
Rosie	I know. Don't call me Rosie.
Caleb	I'm sorry.
Rosie	I'm your mother.
Caleb	My son Bernie is in his room.
Rosie	I heard.
Caleb	He doesn't come out.
Rosie	Right.
Caleb	He set fire to his television set.
Rosie	How can you do that?
Caleb	I don't know how.

Rosie	It's dangerous.
Caleb	This is your grandson we're talking about.
Rosie	Not a smart idea.
Caleb	No. So I took it away from him.
Rosie	Good.
Caleb	I told him I would talk to you.
Rosie	Why?
Caleb	I don't know why.
Rosie	What can I do?
Caleb	Talk to him. He talks to his relatives.
Rosie	Think about it.
Caleb	What does that mean, "think about it."
Rosie	I don't know. It must mean something.
Caleb	It's completely meaningless.
Rosie	Have it your way.
Caleb	I think I'll change the subject now.
Rosie	See if I care.
Caleb	David asks me to have a meeting with Chrystal.
Rosie	David? Chrystal?
Caleb	That's your other grandson and his wife.
Rosie	About what?
Caleb	About having a child.
Rosie	Nice. And?
Caleb	I avoided the meeting. I pretended I didn't hear him.
Rosie	Why?
Caleb	I have my own problems.
Rosie	You can't interfere.
Caleb	Exactly.
Rosie	On the other hand, he's your son.

Caleb	I thought he meant something else, David. I said that. And then I said, of course.
Rosie	You lied.
Caleb	I half-lied, because I was actually confused. I thought I should.
Rosie	But you didn't want to.
Caleb	Right. I wanted to go home and watch the news and deal with Bernie.
Rosie	Not deal with Bernie.
Caleb	And not deal with Bernie. I was divided in two.
Rosie	I have had that. Experience.
Caleb	All I could do was lie.
Rosie	You tend to do that.
Caleb	There was two of me. Meanwhile, I pretended there was a third one.
Rosie	Who couldn't hear?
Caleb	Right, confused by early Alzheimer's.
Rosie	And you liked the power of being asked, the attention?
Caleb	Right.
Rosie	So you were tempted in the first place?
Caleb	Yes, but I didn't want to seem too eager. Being asked for help.
Rosie	The helpful Dad.
Caleb	Yes. Even though my heart was pounding. I lied.
Rosie	What did you say?
Caleb	I said Bernie was waiting for me at home.
Rosie	They had invited you for dinner?
Caleb	Yeah. I said, let's have coffee another time, because coffee is less serious.

Rosie	But they had invited you for dinner?
Caleb	Yes.
Rosie	Now what?
Caleb	I'll talk to Chrystal.
Rosie	What will you say?
Caleb	I'll say nobody knows, and nobody will ever know.
Rosie	What?
Caleb	Anything.
Rosie	Anything?
Caleb	Neither the future nor the past. Meanwhile, there's Bernie to consider.
Rosie	You remember Rabbi Nachman?
Caleb	Of course.
Rosie	He also never came out of his room.
Caleb	There's no comparison, the kid is an idiot. (*Silence*) I'm sorry.
Rosie	What do you want from me?
Caleb	Talk to him. Get him out of his room.
Rosie	I'll talk to Bernie, you talk to Chrystal.
Caleb	It's a deal.
Rosie	Not that it will do any good.
Caleb	Why do you say that?
Rosie	We have passed the point of no return, David.
Caleb	Caleb.
Rosie	What's the matter with you?
Caleb	Nothing.
Rosie	And the other one?
Caleb	Bernard?
Rosie	He shouldn't play with those things.

Caleb	The TV?
Rosie	Right.
Caleb	I agree, Mom. I took it away.

Rosie and Chrystal

Rosie	This is Rosie, who is this?
Chrystal	Chrystal. You dialed my number.
Rosie	Are you all right?
Chrystal	What do you mean by that?
Rosie	Are you all right?
Chrystal	No. At the moment I feel more wrong than right.
Rosie	What did you do wrong?
Chrystal	It doesn't matter what.
Rosie	It's Kafkaesque. You feel it's your duty.
Chrystal	My duty?
Rosie	To be wrong. It's something in the Ashkenazi genes.
Chrystal	It can't be, I'm a convert.
Rosie	Then you got it from David.
Chrystal	Okay, Rose, maybe I did.
Rosie	That's the only explanation I can think of.
Chrystal	Bernie thinks it's because we declared war on Nature.
Rosie	Not us! That wasn't us! That was the Gentiles!
Chrystal	God talked to Abraham.
Rosie	Bernie said that?
Chrystal	Yes. God talked to Abraham, from outside life.
Rosie	What was he supposed to do?
Chrystal	He did the best he could.
Rosie	Abraham or Bernie?

Chrystal	Both.
Rosie	Bernie could be confused.
Chrystal	He listens to the Hopi.
Rosie	They talk to him?
Chrystal	Like God talked to Abraham.
Rosie	Oh, I can't believe that.
Chrystal	It's the end of the Fourth World.
Rosie	Why Bernie?
Chrystal	He agrees with the Indians. And I agree with the Indians. They didn't get enough credit. They took care.
Rosie	You didn't answer the question.
Chrystal	I don't know why Bernie.
Rosie	Maybe he's imagining things. He's Jewish, for God's sake!
Chrystal	His parents separated, or his mother drowned, he broke in two, and now a third party joined in.
Rosie	Who is that?
Chrystal	A Coyote. Mr. Coyote.
Rosie	Indeed. He talks to a dog?
Chrystal	He's not exactly a dog.
Rosie	The dog talks back to him?
Chrystal	He says a mega-volcano is about to erupt.
Rosie	Where?
Chrystal	Somewhere in Asia.
Rosie	When?
Chrystal	Soon.
Rosie	Great.
Chrystal	Sulfuric acid will take the place of oxygen in the air.
Rosie	Great talking to you.

Chrystal	So what should we do?
Rosie	Talk to Mr. Coyote?
Chrystal	He's not a person.
Rosie	Of course he's not a person!
Chrystal	He's a spirit. He lives in the Spirit World.
Rosie	So how do you talk to him?
Chrystal	I don't. Bernie talks to him.
Rosie	I'll call him. Walkie-talkie.
Chrystal	Coyote?
Rosie	No, Bernie, obviously, Sarah.
Chrystal	It's Chrystal, Rose.
Rosie	Obviously.
Chrystal	You have to go over there yourself.
Rosie	All right, then. I'll go.

Bernie and Rosie

Rosie	Hello, Bernie.
Bernie	Hi, Rose.
Rosie	Don't call me Rose. I'm your grandmother.
Bernie	Grandma.
Rosie	You're mad at your mother because she went to hell?
Bernie	Wouldn't you be?
Rosie	Hell is a state of mind, like Rosie in Rio.
Bernie	You're talking about yourself in the third person.
Rosie	So what? This bothers you?
Bernie	Not really.
Rosie	That's the trouble with the Ashkenazi.
Bernie	What is?

Rosie	They're bothered by something they can't put their finger on it.
Bernie	I know what it is.
Rosie	That's why I wanted to talk to you. (*Silence*) So tell me, already.
Bernie	It's because God talked to Abraham.
Rosie	How do you know this?
Bernie	It's in the Bible.
Rosie	Noah's Ark is also in the Bible!
Bernie	So?
Rosie	You believe that, too?
Bernie	It depends on how you look at it.
Rosie	Let's get back to the original question.
Bernie	Why God talked to Abraham?
Rosie	No, why you're mad at your mother.
Bernie	I'm not mad.
Rosie	What are you?
Bernie	I'm sad.
Rosie	I'm sorry. (*Silence*)
Bernie	Why did you do it?
Rosie	Why did I do what?
Bernie	Go to Brazil.
Rosie	I wanted a second chance. I didn't realize. I had no more chances. (*Pause*) Brazil is going fast.
Bernie	Why is that?
Rosie	Nobody has their own money. Everyone has other people's money.
Bernie	I see.
Rosie	So, anyway. Who is this Coyote?

Bernie	He's not a person.
Rosie	What is he?
Bernie	He is what's left over when the world is destroyed.
Rosie	Where will he live?
Bernie	In the wind. In the waterfall. He's also known as Trickster.
Rosie	What will he do?
Bernie	He'll trick one of the cosmic heavyweights to send an arrow down here.
Rosie	A what?
Bernie	An arrow. It'll stick in the ground and bring new life.
Rosie	I see.
Bernie	He'll challenge one of the Gods to a bow and arrow context.
Rosie	You mean contest.
Bernie	Contest. And Earthmother will get one in the butt.
Rosie	Okay, Bernie. I miss you.
Bernie	Come home then.
Rosie	I'm thinking about it.
Bernie	I'll have Coyote give you a call.
Rosie	I don't know about that.
Bernie	It won't be like a regular phone call, Rose.
Rosie	Okay.
Bernie	It'll be like a balloon or something, or a kite, or a cloud.
Rosie	Okay.
Bernie	Or a shining in the sky.
Rosie	Okay, Bern.
Bernie	So watch the sky.

Rosie	I will. I'll watch the sky.
Bernie	Look up once in a while, like every hour of every day.
Rosie	Okay, Son.
Bernie	And you'll see something. Something weird and interesting. (*Pause*)
Rosie	I guess I've given up.
Bernie	What?
Rosie	Getting you out of your room.
Bernie	Don't worry, Grandma. You'll be the first to know.

David and Chrystal

David	They say the earth has died three times already. Once by ice, once by flood.
Chrystal	Who says?
David	The Hopi. I forget the other, maybe ashes. Volcanoes and earthquakes.
Chrystal	Bernie's into fire.
David	Yeah, he's into fire. And you? What do you think?
Chrystal	I think we'll suffocate for lack of oxygen.
David	Oh, for God's sake.
Chrystal	That's a good one. For God's sake. The magma is not far down.
David	What do you mean?
Chrystal	The magma of the earth, molten iron. It's not that far below the crust.
David	Why suffocate?

Chrystal	The oxygen is draining away. Fire can do it. Heat. Sulphur.
David	You're unbelievably pessimistic.
Chrystal	I have a head on my shoulders and something between the ears. You don't have to be a genius to see what's coming, just average intelligence.
David	I get it. It's not that I disagree.
Chrystal	Of course not. You're not stupid.
David	We could get hit by a meteor.
Chrystal	If you throw shit into the water it becomes shitty water.
David	We could lose our fertility.
Chrystal	Same with the air.
David	Do you have no hope?
Chrystal	None. You take me for an idiot?
David	No, I'm sorry.
Chrystal	And I won't perform a sex act.
David	Why not?
Chrystal	It's feeding the beast.
David	It'll be a new life, Chrystal.
Chrystal	It's creepy. And what'll it eat?
David	Milk.
Chrystal	I'll have no milk. It'll be contaminated by things like chromium and rust.
David	Then I won't go on living.
Chrystal	Neither will I, David. Radioactive dust.
David	Did you hear me? What should we do?
Chrystal	We don't need to do anything. Just wait. And be kind. And I'm glad you're kosher, finally.

David and Chrystal, and Caleb

David	It's my father on the phone.
Chrystal	What's he want?
David	I don't know. Ask him.
Chrystal	He wants to put his two cents in.
David	She says you want to put your two cents in.
Chrystal	Tell him I talked to his mother.
David	She said she talked with your mother. Here, you talk to him.
Chrystal	Caleb?
Caleb	This is not a movie. The Messiah is not coming.
Chrystal	Who said the Messiah is coming?
Caleb	Excuse me?
Chrystal	He's not coming, Caleb.
Caleb	How do you know?
Chrystal	Keep an eye on your younger son. He's a pyromaniac.
Caleb	I never said he was coming in the first place.
Chrystal	Bernie or the Messiah?
Caleb	The Messiah.
Chrystal	Where's Bernie?
Caleb	Bernie is home with his books and his DVDs and his iPad.
Chrystal	The Messiah is not God. The Messiah is the King of Israel. We keep on dying, generation by generation.
Caleb	You mean we keep on living?
Chrystal	Living and dying. It passes the blood. Is the blood immortal?

Caleb	Yes.
Chrystal	Excuse me, but I don't think so.
Caleb	Our blood is us, our ancestors and our future.
Chrystal	No longer, Caleb. Do you know why? Too much carbon in the air. They thought they could just suck it up, between the magma and the crust.
David	What was that? I didn't get that.
Chrystal	Suck up the oil and burn it, cook the atmosphere. But the magma is boiling. (*Pause*)
David	I don't think he heard you, Chrystal.
Chrystal	The magma is boiling, Caleb, meaning earthquake and volcano.
David	Storm and flood. Hurricane and cyclone. Tsunami.
Chrystal	That's right, David. Caleb, are you there? Well, the line is dead.
David	There's a dead zone there on his balcony.
Chrystal	Okay. I'll call him back later.

Bernie and Caleb

Bernie	The Hopi will go into underground caves, Dad.
Caleb	Is that where you're going?
Bernie	Yes. They have magical pictures of bison and antelope and little horses.
Caleb	Well, that won't save them.
Bernie	We are creatures which make sunlight into intelligence. We're like sensitive wires.
Caleb	Who told you this?

Bernie	Coyote. But when the oxygen is gone, they'll go down, down into the ground. The Hopi. They'll come up again with eyes the size of beach balls.
Caleb	You're out of your mind.
Bernie	No bodies at all. And they'll eat the sulphur.
Caleb	Am I responsible for this atrocity?
Bernie	You and everybody else.
Caleb	God help us. You especially.
Bernie	Pray, Dad, or praise. Whatever that is. Praise and praise.
Caleb	I'll go to the synagogue and *daven*.
Bernie	Too late. Go to a cave and hide your face. Put on a holy garment.
Caleb	You come with me.
Bernie	No.
Caleb	Where are you going?
Bernie	I'm going with Coyote to the Land of the Dead.
Caleb	Where is that? (*A pause*) Bernie!
Bernie	What?
Caleb	Where is that?
Bernie	I don't know. Brazil, maybe.
Caleb	Oh, for God's sake!

Rosie and Caleb

Rosie	Rosie, your mother.
Caleb	Caleb.
Rosie	I know.
Caleb	Bernie's not in his room.
Rosie	Uh-oh.

Caleb	Who knows where he is or what he's doing.
Rosie	He's setting fires is what he's doing, the fucking arsonist.
Caleb	Who knows?
Rosie	Good God, they'll blame the Jews for everything.
Caleb	There'll be no everything.
Rosie	There'll be no Jews.
Caleb	There'll be no nobody.
Rosie	When the Jews are gone, what's left?
Caleb	The earth itself will die. It says so in the Talmud.
Rosie	Where in the Talmud?
Caleb	I forget now. It's carbon. When there's too much carbon you can't breathe.
Rosie	I see.
Caleb	So we'll say good-bye.
Rosie	Good-bye.
Caleb	Bye, Mom.
Rosie	Bye, bye, Baby.
Caleb	Bye.

Coyote

Coyote	(*Off*) Coyote, who is I, looks at the audience. They resist the impulse to applaud. What does this have to do with the fate of the Jews, they wonder. The Jews are us, says I, Coyote, calmly, in Lakota—we are all Arabs. It's all right if you don't think so. Me and my Hopi friends are not Arabs and you are all shit and not too bright. I'm escorting the Hopi to their special caverns set aside for

them by Earthmother. We'll clean things up eventually
and then we'll start over. Meanwhile, we thought we'd
take a few righteous Jews with us to the center of the
Earth. Those of you who qualify, and want to come,
follow me. Oh. The gentleman over there asked how you
qualify. Well, you have to be an American, of course, and
have harbored no resentments for the last ninety seconds.
Okay? Let's go.

MONTAGE OF COYOTE AND BERNIE SETTING
FIRE TO THE CITY.

The End

Adele

Characters

ADELE	*Fifties, slim, anxious. An actress.*
SAMUELSON	*Sixties. A psychologist.*
DR. SCHINE	*An M.D.*
JANE	*Adele's older roommate. A healer and masseuse.*
GRACE	*Adele's younger roommate.*
EVE	*Another roommate.*
NORMAN	*A theater director.*
OTHER VOICES, OFF	*Adele's MOTHER. Son, NATHAN. Two DOPE DEALERS.*

SCENE	*STAGE is more or less empty, except for chairs for the actors. No entrances or exits. Scene changes are made by standing, sitting, moving seats, postures, etc., and quick light changes. Stage directions, not spoken, are in parentheses. Lines V.O. are in bold.*

1. (*Lights.* ADELE *and* SAMUELSON.)

Adele	Why do I feel that I'm not entitled to my own respect? (*Pause*) Are you going to tell me? Now? (*Pause*) Makes no sense at all.
Samuelson	Are we trying to make sense?
Adele	I'm trying to understand. It's so important that I understand. So I stop having these. . . panic attacks. (*Pause*) I know it's anxiety. I know that. That's common knowledge. My blood pressure goes up, which causes an anxiety attack, which causes my blood pressure to go up. I think that's what happens. I looked at the computer. In the doctor's office. And it said "essential hypertension." I thought, Jeez, what the hell is that? Look what's happening. I just want it to go away. I still can't believe it's all happening to me. I want it to stop. He gave me blood pressure meds. They have side effects. Headaches. Chest discomfort. Constipation. "Stay with it for a while." That's what he says. And call your shrink, he says, that's part of the prescription.
Samuelson	So?
Adele	So what?
Samuelson	Do you want to give it another try?
Adele	More psychotherapy?
Samuelson	Yes. Your doctor did call me. Dr. Schine. He called me.
Adele	Yeah, he thinks I'm falling apart.
Samuelson	Are you?

Adele	I've been having. . . panic attacks. But I already fired you once.
Samuelson	Yes, you did.
Adele	And I don't know if I want to do this anymore. Get myself over here and talk about myself endlessly and then figure out a way to pay for it.
Samuelson	It was Dr. Schine's prescription, the meds and therapy together. They had to go together.
Adele	I'm an artist, an actress. As you know.
Samuelson	Yes, I know.
Adele	God, what a mess. (*Pause*) Should we go back as far as high school?
Samuelson	Why not?
Adele	Remember? A long time ago. He meant well, the principal. I was getting into fist fights with boys and I refused to speak about it. Once, I got all the way to the principal's office, blood on my mouth, leaning against the walls. He looked at me, like what's up with this? I didn't say nothing. Ward R. Young was his name. A Gentile. My teachers, they all meant well. Jews, mainly, socially conscious types, like it used to be in the old days. They knew my situation. I was reading all night and getting to school late in the morning. Dr. Young said it was okay. Said I could come to school at lunch time. And the teachers gave me a scholarship when I graduated, so I would become a teacher and my life would be saved. Albany State Teachers College. They were very kind. But I didn't go there. I wanted to act. No way I was going to

Albany State. Brooklyn College was where I went. I was an honors student there, believe or not.

Samuelson Why wouldn't I believe it?

Adele I kind of messed up, though. I was going to auditions, when I should have been going to class. Working as a waitress. No one was interested. Amateur stuff.

Samuelson You see what you did?

Adele No.

Samuelson You took it back. You were an honors student.

Adele I don't know what I meant by doing that. This is something I always do? Take it back?

Samuelson Yes. You'll say something good, and then you'll take it back.

Adele I should feel worthy of my own memories and thoughts.

Samuelson Yes. The teacher of my teacher thought of it as a plague. You don't feel equal. So you can't have problems. You can't have a hair out of place. You have to be buttoned up at all times.

Adele Oh.

Samuelson You don't feel worthy of your own intelligence.

Adele Why don't I?

Samuelson There could be many causes: education, family, rank, class, race—

Adele It's a political question, isn't it? It's political.

Samuelson You could say that, yes. It's about power.

Adele It's like Kafka, isn't it? It is like Kafka. His accusers were his superiors.

Samuelson They were superiors, yes. Authorities.

Adele	That's how I'm going around! (*Pause*) Where did that come from? The harsh judgment, followed by a feeling of shame? Damn! I hate that! I'm intimidated. It's true. I think that's true. I'm looking at myself and I think that's true. On the other hand, I can't believe it. But it seems like it's true. It's painfully true. (*Pause*) I don't want to be that way. Maybe you have a pill, Doc? (*Pause*) Why not? I think I'm a lower class of person. So I don't have the right to feel equal. Why not? You should have a pill for inferiority. I feel inferior. I feel ashamed. I feel like there's a light on me, like I'm on stage, in a performance.
Samuelson	And you'd better know your lines.
Adele	Yes. And I have to get it right. Actually, I don't know what I was trying to say there. I want to change now. I want change now, because I'm going to forget. I'm going to forget what I said, what I myself said, forget what I said or understood. I'm going to forget. I was having. . . panic attacks, panic attacks. I never had them before, before maybe a month ago. I never had them before.
Samuelson	When do they start?
Adele	There's no trigger. There's no trigger, they happen by themselves, for no apparent reason. No apparent reason. Stress. Yes, stress. I don't like stress. I never liked stress.
Samuelson	Who likes stress?
Adele	I'm alone. I feel alone. Maybe that's a trigger, right there. Maybe that's a trigger, for the panic

attacks. I walk into my apartment and I'm alone. And I think—"My God, I'm alone. My life is a failure." And then my blood pressure goes up and I start to sweat, a cold sweat. And then my blood pressure goes up. I think I'm having a heart attack. It's like Cinderella and her evil stepmother, only the evil stepmother is in me. And my real mother was not, shall we say, nurturing. Damn. You've heard this before, no? Cinderella? No. Yes? I heard it years ago. That's her. I just heard her talking, my original mother. Huge sweats. Cold sweats. Terror. Why do I have them?

Samuelson   Nobody knows why. But it figures to go back to childhood. Childhood. Where people looked down on you.

Adele   Lousy bastards.

Samuelson   So that's a true possible cause there. Stands to reason. And your father was also a problem. So that's all in you. Take a look at Erikson, Eric Erikson. *Childhood and Society.*

Adele   My father and my mother and the people. Stands to reason. My father and my mother and the people. I got intimidated. Damn. "**They have it harder in China. They have it harder in India. They have it harder than you. All you have to do is obey your mother. They stacked us up like cordwood and now they're doing it again. Would you have got on the trains? You. I'm asking you.**" It's a question she was always asking. My mother.

Samuelson	Which question?
Adele	About the trains. "The Vatican Bank kept the money of the dead Jews of Europe. Insurance money. They still have it." You know, to the death camps. And the Vatican Bank. . .
Samuelson	Yes, I do know.
Adele	"People are animals. Animals don't do the shit we do. They just eat. What do you think you're doing? Trying to be sane? Trying to be normal?" That's her, doc. I don't know what's happening to me. I don't know who I am. And I'm feeling sorry for myself, which I know is a form of looking down on myself. "You go over to the Bronkowskis and you eat over there and you don't bring anything home for me to eat, not a bone, not a piece of meat or glass of milk! A piece of fruit! Your own mother! What's wrong with you? There's something wrong with you, you don't bring home anything for your mother! Look how they treat you, look how they treat you! Like a nobody, like a piece of shit, they're like the fucking Nazis! And look how they treat your mother!" She thought I was a hot little piece of shit. (*Pause*)
Samuelson	What are you thinking?
Adele	I was thinking, I'm not aware, I'm not aware that I'm obedient to everyone else, look up to everyone else. I see it a little bit, especially sexually, where people, you know, take advantage. There was this guy, we'd have sex and then he cursed me out and beat the crap out of me. Called me a bitch and a whore and all

kinds of bad things. And then he'd call a few days later and apologize and invite me out again, and I'd go along with it. He had to feel superior. And I went along with that. Because I agreed with him, that I'm lower than him. Apparently. Is it a question of class? Yes? No?

Samuelson More like rank.

Adele I tried to please. Now I'm worried. I'm almost depressed. I don't know if I can do it. Have confidence. You know, I'm up there on stage and I'm pretending that I know what I'm doing. Well, I shouldn't have said that. I'm not sure about that. I *do* know what I'm doing. The play takes care of you, if you're prepared, if the language is good, if you obey the rules. I'm always obedient. I'm always obedient. Anyway, the question is moot.

Samuelson Moot?

Adele I was going to say, it's a lie. I'm really not. Obedient. I don't know what I am or who I am. And I'm not so vulnerable, either. Okay? I sent her checks for years. I was working as a waitress. Years and years of the same letter, every month, word for word. What is that? I wanted to do the right thing. The same letter, month after month. The woman was mad. I feel at home in the theater. I feel okay. I feel happy in a theater, any theater, more happy than at home.

Samuelson Because you're good at it, and you have self-respect there. You respect your ability. Have I told you the story about Bruno Bettelheim?

Adele	Yes.
Samuelson	I'll tell you again. He was my teacher at the University of Chicago. One thing he was very angry about was that the Jews didn't fight back. So he used to tell this story. This was in '42 or '43, before he was ransomed. He was in a camp, and they were rounding people up for selection—who would go directly to the gas chambers—and one of the German guards recognized one of the young Jewish women they were about to murder, that she was a famous ballerina, and he singles her out to do a dance for him. At first she's confused. She doesn't know what to do. She's half-naked, she's on line to be killed, but the German guard insists and pushes and prods and hits her, and she starts to dance. And something awakens in her. She remembers who she is. She dances next to this German officer, grabs his gun and blows his brains out with it.
Adele	Yeah!
Samuelson	He told that story a lot. If you are nothing, if you have no identity, no reason to live, no family, no occupation—you don't defend yourself, you don't fight.
Adele	You see what a total mess we live in? It's murderous, and they made all these free-trade agreements and hollowed out the country. Whole towns fell into a sinkhole of poverty. What was that all about? The Government lies. The Supreme Court is a right wing—is—what is that? People won't see a play unless there's a TV star in it. And they have to say in one word what the play is about, or they don't understand it. The

country is like on a third-grade level. And then you got all these murderers and racketeers running around destroying the world in the name of God and religion. What's going on? You got these idiots in congress—they don't believe in climate change! We elected these guys! (*Pause*) Okay, I'll stop. The whole thing is so stupid, I can't fucking believe it. (*Pause*) Sorry. Sorry about the cussing.

Samuelson You're allowed, Adele. I work for you.

Adele Sorry. It's my mother. I got it from her.

Samuelson Anyway, that's what they did, that's how they did it. They stripped away everything until you were ready to die, in a kind of trance.

Adele Motherfuckers. Sorry. (*Dim out.*)

2. (*Lights up. They've changed positions—time has passed.*)

Samuelson So, what happens when the anxiety attack begins, Adele?

Adele I don't know what happens. (*Pause*) My blood pressure goes up, I get anxious and my blood pressure goes up. I'm not usually that way. You know, where I break into a sweat and I think I'm going to die. And I need a doctor and someone to hold my hand or take my blood pressure or give me intravenous Ativan, or whatever it was. (*Pause*) And I get confused. In these so-called panic attacks. Panic attacks. It's humiliating. On the other hand, I can teach my class. I can teach my acting class. I don't have a problem with it. I'm on, and when I'm on, I'm on. I mean, I'm functioning well and my mind is working fine. There was only one thing that was odd, which is that I missed a call. I somehow made it up in my mind that I hadn't been called, and I had been. An audition. That was scary. I sort of talked myself into something, and then I heard my name called. It was a reading, and I did the reading, and I did it well. I can still do my auditions. And I can do them well. Right now, I'm waiting for a call.

Samuelson   Good. From whom?

Adele   The casting director.

Samuelson   That sounds almost Kafkaesque.

Adele   It does. Again. His name is Norman something. I'm hoping for serendipity as I find my way. Not an event, perhaps an understanding. (*Pause*) I'm okay on stage, but the rest of me is me.

Samuelson   You still have the Spinoza Society.

Adele   In the first place, I'm Jewish. As you know. I was a convert, you know. So was Spinoza. They say. Not an easy thing to do. It was hard. When they took me away from my mother, I joined the goodness of another tribe, Jane's tribe, one of my roomates's tribe. Gentiles. When I converted back, the Rabbi wasn't easy on me. I learned a lot from him. I'll tell you about it sometime. No, I'll tell you about it now. The Law and the Covenant. You make a deal with Yahweh, or the Lord. So you and Him are tight and He'll take care of you. So then the Europeans killed a third of the

Jewish people. So it can't be about that, right? I mean, I converted back because of my blood, because of my soul, because of my name, my ancestors. (*Weeps. SAMUELSON hands her a tissue.*) Thank you.

Samuelson Of course.

Adele I don't know why. It's impossible to explain any of it. It makes no sense.

Samuelson And on stage?

Adele On stage, I ride the audience attention. It's like surfing, like a magic carpet. If it's a good play, you ride it. You ride, and your mind is active, you're alert. That's how it is for me, anyway. (*SAMUELSON gestures that the session is over. Quick dim out.*)

3. (*Back up. ADELE is alone. Her posture is slightly different.*)

Adele I'm a survivor. I don't know how else to say it at the moment. It's like a part of essence—the essence of persecution, intimidation, fear of the superior. It happens by itself. Something serious. It's been called a plague. Why mankind is destroying itself and the earth. When it goes down, we all go down. We're all going down. The animals know. The spirit world knows. My grandmother's entire family was murdered in the Ukraine. Their neighbors locked up the whole town's Jews in a barn and then they burned the barn down. Talk about panic. Imagine. With kerosene. They needed no help from the Germans. The Shoah was the beginning of the end of the civilized world. The final devolution of Man. (*Pause*) Let's go on a shooting spree. To the Ukraine. We'll knock on doors and shoot some of those idiots. That's my mother talking. "*Now.*" Too late now. Conversion is not going to help. Going around being cool is not going to help. Revenge is not going to help. (*Pause*) I wouldn't mind a taste. Bullets into those stupid heads. **"They're not like us, the Gentiles,"** she says. **"They have different beliefs. Like an automatic afterlife."** (*Pause*) For there to be an afterlife, we'd have to have an attention as hot as the sun, an attention as hot and fine and vibrant as the heat of the sun, an attention that corresponds with sunlight. (*Pause*) I don't think you got that. It's right there in the First Cause. **"So. Why did you become a Jew again?"** You know why, Mother. Because I am a Jew. Because the Jews are Chosen. Yes. There are entities who watch over the Jews. . . . (*Standing*) I'll tell you how I know. Last night before I went to bed, I got down on my knees and I said a prayer for all the Jewish children at Aucshwitz. And I went to bed. I slept wonderfully well, and when I got up—usually I'm a mess when I get up in the morning, as you know—but I felt great, wonderfully well, and at peace, like I never do. I had had a dream. In my dream there was a Being, a black Being, who had wings. (*Falls to her knees*) The wings were pointing down, and he was looking at me with these kindly eyes, and communicating, not talking, but telling me something with his Being, like an angel, a black angel—he was saying that all those murdered Jewish children were all right, that they were being taken care of, and they were all right. That everything was all right. And I believed him. (*Rising*) I was on my knees. . . One problem is the past. I have a lot of bad memories. What do we do with the past? The humiliations of the past? How do we make all our memories good ones? That's a real question, a moral question. A religious question. (*Sitting down*) You didn't get it. You didn't get what I was saying. (*Pause*) You can't go around having panic attacks. It's not good for your career. It's not good for the family. It's a medical condition. It's not a spiritual or a family condition. It's not a career condition. Anyway, you can't control it. It's not like you have any control. You can't meditate yourself out of it. Like some people think they can. I won't mention any names. Maybe a swami or a yogi. A Buddhist. A Spinoza person. (*Pause*) This is what happened with my doctor, Dr. Schine.

4. (*Enter* Dr. Schine, *who takes her pulse.*)

Dr. Schine	Your pulse is fine. Any fibrillation?
Adele	What's a fibrillation?
Dr. Schine	Irregular heartbeat.
Adele	No. I broke into a heavy sweat.
Dr. Schine	Chest pains?
Adele	A little. Yes.

Dr. Schine	Now?
Adele	No.
Dr. Schine	You are a little clammy.
Adele	Yeah.
Dr. Schine	But I think you're having an anxiety attack.
Adele	You're kidding.
Dr. Schine	Where you have symptoms is all.
Adele	I feel like a complete idiot.
Dr. Schine	You've felt like that since I've known you. Which is most of my life.
Adele	I'm sorry.
Dr. Schine	Don't be sorry. It happens.
Adele	A complete idiot.
Dr. Schine	Stop that.
Adele	Okay.
Dr. Schine	I'll give you a prescription for Ativan, and a blood pressure med, but you'll also have to see a shrink. Will you do that?
Adele	Yes.
Dr. Schine	Call him tonight and ask him to call me.
Adele	Why?
Dr. Schine	Never mind. I want to talk to him.
Adele	Okay. I'll call him tomorrow. What about the Ativan?
Dr. Schine	Take it if you feel something coming on. Don't take too much of it. I'll call it in. Rite-Aid.
Adele	Thanks, Doc.
Dr. Schine	(*To someone off*) Take her home. No, take her to Rite-Aid, then take her home. (*Exits*)
Adele	Humiliation. (*Quick* Dim out.)

5. (*Lights back up.* ADELE *is alone.*)

Adele   I might have an audition. It's a special, by invitation. I never miss an audition. I think it's a movie. About Cinderella. Disney. I have to be there. It's a special event, and I'm very competitive. There's competition amongst actors. I want to be one of the chosen. The chosen few. The chosen. (*As* MOTHER) **"The Accused. The murderers of God."** I accuse myself. I'm self-accused. Why do I do that? Because I think I'm low. Low down. So. Cinderella goes to the ball. Who is to be her true love? Trials and tribulations, not unlike Kafka, only more personal, just as drastic, but subjective, because of inferiority and persecution. (*Pause. Stands. In tears.*) So I go to this fucking audition. Excuse me for cursing. It's a big part. It's not *Cinderella*. It's a comedy on ABC. It could change my life. I'm sitting there and nobody is there. Nobody else is around. Finally, I go up to the desk and I ask the girl what's going on. She looks me up and the auditions are already over. My manager sent me at the wrong time. So humiliating. I call my manager and the man says he made a mistake. I say how could you make this fucking mistake when my career is on the line? All my life I've been waiting for this, you asshole. And then he says—I don't know why he says this— "I think I'm afraid that if you get something good, you'll leave me." I couldn't fucking believe it. Can you imagine? I started crying and I cried for a whole day.

My roomate, Jane, had to get hold of me and calm me down. I fired the sonofabitch immediately. Now, I'm not sure what I'm going to do. (*Quick D*IM OUT.)

6. (*Lights up.* ADELE *is alone.*)

Adele   I was born Jewish. I don't have to take that back. We don't know why this all happens, but you can't rule out cause and effect. It has a lot to do with childhood, and culture, and other things. History and time. (*Pause*) But it's not the whole picture—you're no mark in the theater, Adele, as an actress. You'll fight for a part. You'll show up for a part and you'll fight. (*Pause*) I'm happy in a theater. Any theater. Auditioning or not. Because I have an identity there. I've told you the Bettelheim story? I have an identity there I respect, like the ballerina. She realized who she was and shot the Nazi sonofabitch. Which brings me to the fear of death. I don't want to die like a dog.

Samuelson   You have a prejudice against yourself.

Adele   My mother never looked me in the eye, never touched me except to hit me. She used a broom or a coal shovel. The shovel had sharp edges. The wicked witch. I got up with her in the freezing cold to help her to get the stove going in the kitchen. She was often ill-tempered. It was so cold. We'd go outside to get the coal and bring it in and kindle the coal fire in the kitchen. And then we'd light the other stove in the front room, which was a wood burner. We slept with all our clothes on. Sometimes she'd get pissed off and hit me with the shovel. One day, when I was about eleven, I defended myself. I held her arm before she could strike me. I said, "If you ever do that again, I'll kill you." And I think I meant it. She never hit me again, not with the coal shovel. I moved up into the attic, which had no heat. There I would read, when it was quiet, until four or five in the morning. The principal let me come to school late, in the afternoon. No problem. Maybe I'm getting this mixed up. He was very kind. And so were the teachers. Very kind. They gave me a scholarship. Their own money. And the synagogue gave us food and clothes and money. Very embarrassed old men with beards. At Passover, they brought boxes of ammo. There's a slip for you, Doc. Matzos, not ammo. They'd come and go quickly. Leave the boxes at the door. For Jews to be in that miserable situation. It's a *shondah*. Though it wasn't uncommon in the old country. They collaborated. The motherfuckers collaborated. The *sheyna yidn*, the leadership, the big shots, they collaborated with the Germans, the French, everybody. That's why no one talked about it. No one wanted to know. I do have a prejudice. They collaborated. The motherfuckers collaborated. No one wanted to say. No one wanted to know. (*Dim out*)

7. (*Lights up on* ADELE *alone.*)

Adele
All religions are the same. I don't even think of Judaism as a religion, though they made it tough to

get back in—it's a collection of tales and precepts and sayings and arguments. A way of life, a tribe. A race. A culture. Holidays. You put ten Jews in a room and you got ten different forms of Judaism. This was true even in biblical times. Like Maimonides said, in *A Guide for the Perplexed*. That certainly fits me.

Grace You wouldn't acknowledge our Savior. There's the problem right there.

Adele Fuck you.

Grace *No, fuck you.*

Adele You're an ignorant, mean piece of shit, Grace. (*To audience*) That's one of my roommates, Grace. (*Dim out*)

8. (*Lights up on* SAMUELSON *and* ADELE.)

Adele There's another person in me. An entity. She's me. And she scares me. She continually attacks me. She sounds like my mother. Harsh. And the village and the neighborhood and the relatives. I'm writing a play about this. *Cinderella*. I am okay then. When I'm writing. When I am acting. I was always okay, then. And now. On the stage. Because I respect that in myself. I was always all right, intellectually speaking. And a talented actress. I was always all right on that end of things. It's all the other stuff, the social stuff, where this harsh other person is in me, who feels like me. When I'm writing, or acting, she's not there. So far. I have a couple of hours, when writing. Then, at a

	certain point, I know the rest is bullshit, so I stop. Then this other person comes back. She comes back in my head to attack me.
Samuelson	You think of yourself as lower class, a second-class person.
Adele	I'm not aware of it. It's subtext. I don't feel I can stop her. So I'm frightened. I can't stop her from attacking me. And it's me, it's in me. (*Silence*) And she never had a kind word for my father. I don't think she liked men very much. She hated my father, I can tell you that.
Samuelson	They were lucky to be able to have time together. Your parents, I mean.
Adele	Oh, bullshit. They had no clue. In my mind they are the same person. My mother, my father. They get all mixed up in my mind. I hate people, actually. I hate them all.

9. (GRACE *and* EVE)

Grace	She has an idea about herself, some kind of superiority.
Eve	How far off is that?
Grace	Some sort of Jewish thing. Intellectual and talented.
Eve	That's the trouble with the Jews.
Grace	Well, that's part of it.
Eve	And she's a reverse-convert.
Grace	What is that supposed to mean?
Eve	I'm just saying.
Grace	Meaning she has all the racial characteristics.

Eve	Right.
Grace	So she doesn't need to be so proud in the first place.
Eve	Right. Smart and talented are also Christian virtues.
Grace	Of which she has none, really. She's an anti-Christian.
Eve	It's to spite us. They're full of spite.
Grace	The Christians or the Jews?
Eve	I meant the Jews.
Grace	You can be very confusing.
Eve	Life is confusing.
Grace	I know it is. Like panic attacks.
Eve	She's not that old.
Grace	Right. She's old enough to not have panic attacks. We can't have panic attacks. She needs to have more poise inside. More quiet. For the young in her acting class. For her family and friends. Though she doesn't have many friends.
Eve	She has a few in the theater world.
Grace	The theater world.
Eve	The theater world.
Grace	What kind of world is that?
Eve	Egotistic and attention-getting.
Grace	Attention is everything. Where she's not a star. No, she's no star. Though she thinks she is one. And she's alone, and she hates it. And she hates us.
Eve	You took the words right out of my mouth. (*Knock at the "door"*) Oh, that's Jane. (*Enter* JANE)
Grace	Hi, Jane.
Jane	Where's Adele?
Eve	She's not here.

Jane	The little bitch. Why not?
Eve	She didn't say.
Jane	Well, she can't complain now that we never invite her to talk. Can she?
Grace	She'll complain anyway. Complaining is one of her things. Attributes. I was going to say. . . never mind.
Jane	What, that it's a Jewish trait? Complaining?
Grace	Yes.
Eve	We know each other's minds, don't we?
Jane	No, we don't. It's the usual baloney, Eve. (*JANE and GRACE exit. ADELE turns downstage where she joins EVE.*)
Eve	How's it going?
Adele	It's tough to be sick all the time. Depressing. It's depressing. What does that mean, spiritually? Is it a kind of crime? The shrink is helping me. All that self-deprecation. Must be some kind of crime. A criminal offense. You're supposed to be happy. Happy, happy, happy. Otherwise, you're dead. I was having panic attacks, and I lost faith. I lost faith in myself. My blood pressure took it away. I got the blood pressure meds, finally.
Eve	Are they working?
Adele	They seem to be.
Eve	What's the count?
Adele	135, 140, around in there.
Eve	That's almost normal.
Adele	Yeah. And I'm still seeing my shrink. It was part of the prescription. Hysterical woman having an anxiety

	attack. He wrote the prescription and he made me see my old shrink and he talked to him on the phone. I don't know what they said.
Dr. Schine	She's panicking. You know her background?
Samuelson	Yes, I do.
Dr. Schine	She needs to be talking to someone. She could be having a breakdown.
Samuelson	I understand.
Dr. Schine	Her blood pressure is very high, which could lead to a stroke. I gave her pills for that, but she really needs the therapy to go along with it.
Samuelson	We'll see if she calls.
Dr. Schine	She'll call.
Adele	So I called.
Eve	Seems good, Adele.
Adele	Why?
Eve	Is it helping you?
Adele	Yes.
Eve	So, it's good.
Adele	You're so rational, Eve. Apparently, my mother was not my friend. Never a kind and encouraging word. Never even gave me a look. A hitter. But it wasn't just that. You want to hear more?
Eve	I'm not sure I do. No.
Adele	It was the rest of the society, also, who looked down on this poor, fucked-up kid.
Eve	You seem much better now.
Adele	Then what?
Eve	Than before.

Adele	No more panic attacks.
Eve	Good. We need you back at the Spinoza Group.
Adele	What for?
Eve	We need everybody. People who can think. Obviously.
Adele	Yeah, yeah. It's ironic, no? I converted in the other direction. I was a Jew who became a Gentile who became a Jew again, and Spinoza was a Jew who went the other way.
Eve	No one knows for sure. He could have been practicing in secret.
Adele	I doubt it. He lived in solitude. Like me. I imagine him that way. A great example of the Jewish mind. Him and Maimonides. Some people thought he was a convert also. But he wasn't. Not Maimonides. That was just a rumor, I think. (*Awkward pause*)
Eve	How's the writing?
Adele	I'm trying to say everything I possibly can. It's too much, probably. But who knows when I'll get another chance?
Eve	Can you come to a meeting soon?
Adele	I don't know. (*Pause*) I don't believe in God.
Eve	(*Ironic*) I'm shocked. What do you believe in?
Adele	Nature.
Eve	Nature is in the image of God.
Adele	Life is too random for that kind of reasoning.
Eve	Not for people like us.
Adele	We're not the same kind of people. You're a Christian and I'm a Jew. I don't know if I believe in anything, to tell you the truth. Seems foolish. Even Nature, which

will vanish, eventually. So what is reality? A mirage? A visualizition? A trial? A dream? A silence? An electrical phenomena? What is it? During a panic attack, it's all suffering, that's all it is, pure suffering. The earth is failing, and it's because of us, and it has no meaning at all. (*Pause*)

Eve I don't agree with you.

Adele Not after the Shoah.

Eve I don't agree.

Adele No, you wouldn't. (*Steps away.* JANE *with* GRACE)

Eve The woman has a problem.

Jane We all know that.

Eve Personally, I think she's schizophrenic.

Jane You don't know anything about it.

Eve I know all I need to know. She's at least two different people.

Grace Plus the Actress.

Eve What's with the panic attacks?

Jane Nobody knows, really. It may have had something to do with blood pressure. She gets stressed, her blood pressure goes up, she gets anxious about being anxious, and her blood pressure goes up.

Eve I think the stress is because she doesn't want to do what she's doing. She doesn't want to go to the Spinoza Society, and she doesn't want to be with us, and she doesn't want to act.

Grace She's writing a play now.

Eve And she doesn't know if she's a Gentile or a Jew.

Jane She knows. She's a Jew.

Eve	Which is pretty heavy.
Grace	And she has all these strange ideas.
Jane	Remember, she lost a son. (*Pause*) And before she came to us, her mother was a madwoman. And she's converted twice now.
Eve	I think she needs help, Jane.
Jane	She's doing that. She's getting help.
Grace	What's this play she's writing all about?
Eve	Probably about us.
Grace	Yes. No question.
Jane	The first conversion was because of the Resurrection— she wanted to see her son again. It was something she wanted desperately to believe. And the second one was also about Resurrection—
Grace	Because she couldn't believe.
Jane	Right.
Eve	And now?
Jane	Now, I don't know.
Grace	I think she's nuts.
Jane	No. She thinks she's supposed to serve. The inferior serves. So she thinks she's supposed to find a solution. (*Re-enter* ADELE)
Grace	Oh, look who's here.
Eve	Speak of the devil.
Jane	Are your ears ringing?
Adele	Yes, they are. You were talking about me.
Grace	You're the only person worth talking about.
Eve	On earth.
Jane	How are you?

Adele	Actually, I'm the finest actress in the city. It's not only a question of talent, although that's true—talent is important, talent is a given. It's a question of skill. Skill is better than talent, because I know what I'm doing, and that's why I can write a play, as well, because I know what to do. I'm a triple threat.
Jane	I didn't follow that. Did you, girls?
Eve	No.
Adele	There's me watching me and then there's my character, based on me. (*Pause*)
Jane	I don't know if I like this particular Adele.
Samuelson	**When you say "actually," it's apologetic. You're not supposed to be equal, or more than equal.**
Adele	Oh.
Grace	What?
Adele	Nothing. (*Pause. To* JANE) You remind me of my mother. She never liked me. She never actually looked at me. Actually. Which is odd. To never look at a person. Your own daughter. But character counts. Everything counts.
Jane	Excuse me?
Adele	So, in that sense, you're responsible for who you are. One is. If you drink too much, or take drugs, or fool around, or steal, whatever, or have a panic attack, even so, it's your responsibility. No excuses.
Jane	I'm not like your mother.
Adele	No, definitely not. (*Aside*) You're like one big-time high-functioning, greedy kraut.
Jane	I didn't hear that. Did you, girls?

Adele	My mother couldn't hardly function. You function like gangbusters. You make a good living and do your spiritual thing with your dying cancer patients and my mother was picking in the garbage and sending me out to beg.
Jane	Don't start resenting me now.
Adele	You have such a classic German face. And you overcharge. It's like a borderline con. Taking advantage of the old and the sick.
Jane	Did you hear me, Adele?
Adele	While you preach them your spiritual salami.
Eve	Adele.
Adele	Spinoza, indeed. I'm not just resenting you now. I've been onto you for a while.
Jane	That's enough.
Adele	It's never enough. (*Long silence*)
Eve	This is new.
Grace	This is definitely new.
Jane	Hopefully, it'll pass. (*Pause*) You're not being fair, Adele. Or just.
Adele	I'm sorry. (*Pause*)
Jane	We'll let it pass. (*Pause*) How's your blood pressure today?
Adele	I didn't take it today.
Jane	Would you like a session? A freebie?
Adele	No.
Grace	You should take your blood pressure. Every day.
Adele	No. I'm too agitated now.
Jane	A massage?

Adele	No.
Jane	A freebie.
Adele	No. I'm all agitated now. (*Turns away.*)
Jane	Okay. Maybe later.
Grace	I can't believe this. I can't believe I heard this.
Jane	She's agitated.
Eve	You can't take that shit from her, Jane.
Jane	It's alright. She'll calm down with my therapy massage.
Adele	Therapy, indeed.
Jane	She always feels better afterward.
Adele	(*Turning back*) She puts her hands on their heads and then she caresses them a little—arms, legs, shoulders— and then she holds their hands and tells them death is just another thing that happens and God is always with them, so death is just a transformation of energy.
Jane	That is exactly what happens.
Adele	You don't know what happens. God is watching and everything is okay. No need for anxiety or panic attacks. Go ahead and die. Her hands are warm, though. It really is very nice. And then you get up and wonder, "what just happened?" A hundred-and-seventy-five bucks just happened. Where'd you learn that stuff, Jane? (*Exit JANE*)
Eve	Now, you did it.
Grace	Why'd you call her a kraut?
Adele	She is a kraut. You're all krauts. You should get down on your knees and wash my feet, like your famous God. And then you should repent, like the pieces of shit you are.
Grace	I could slap you.

Adele	Go ahead.
Grace	I won't.
Eve	Maybe I will.
Adele	Go ahead. (*Pause.* EVE *punches* ADELE *to the floor, exits. Quick* BLACKOUT.)

10. (*SAMUELSON and* ADELE)

Adele	So, she punched me in the mouth.
Samuelson	Oh. You punched her back?
Adele	No.
Samuelson	Why not?
Adele	She fled.
Samuelson	I see.
Adele	She fled. Otherwise, I might have.
Samuelson	I see.
Adele	Punched her back. Probably not. Otherwise, maybe I would have. Stood up to her. High blood pressure or not.
Samuelson	You might have.
Adele	A change in behavior for sure.
Samuelson	It's not the blood pressure.
Adele	What is it?
Samuelson	Psychological. Confrontation. You avoid confrontation.
Adele	I did call them krauts.
Samuelson	Right.
Adele	So that's good.
Samuelson	You do think you can fix yourself.
Adele	I do?
Samuelson	But that's what you hired me for.

Adele	I think I can fix myself?
Samuelson	Yes.
Adele	Where'd I get that idea?
Samuelson	It's common. But it doesn't happen that way.
Adele	Why do I think I can fix myself?
Samuelson	It doesn't happen that way.
Adele	That I should fix myself. That I'm responsible.
Samuelson	It happens by itself.
Adele	That I can't brag? That I can't have an ego?
Samuelson	Because you don't feel equal.
Adele	How much of that is a moral question?
Samuelson	Moral?
Adele	About character.
Samuelson	Because you don't feel the right.
Adele	Why not?
Samuelson	We don't know, really.
Adele	I was thinking I could find a solution. But there is no solution.
Samuelson	This is the solution.
Adele	People believe in things. Solutions. (*Pause*)
Samuelson	*The Interpretation of Dreams.*
Adele	Is what?
Samuelson	Is the first book of modern psychology. A hugely important book. And Freud knew it. So he held off publication for a year, or so, until it was 1900. Because it was significant that way. 1900.
Adele	You're saying this is new.
Samuelson	Yes, this is a relatively new science.
Adele	Nobody knows anything.

Samuelson	Maybe not.
Adele	About anything.
Samuelson	I didn't say that.
Adele	Let me try this on you.
Samuelson	Okay.
Adele	My son was a junkie because I was a junkie. He died from shooting up. Of AIDS. Dirty needles. Now it's all revealed. But what does it mean? According to celebrity junkies, it means they didn't love themselves. Low self-esteem. Plus something nagging them inside. Something was definitely nagging me inside. I always thought it was a class issue. And now I'm thinking it was a class issue. And now you're saying it's a class issue—
Samuelson	Not feeling equal, not feeling the right.
Adele	I have to think about that. I don't know how to think about that. How is it connected to panic attacks? It's intolerable to lose a son. It's a bottomless sorrow that never ends. Why do people send their sons to die? It's so messed up. Abraham and Isaac. Gone to the slaughter, one reason or another—territory, pride, water, land, clean air, God, you name it—
Samuelson	Slow down, Adele.
Adele	I can't slow down. My heart is going too fast. And it's all so crazy.
Samuelson	Slow down.
Adele	I have an audition today.
Samuelson	More's the reason.
Adele	Why did I become a junkie? Why? A nice Jewish girl like me? (*Laughs*) An intellectual! An actress!

Samuelson	You wanted to feel equal for a minute.
Adele	Yeah, it all goes away then. It all goes away. (*Breaks into tears*)
Samuelson	Adele.
Adele	But I don't exactly know what I mean by that. Sorry. I live a lonely life. (*Pause*) I don't know how to accept it. I blame myself for it.
Samuelson	It's not a crime.
Adele	Holy shit. (*Silence*) I don't know what I meant by that. (*Silence*)
Samuelson	What's with the Spinoza Society?
Adele	What's with what with the Spinoza Society?
Samuelson	How did you get involved?
Adele	Here was a smart Jewish guy who got excommunicated. Baruch Spinoza. Rang a bell with me. I was always converting or re-converting. In my head. I don't know how they could excommunicate anybody. There is no such thing in Judaism. All synagogues are local. They just said to Spinoza—you're an atheist—take a hike. So he lived in a room somewhere like an ascetic and kept his nose down. It was his rhythms, the way he reasoned his way mathematically. Created a rhythm. If this is true then such and such is self-evident. (*Pause*) I don't know, actually.
Samuelson	You're taking it back again.
Adele	I think I was attracted to his rhythms.
Samuelson	What about his ideas?
Adele	I think he was too much in his head, actually. He should have fought it out with the rabbis. I don't know what I meant by that.

Samuelson	You're doing it again.
Adele	Debate. Dialectic. *Davening.* The three D's.
Samuelson	The three D's?
Adele	I just made that up.
Samuelson	Go on, though. Don't back off.
Adele	The whole Jewish community had been expelled from Spain, as you know, and they had barely created this community in Holland, and they were scared of losing it. They kept their heads down. Spinoza comes along, who is very smart, and he has a whole new idea about God, based on nature, the laws of nature, which is heretical to the rabbis. Which it was. God is above nature for the orthodox. Anyway, there's a word for what he did. Syllogisms. To love God doesn't mean that God exists. You could be loving the idea of God. Actually, he goes into that a little. For him, that was a kind of proof.
Samuelson	Thank you.
Adele	The rabbi, when I was converting back to my religion of birth, was a hard-ass and a shmuck. Rabbi Pelsenberg. It was all memory and midrashic argument and prayers three times a day, and what was for men, what was for women, and what was kosher, and so on. I don't think Spinoza was into that stuff and neither was I. I just stopped it and identified myself as a Jew again and forgot, mostly forgot, the virgin birth and the Resurrection and all that. . . . Spinoza didn't become a Gentile, either. He kind of got it from both ends.

Samuelson	So what did you do?
Adele	At the Society?
Samuelson	Yes.
Adele	Meetings. Talks. Discussion. Nothing too serious. This was after I had cleaned up and it was kind of a relief. No more rehab. Not to talk about drugs for a change. I used to feel shy with my own son. I was shocked by that. This urge to perform, to please. Embarassed by that, by my own insecurity with my own son.
Samuelson	Teenagers are hard to deal with.
Adele	I feel bad about it right now. He wouldn't say much. I couldn't get him to talk. He was always hustling me for one thing or another. Money for gas, money for clothes, money for dope. On and on. Never asked me how I was or what I was doing. Selfish sonofabitch. Junkies are like that. I know. I was one myself.
Samuelson	Not for long.
Adele	No. Long enough. Too long. Definitely hurt my so-called self-esteem, such as it is, such as it was. Like none at all. Such a cliché. Nice Jewish girl, talented actress, shooting up in hallways, backstage, filthy bathrooms, throwing up in cabs. Lots of fun.
Samuelson	It helped you to feel equal for a minute.
Adele	It got me off the anxiety train for a minute. And now I'm in danger of panic attacks.
Samuelson	And feeling sorry for yourself.
Adele	That's what my older roommate says. Jane.
Samuelson	I don't think that's so bad. Pitying yourself maybe is in the right direction.

Adele	What do you mean? (*Pause*)
Samuelson	You loved your son?
Adele	Yes.
Samuelson	You had compassion for him.
Adele	Sometimes. Sometimes I wanted to shoot him. Sometimes he'd get this look in his eye and I had no idea where he was. Somewhere else entirely. And I'd panic. And ask him what he was thinking. And he wouldn't answer me. I'd panic, and ask him again.
Adele	**What are you thinking about?**
Nathan (off)	**Nothing.**
Adele	**You must be thinking about something.**
Nathan (off)	**I'm not.**
Adele	**You're not here.**
Nathan (off)	**Mom?**
Adele	**Yeah?**
Nathan (off)	**Don't ask me shit like that. Everything's fine.**
Adele	And then I'd feel my heart sink, in absolute shame. (*Pause. BLACKOUT. SAMUELSON withdraws.*)

11. (*Lights. ADELE is standing. The CASTING DIRECTOR, NORMAN, enters and takes a seat.*)

Norman	Hello.
Adele	Hi.
Norman	Nice to meet you.
Adele	Thank you.
Norman	Thanks for coming over.
Adele	Sure. (*Pause*)
Norman	Have a seat. (*ADELE sits.*) Relax.

Adele	I am relaxed.
Norman	Sorry. (*Pause*) So, to start with: Don't act.
Adele	What is that supposed to mean?
Norman	Sorry. I'm worn out. I've been seeing a lot of actors and they all act too much.
Adele	I'm not that kind of actress.
Norman	You know, they feel like they have to write the play. They feel like they have to sell it, show it, interpret it, because the writing is so bad, the actor has to fill in the meaning. We're not doing that kind of play. We're doing a play where the writing is perfect, where the actor needs to be behind the writing, not in front of it.
Adele	I think I agree with you.
Norman	You think?
Adele	I agree with you.
Norman	Good.
Adele	I'm writing a play myself. And I want the audience to hear the writing.
Norman	Yes, I've heard about you and your career.
Adele	Some career. From whom?
Norman	The Spinoza Society. I used to be involved over there.
Adele	Jane?
Norman	Jane something.
Adele	My condo partner.
Norman	Yes.
Adele	Interesting.
Norman	Did you bring anything to read?
Adele	Read?
Norman	For the audition.

Adele	No. Don't you have sides?
Norman	No. We ask people to bring something in—something they know, something they like.
Adele	I don't have anything. I didn't actually realize—
Norman	Okay. Maybe we can find a script—
Adele	Wait a minute. I can do something from my own, uh, work in progress. From memory. Do you mind?
Norman	No. Please.
Adele	Should I do it here?
Norman	No. Take that chair if you like. More light there.
Adele	Okay. I'll stand.
Norman	Fine. (*Pause*)
Adele	This is from something called "Cinderella."
Norman	That you're writing.
Adele	That I'm writing. It's an abstract version of "Cinderella," and this is someone talking about Prince Charming.
Norman	Go.
Adele	"The Prince of the Kingdom is on another level—the level of myth, or symbol—goodness and truth—and accuracy. That is: His aim is sharp and persistent. He will find the right bride, or he will live the rest of his life alone. He'll make that sacrifice, rather than the wrong choice, and be lonely, and uncomfortable with his attendants, who will lie to him and create obstacles in his way—political, romantic, family obstacles. His life will be difficult and dangerous, because he can't trust those around him, and he's isolated from the truth, and from himself. And so he will pity himself, and loathe himself for pitying himself, and be afraid of

the so-called authorities that he has himself placed above him, who scrutinize and judge him, so he is embarrassed to open his mouth in order to utter his despair." I think I'll stop there.

Norman	Interesting.
Adele	Thanks.
Norman	Reminds me a little of Kafka.
Adele	Yes, that's what people say. Maybe it's partly true.
Norman	You memorized it?
Adele	Mainly. Actually, I have a genius level photographic memory for dialogue.
Norman	Congratulations.
Adele	I made that up. Sorry.
Norman	No problem. Are you writing about yourself?
Adele	We all write about ourselves. That's all we write about. Don't you think?
Norman	Probably, yes, I would think so.
Adele	Is that it?
Norman	For now. I'm very encouraged.
Adele	Thank you.
Norman	You're welcome. We'll be in touch. (*Quick* DIM OUT. NORMAN *withdraws*.)

12. (*Lights up.* SAMUELSON *and* ADELE. *They settle.*)

Adele	I'm not feeling so good.
Samuelson	What happened?
Adele	I got whacked.
Samuelson	Whacked?

Adele	Whacked. I got killed.
Samuelson	What happened?
Adele	I went to get my ears cleaned. This is a doctor I know, a surgeon. She cleans my ears. I have a lot of ear wax, so I know her. (*Silence*)
Samuelson	Go on.
Adele	So I rush over there because I couldn't hear anything well—but my pulse, I was hearing my pulse, which is really weird—and at first she said she wasn't there, then I get an e-mail saying she's there, if I want to come over—which was a warning sign—and I get there, and she's alone. First, the door won't open, I start to leave, the door opens, and there she is in her white coat—Marie—forty-five, fifty—wild eyed, messy hair—alone.
Samuelson	She's a doctor?
Adele	She's a surgeon, eye, nose, mouth. And she starts talking. She's still a good-looking woman, charged-up, she says, by the drugs she took earlier because her brother-in-law and her father-in-law threw her to the ground and hurt her neck. They threw her onto hard concrete. Her husband had just died. They were trying to get her house away and had taken her into court. They were trying to destroy her. Litigation was the worst thing you could go through, and America was the worst place in the world to endure it, although Canada wasn't so great, either. I hadn't sat down in the chair yet. She had a French accent, she's from Montreal, and had spent a lot of time in Paris, where

she learned the art of surgery. But first she told me
about the north of Canada, the wilds of Canada,
where she learned surgery the hard way, because it was
so primitive up there and you had no choice, you had
to do it. She took a penny out of a kid, with no
knowledge of how to do it. She just did it. Kid
swallowed a penny and they told her to get the penny.
I still hadn't sat down. I was standing there. Her
brown eyes darted around, glancing into mine once in
a while. It began to dawn on me that maybe she was
stoned. But I don't think that was it.

Samuelson What was it?

Adele I think she was flipping out. I think she was Mad, with
a capital M.

Samuelson And you were intimidated?

Adele I was more and more intimidated, and more and more
aware of it happening to me. It was almost like I began
to shrivel. She began to loom over me and I got smaller
and smaller. She couldn't stop talking.

Samuelson She was hysterical.

Adele She was more than hysterical.

Samuelson You were frightened.

Adele I was terrified.

Samuelson Your mother.

Adele My mother, and God knows what else.

Samuelson Like what?

Adele Aging, something to do with aging, or blood pressure,
or something. She went on and on—about this huge
tumor she cut off of this guy's neck when nobody
would go near it, about a knife she took out of a man's

head—all kinds of circus-like surgical episodes she had accomplished with derring-do and panache, and how she was born to be a doctor since the age of eight, and on and on from there. Finally, I get into the chair, and she does my ears while she continues to talk. My blood pressure was 143 over 80.

Samuelson   Not bad.

Adele   No, high, but not bad. I'm feeling pain in my head and my heart was pounding and I'm worried about having a panic attack, but I was also fascinated—I was watching a madwoman. And I was trapped.

Samuelson   Intimidated.

Adele   You said that. Yes, I was. I couldn't get out of there. And she was the one who'd told me about the blood pressure in the first place, last time I was there. It was her. She had taken my blood pressure and freaked out and freaked me out. Yes. I was intimidated by a woman, a crazy woman, and earlier I had been intimidated by Eve.

Samuelson   Why?

Adele   Well, she kept hanging around and hassling me about things like men and marriage and sex and all that crap.

Samuelson   You had two confrontations in a row. Eve and the ear doctor.

Adele   I can't stand it anymore, being intimidated by everyone on earth.

Samuelson   You're not allowed to have problems because you don't feel entitled to your own respect.

Adele   I wish you'd stop saying that.

Samuelson   Not a hair out of place.

Adele	She had to cope with one tumor on the side of a guy's head in Paris, a huge lump, nobody would deal with it, until she stepped up as the French Canadian champion of fearless surgery, and just cut the guy's lump off, blood streaming onto the floor while the nurses looked on aghast and admiringly, or so she said. On and on, feats of heroism supported by God.
Samuelson	Tumors?
Adele	Yes, there were a few of them. Tumors. She wasn't afraid of them. "Do you believe in God," she asked. "Sometimes," I said. "I do. He's the only one you can talk to. There is no one else. You can't trust them. Only God. I talk to him and I pray. It's the only thing that helps. Everyone else is trying to hurt you." She had a point there. Her relatives were claiming she was crazy and couldn't handle things and was not entitled to the community property. (*Pause*) And then she checked me for tumors and I almost jumped out of my seat.
Samuelson	Did she clean your ears?
Adele	Yes, somewhere along in there. I'm not sure what she did. But I feel like I've lost my mind. I have no idea who is talking now. I absolutely loathe not being able to stand up to people. I can't bear it anymore.
Samuelson	It's getting better.
Adele	No, it's not.
Samuelson	Yes, it is. You're allowed to have problems.
Adele	I can't stand up to Eve, who wants me to get out of the house, and I can't do it.
Samuelson	But you did stand up to her.

Adele	I held her off. Barely.
Samuelson	But you did it.
Adele	I guess. Sort of. And then I did a monolgue for Norman and it was an absolute lie. A total fake.
Samuelson	When was this?
Adele	Yesterday.
Samuelson	You told me before that it was an excellent monologue.
Adele	I was wrong. I should go back to Eve and tell *her* to get the fuck out.
Samuelson	Maybe so.
Adele	But I can't. Because everyone in the world is superior to me.
Samuelson	It's neurosis. You're allowed.
Adele	It was fake.
Samuelson	What was fake?
Adele	The monologue was fake. The whole thing was fake. My whole career is fake.
Samuelson	You don't believe that.
Adele	I do right now.
Samuelson	You had two confrontations and it set you back a little.
Adele	It definitely set me back. I felt trapped. (*Pause*)
Samuelson	Do you need the rest room?
Adele	Yes, thank you. (*Quick dim out. SAMUELSON sits.*)

13. (*Lights. ADELE and JANE.*)

Jane	I don't remember this person.
Adele	He mentioned your name.
Jane	I still don't remember this person.

Adele	The Spinoza Society.
Jane	Does not ring a bell. I'm not that involved anymore. Your friends still go.
Adele	They're not my friends. They're my roommates.
Jane	Right. Roommates. What's his name?
Adele	Snow Storm.
Jane	That's a name?
Adele	Not a real name. He's one of those futuristic code guys who are going to change the world with computer codes. Intelligent machines that will make a new world. People will have new names, like "Snow Storm." Like the Indians. If there are still people around. They're freaks, these guys. They're dreaming. People are already machines. They've made a lot of digital money, so their bells have been dinged.
Jane	People are machines?
Adele	Yes.
Jane	Okay. What's the point?
Adele	These kids are right in a way. Their aim is to be more intelligent. But whoever or whatever programmed the evolution thing made some mistakes. Didn't work out too well. So these silicon kids want to reprogram the whole operation.
Jane	Good luck with that.
Adele	They're full of shit.
Jane	Like everything else?
Adele	Right.
Jane	How's the therapy going?
Adele	Great. You don't have to help me find a gig, Jane.

Jane	I had nothing to do with it. I don't know this guy, Norman. Really. Is he an actual theatre person?
Adele	I think he is. He seemed to know what he was talking about. And he knew my history. He researched me. Apparently.
Jane	Well, that's interesting.
Adele	Why?
Jane	Means he's seriously looking for someone.
Adele	Someone weird.
Jane	I wouldn't say that, necessarily.
Adele	No, but it's what you were thinking.
Jane	Hostile, Adele?
Adele	I hate that word.
Jane	What did I do this time?
Adele	Deep down you have contempt for me.
Jane	That's your neurosis talking, your inferiority complex.
Adele	Skip the jargon. It's because I'm smarter than you.
Jane	Yeah, I was studying Spinoza while you were shooting up in johns.
Adele	Look where it got you.
Jane	Look where it got you, smart-head. Panic attacks. Therapy. Hypertension.
Adele	I hate that word.
Jane	You hate a lot of words.
Adele	And I'm Jewish.
Jane	That's sheer paranoia. A phobia.
Adele	No, it isn't. We've earned it. Hatred for Jews has become organic to the planet earth. Because of envy. That's why these silicon idiots are idiots. Hitler and his

thugs didn't think they were wrong. They thought they were making a change for the good. They wanted to clean up the gene pool, change the programming. Purify. And, after two thousand years of Jew-hating, most of Europe went along with it. America went along with it. Never forget that. And now we got these Islamic imbecile freaks to deal with. The purification of the earth. And now these digital maniacs.

Jane Well, I didn't follow your reasoning entirely, and I don't entirely agree.

Adele Which is it? You didn't follow, or you don't entirely agree?

Jane Both.

Adele Anyway, what did we do? We sang the *Sh'ma* in the gas chambers. "Hear O Israel, the Lord is God, the Lord is One." The Muslims stole that formulation from us, by the way.

Jane You don't have to project that paranoia on to me. You know I'm not an anti-Semite. And neither are the girls.

Adele Yes, they are.

Jane It's just talk.

Adele Talk will do it.

Jane Take it back.

Adele For you, I will. I'll take it back.

Jane Spinoza was a Jew, after all. And so was Christ.

Adele And so were Einstein, Freud and Marx. Who created the modern world.

Jane True. I admit that.

Adele	Sorry. (*Pause*) I am, Jane. (*Pause*) I don't think you're an anti-Semite.
Jane	Thank you. What was the play about?
Adele	Which one? Norman's?
Jane	Yes, the one you read for.
Adele	I didn't read anything. They didn't have sides. I did something from my "Cinderella."
Jane	How'd he like it?
Adele	He seemed to like it. Hard to tell. I liked it. (*Pause. DIM OUT. JANE withdraws.*)

14. (*Lights up on ADELE.*)

Adele	(*To audience*) So, I've been having strange sleeps. (*Pause*) Not easy to talk about. (*Pause*) Not dreams so much as sensations. Heavy blocks of wood or ice. (*Pause. Enter SAMUELSON. He sits.*) Before I'd go on a date, I'd be sure I'd find a way to do a little performance for this person. It could be only a second or two, like a bright smile, or a giggle, or a laugh. I'm sure this is really common. Guys fall for it all the time. It's a signal, you know, that it's all right to make a move. Go on to the next moment.
Samuelson	Totally normal.
Adele	I'd have felt better if my son was in the same city. I didn't have to see him. But I'd feel better if he was merely in the general vicinity.
Samuelson	Also totally normal.

Adele	He never called. Unless he needed a ride, or money, or a place to stay. Otherwise he was completely indifferent. He didn't give a shit about me, really.
Samuelson	He was a junkie.
Adele	I know what it means to be a junkie.
Samuelson	It wasn't the same for you.
Adele	How so?
Samuelson	It was more experimental for you, a life experience, and you were able to quit. He wasn't.
Adele	I wanted to get into the Spinoza Society. They would have taken me anyway. They take everybody. It was all in my imagination.
Samuelson	Maybe not.
Adele	It took eighteen months to kick the methadone. Eighteen months of no sleep and pain in the central nervous system, in the solar plexus.
Samuelson	Shows character.
Adele	There is evil in the world.
Samuelson	Pardon?
Adele	Because methadone is in it, among other things. The world. Evil stuff, invented by the Germans. I could go on, but it's not what we're talking about.
Samuelson	We can talk about anything here.
Adele	We're talking about high blood pressure and hypertension and panic attacks. Approaching the theory that they are connected to anxiety, due to low self-esteem and the stress of living.
Samuelson	Is that what we're talking about?

Adele	Everything seems to have gotten worse since I've had these attacks. I feel like a complete idiot.
Dr. Schine	You've felt that way before. I'll give you some pills for the blood pressure, but you also need to see your therapist. Will you do that? And ask him to call me.
Adele	It's so humiliating. Dr. Schine making me see you.
Samuelson	I know it is.
Adele	I can't stand it anymore. (*Pause*) I guess I can. (*Pause*) No, I can't face it.
Samuelson	You are facing it.
Adele	Alone.
Samuelson	No, with me.
Adele	I'm alone.
Samuelson	Your son loved you. And you loved him. And you loved your mother.
Adele	No, I didn't. None of that is true.
Samuelson	As children we identify with our parents.
Adele	Isn't that weird?
Samuelson	No, it's normal.
Adele	I feel like I've been alone my entire life.
Samuelson	Very dramatic.
Adele	Yes. That's what I do. Went to an audition the other day, in fact.
Samuelson	Good!
Adele	They haven't called back yet.
Samuelson	Interested?
Adele	I think so. Yes.
Samuelson	What is it?

Adele	A guy named Norman. Something "experimental." We'll see. (*DIM OUT.*)

15. (*Lights. "ENTER" GRACE and EVE.*)

Grace	Panic attacks lately?
Adele	No. Fuck off.
Grace	I was reading somewhere, there's danger of a stroke.
Adele	Did you hear what I said?
Grace	Yes. "Fuck off."
Adele	Fuck off.
Eve	No, you fuck off.
Adele	Brilliant.
Grace	Stroke danger.
Eve	How's the theater business?
Grace	Mom told us.
Adele	Great.
Eve	What's up?
Adele	Sky's up.
Eve	Brilliant.
Grace	You never know.
Adele	Fuck off again.
Grace	Thank you.
Eve	How old was Nathan?
Adele	I'm not telling you.
Eve	When he died.
Adele	Seventeen. I was thirty-four. His father left right after. Okay?
Eve	He was a drunk. The father.

Adele	Ned. He was definitely a drunk. He broke all the windows and left. Thanks for bringing it up.
Eve	You're welcome.
Grace	And you?
Adele	Me, what?
Grace	What happened to you?
Adele	I had gone back to school. I was an honors student at Brooklyn College.
Grace	In what?
Adele	Theater. Then I left.
Eve	You became a junkie.
Adele	No, I had already been a junkie. Thank you, very much.
Eve	Well, it can be confusing.
Adele	Me, too. It's confusing to me, too.
Eve	I'll bet.
Grace	And then you converted.
Adele	Yes.
Eve	Why?
Adele	I was following Spinoza, who had never actually converted, as far as we know, and I wanted to see my son again. It was no big deal. It was mainly an acting thing. An inner performance, so to speak.
Eve	And then you converted back? (*ADELE nods*)
Grace	How did you do that?
Adele	I stayed who I already was.
Eve	Boy, is that confusing.
Adele	Yeah, it is.
Grace	Could lead to panic attacks and/or stroke.

Adele	Fuck off, Grace.
Grace	I'd be careful, if I were you.
Adele	You're not me.
Grace	Luckily for me.
Eve	Sure you want to be on stage?
Adele	I'm sure.
Grace	If you get the part.
Adele	I'll get it.
Eve	Because of the stress.
Adele	I don't know what the part is yet.
Grace	I couldn't do it.
Adele	No, you couldn't.
Grace	I could if I tried.
Adele	I don't think so.
Grace	Why not?
Adele	Acting is not pretending.
Grace	You were pretending to be a Gentile.
Eve	She's got a point there.
Adele	Acting is about intelligent speech, which leaves you out. Oh, forget it. I wanted to be myself. A Jewess. They tried to exterminate us. Remember? It's a reason for Jewish solidarity forever.
Eve	What about the religion?
Adele	Religion has nothing to do with it.
Grace	What's "intelligent speech?"
Adele	Not like yours. It's a learned art.
Grace	Okay, okay. Talk straight for a change.
Eve	It was a simple question.
Adele	I am talking straight. You don't give me any credit.
Eve	We try.

Grace	Give an example.
Adele	Take Spinoza. You know something about Spinoza.
Eve	You know we do.
Grace	Continue.
Adele	You have these guys I was telling you about, physicists, moderns, figuring out the origins of the universe. In Kabbalah, which apparently Spinoza knew, above the Tree of Life and below the Tree of Life, is Absolute Nothing. *Ein Sof.* The modern view is a combination of quantum theory and Einstein's theory of relativity.
Eve	Another Jew.
Adele	Right. Where was I?
Eve	Spinoza.
Adele	Spinoza was trying to use geometry—theorems and axioms and propositions—to prove the mind of God. Based on the laws of nature. Including the laws of ethics and morals and so on. In modern mathematics, the universe began with the Big Bang by itself, out of Nothing, which is inherently unstable, and then expanded, balanced by the relation of energy of movement and gravity. So. . .
Eve	So?
Adele	I got lost there.
Grace	Take a breath. (*Pause*) Take another breath.
Eve	Avoid stress.
Adele	The mind of God. (*Pause*) I think what he meant was that God was existence itself. Which arose out of Nothing. (*Silence*) Sorry. I made a jump there. I'm not sure what I'm saying. Sorry.
Grace	You apologize a lot.

Adele	I know I do. It's a bad habit. Sorry.
Grace	Nothing to do with acting, per se. Though it sounded intelligent.
Eve	Incomprehensible.
Grace	Really. (PAUSE. DIM OUT. "EXIT" EVE and GRACE.)

16. (UP ON ADELE.)

Adele	(*To audience*) I was talking to my roommates. Grace and Eve. For some reason, I was trying to explain the origins of the Universe. They didn't get it. I didn't get it, either, so I started apologizing, which I do all the time. I apologize for my very existence. It's a joke. No wonder my son ignored me. I wasn't important to him at all, except for being a money source and providing a place for him to hide out, to chill. So what's the point? Excuse me? He shot up with his girlfriend. He was very deferential and easily influenced. Like me. Amazing how the human mind works, if it works at all. People are people, and needy. I need to forgive and forgive. Give in advance. Americans like dope, and alcohol. And guns. And cars. And money. And TV. And so does the rest of the world. He, Nathan, ended up dying. In a hospital, tubes coming out all over him, begging to die. With his eyes. Here comes the casting director. (*Light change.* NORMAN *joins* ADELE. *Pause.*)
Norman	What's with the Annunaki?
Adele	I give up. (*Laughs*) They were Sumerian gods. People from another planet. Apparently. They helped

	Mankind form civilization on earth. At the right time, they're going to come back. There'll be a war, and the Annunaki will save us.
Norman	Like the Messiah.
Adele	A lot like the Messiah. Supposedly, I look like them. The Annunaki. I think I do, actually. (*Coquettish*) Yeah. And those little hats. (*Pause*) Your idea of a digital plan and a new world order is also messianic.
Norman	I'm glad you brought that up. I'd like to consider you, if that's all right.
Adele	Consider me for what?
Norman	The lead.
Adele	The lead?
Norman	Yes.
Adele	The lead in what?
Norman	In our play.
Adele	Consider me? What does that mean?
Norman	Consider. Think about?
Adele	Think about?
Norman	My play.
Adele	Where's the play?
Norman	We're not there yet.
Adele	You're not where yet?
Norman	On the page.
Adele	Not on the page?
Norman	Not yet. We're working with code. Algorithms, numbers.
Adele	I have no idea what that means.
Norman	A certain planned randomness.
Adele	Where's the fucking play?

Norman	It's like a recipe.
Adele	Sorry.
Norman	No, I totally understand.
Adele	What do you understand?
Norman	Where you're coming from.
Adele	You're offering me the lead in a play that doesn't actually exist?
Norman	Actually, it exists.
Adele	Where is it?
Norman	It's in my head.
Adele	Great. (*Coughs*) You're offering me the lead in a play that doesn't exist anywhere but in your head. Story of my life. Why?
Norman	You'd be great in it.
Adele	Why?
Norman	I don't know why.
Adele	Well, that's honest. Can you say more? (*Silence*) That's all right. Never mind. But I can't agree to anything that doesn't exist. Even I have written, am writing, a play that's on the page. On the page. You heard some of it.
Norman	Well, that's partly why I'm considering you.
Adele	Thanks a lot. But I can't take you seriously so far.
Norman	I understand.
Adele	Maybe something more substantial next time?
Norman	Yes. (*Pause. DIM OUT.*)

17. (*JANE sits down with ADELE. Pause.*)

Jane	Did you meet? With the casting director?

Adele	Yes. Norman. For nothing.
Jane	I think it's something.
Adele	No. Nothing's there. Nothing at all. Like everything that exists. Nothing. A bubble in time. Time in the bubble. Whatever. Nothing.
Jane	You sure know how to negativize.
Adele	Is that a word?
Jane	Probably not.
Adele	I got mad at myself for having panic attacks.
Jane	Apropos of. . .
Adele	Negatavizing. I have no idea what this guy Norman is talking about. And I don't know who is talking when I speak. So I don't know. Even now. We seem like we're being nice to each other, even though I'm harboring a lot of resentment. At the way he talks. This digital messianic nonsense.
Jane	What else is bothering you?
Adele	Because I couldn't be a Christian. I couldn't live up to it. No matter what I did.
Jane	Spinoza did.
Adele	You don't know that. Nobody knows. Anything. About Spinoza or anything else. Fuck this guy, Norman. Anyway, I'm Jewish, thank God, because you can take it any which way, or no way at all. I mean the Old Testament. The Torah. It's not like a total dogma and you can't misinterpret it, like the Koran, because there's too much of it and it goes every which way. So the result is openness and diversity. We don't go around proselytizing or killing people for not being

	Jews, or the right kind of Jews, or something weird like that.
Jane	There are different kinds of Christians, too.
Adele	Like this guy Norman—the casting director—he's into something else entirely, where he thinks there'll be machines, that we'll evolve, via technology, into a better machine, more rational, more sound mentally, and thus a better world. (*Pause*) I think he's wrong. It's another form of messianic thinking. I'm just saying. I'm thinking aloud. (*Pause*) There I go again—taking it back. It's like I'm not worthy of having an actual opinion.
Jane	I don't know what to say.
Adele	He's really helping me, Samuelson.
Jane	I wonder what Spinoza would think.
Adele	He would say that Nature was a machine and that the brain, the wiring, was God. (*Pause*) Actually, I don't know what he would say. (*Pause*) I did it again. Took it back. (*"ENTER" GRACE. JANE stands.*)
Grace	Where you going, Jane?
Jane	I have an acolyte.
Grace	You still doing that?
Jane	Sometimes. When I'm needed. (*Exits. Pause.*)
Grace	Are you kosher?
Adele	Are you kidding?
Grace	No. I thought that was a legitimate question.
Adele	You'd know it if I was.
Grace	How?
Adele	Never mind. You'd notice. You don't know nothing about it. But I'll tell you one thing. Which is—I was

	thinking about this earlier—I appreciate it more now. Ask me why.
Grace	Okay. Why?
Adele	It creates a path to obedience. People need to be obedient. Because of all the inner chaos. There needs to be something larger to obey. Some order inside. Laws to obey. That's why all the rules and regulations in Leviticus, and so on. It's a lot, all day, food and clothes and behavior. Fasting. Prayer. Holidays. Order and obedience. Makes for a kind of sanity. (*Pause*) I've thought about it.
Grace	Not for you, though.
Adele	So far, no. I'm not so much a religious person. So far. (*Pause*)
Grace	How's your play coming?
Adele	I'm getting there.
Grace	Where?
Adele	I don't know. Somewhere. I don't want to jinx it by talking about it. A certain kind of energy coming down.
Grace	What kind of energy?
Adele	Very fine. Don't interrupt me.
Grace	I'm just asking.
Adele	Don't ask me.
Grace	You're not writing.
Adele	I'm thinking.
Grace	What are you thinking?
Adele	I can't think and talk to you at the same time.
Grace	What's it about?
Adele	Human life on earth.

Grace	Come on.
Adele	Orifices.
Grace	Adele!
Adele	I'm an anal intellectual, according to some people.
Grace	What is that supposed to mean?
Adele	Don't talk to me now.
Grace	What are you going to do with it?
Adele	With what?
Grace	Your play.
Adele	I don't know, Grace.
Grace	Aren't you scared of what people will think?
Adele	No.
Grace	I would be.
Adele	Shut up, Grace.
Grace	You're an actor, but you've never written a play before.
Adele	So what? As soon as they have to think, the game's over. Life on earth: murder and mayhem.
Grace	That's a negative attitude.
Adele	Sorry, but I don't give a rat's ass.
Grace	That's a really bad attitude.
Adele	Go away, Grace.
Grace	No. I live here.
Adele	Okay. Just don't talk to me. (*Pause*)
Grace	Is there any sex in it?
Adele	Good question.
Grace	I think there should be. It's entertaining.
Adele	I agree with you. Orifices. The trouble is I haven't had any lately. Penetration. But I'm thinking about it.
Grace	What are you thinking?

Adele	None of your business. (*Pause*) I made it with two guys once. They were dope dealers, so I sort of had to. Don't believe everything I say.
Grace	How was it?
Adele	It was nice for awhile. Then it got complicated.
Grace	Tell me?
Adele	No.
Grace	I've changed my mind. Sex is stupid, really.
Adele	You've got a point there, Grace. I agree.
Grace	See you, Adele. (*Exits*)
Adele	Bye, bye. (*Pause. DIM OUT. "Enter" NORMAN.*)

18. (*Lights up.*)

Adele	"So. . . Cinderella goes into the woods. . . No. . . Yeah, she goes into the woods. . . basically she's looking to score. . . not the woods. . . she goes up to this apartment in the projects. . . two black guys are there. . . one of them is young, a teenager, and the other one's a big dude in his thirties. . . they can't believe there's this little Jewish woman by herself buying some dope. . . there's like hardly any furniture. . . just a couch and a chair and some packs of dope and paraphenalia. . ."

(*VOICES OFF, from the past: two young black MEN and ADELE:*)

	Where you from, Lady?
Adele	**Long Island.**

	Where in Long Island?
Adele	Great Neck.
	What the fuck you doin' from Great Neck?
Adele	That's were I'm from.
	What the fuck.
	What you want?
Adele	What you got?
	Who followed you?
Adele	Nobody.

Adele   "So. . . she realizes she's scared and she's made a mistake, but she's dope sick, and the boy on the street—another black kid—sent her up there, saying it was all cool, nothing to worry about, and he stayed outside. . . she wonders about that, but she's deferential as usual, believing everybody is above her, including this illiterate doper black kid on the street, so she dutifully follows instructions and now she finds herself in this project hell-hole with two dangerous dopers who don't like her. . . No, it's not that. . . they do like her. . . a woman alone, not too old, and she's fuckable, a white Jewish woman junkie and not bad-looking and fuckable, if she's really alone. . . it's an unusual opportunity. . ."

	Who sent you up here?
Adele	Peewee.
	Peewee?
	Peewee?
Adele	Yeah. I could go now if it's not right.
	We know him.

	Where is he?
Adele	He's downstairs.
	On the street?
Adele	I think so.
	What you want?
Adele	Three or four bags maybe. Are you guys holding?
Adele	"She's using the lingo of the day. . . and trying to act cool, but she's starting to shake, she's starting to tremble. . . they look at her arms."
	She's got marks.
	Yeah.
	Show us the money, woman.
Adele	"So. . . she pulls out some of the money. . . because she knows an old junkie trick, which is you don't show all your money, you just pull out some of it with a movement of your hand in your pocket, separating out some of the money, but these guys know the trick and the kid grabs her arm and takes the money and hangs onto her arm. . ."
	What's your name?
Adele	"She was going to say Cinderella, but instead she says:"
Adele	Rita.
	Take a look in the hall. (Pause)
Adele	Enough of that stuff. My memory isn't what it once was. It never is. One of the flaws in the structure of the human brain. It's a bunch of titillation, mainly. I'm not sure it ever happened.
Norman	A scene from your play?

Adele	Maybe. I have fantasies. I have seen some porn. The decadence of the West. Yeah. These days, I'm not interested in that kind of thing.
Norman	But it still happens, of course.
Adele	How would you know? I'm talking about the street.
Norman	One has friends.
Adele	You have friends? On the street? Junkies?
Norman	Yes. Why?
Adele	I don't know. You don't seem the type. (*Pause*) These Islamic fanatics, they want to cover up the women so they're not distracted from worshipping God, can you imagine what's going on their heads?
Norman	Yes.
Adele	You're going to change that? You're going make a play about that?
Norman	Spinoza was into it a long time ago. The naturalistic universe, based on laws, theorems—back to the First Cause.
Adele	Yeah, yeah.
Norman	You don't sound like you believe in it.
Adele	I don't. I quit. Things just happen.
Norman	You're really not that far from us, spiritually speaking.
Adele	Yes, I am.
Norman	Must be lonely for you.
Adele	Yes, it is. It's lonely as hell. You've got a world war developing between fundamentalist, radical Islam and the West, while people go to basketball games, the stock market rebounds, people look for jobs, actresses go to auditions, and then you've got these freaks, like you, talking about the digital revolution, as if the

human being will turn into a system of equations and algorithms that will create a new world. Did I get that right?

Norman   No.

Adele   It's baloney, anyway. That's what they say over and over again and make a lot of money. Which is what they really want. And the primary target, for these idiots and crazies and fanatics, as always, is the Jews. And I am a Jew.

Norman   It's not as simple as that. It has nothing to do with anti-Semitism.

Adele   Yes, it does. You're talking about the culture. Who created the culture? Who created the world of Commerce, of Thought? Who goes to the theatre? We do. They're going to come after us, Norman. Bearded imbeciles with Kalashnikovs and machetes and tanks. They'll torture and kill right way. Forget the gas chambers. The earth will be covered with blood. Then there'll be a change. The blood will create new substances, the land and air and water will change, and new creatures will appear. Maybe the Annunaki. But, in my opinion, there'll be no justice for people like us, and no revenge, as usual. (*Pause*) Is that what you're getting at?

Norman   No. New codes. New patterns. Ways of understanding. Like Spinoza's mathematical approach, his geometry, but we have a new technology now, that can support the ideas. His and others. Like your idea of the Annunaki.

Adele   Yeah, digital Annunaki.

Norman	Right.
Adele	I'm not inspired.
Norman	No?
Adele	No.
Norman	Can we meet again soon, Adele, and talk some more?
Adele	Yeah, Norman, if you bring something real with you. Something that makes sense. (*Pause. D*IM OUT*. "Exit"* NORMAN.)

19. (*Lights up.* ADELE *changes position.* SAMUELSON *joins her. Pause.*)

Adele	So I got a little over the top there. With Norman. And I don't really give a damn. The thing is, I don't remember key phrases, like "buttoned up," and being "neurotic" or "treated like a pet," or any of that. And I need to express myself.
Samuelson	You don't need to remember phrases.
Adele	Because the situation is dire.
Samuelson	Dire?
Adele	This creature which has evolved for no reason, as some people have observed, like a virus, eating everything around it. A complicated organism with a complicated brain, built to eat and shit and copulate and survive, and that's it. (*Pause*)
Samuelson	That was good.
Adele	What do you mean, "good?"
Samuelson	Eloquent.

Adele	(*Aside*) They pushed us into ghettoes and walled us in until we stank to high heaven. Dropping dead on the streets.
Samuelson	Excuse me? Did you say something?
Adele	Kids these days—they know nothing about the Shoah. My own son wasn't interested in it. He was interested in other things. Like getting high. But he got his own taste of misery. Maybe he learned something. But I don't know what I'm talking about, either. I wasn't there. (*Pause*) There I go again. Taking it back.
Samuelson	You're angry.
Adele	Yes. So what?
Samuelson	You have a right to be angry.
Adele	I know that. And I want revenge. I heard myself say it. I heard myself think it. I imagined certain. . . actions. But what good would it do? They're all dead now. And people's brains are not wired to remember anything. Morally, we are still. . . I don't know what. (*Bursts into tears.*) Sorry.
Samuelson	Why? You're allowed to cry.
Adele	(*Weeping*) At least we, the Jewish people, are interested, at least we care about memory, and thought, and language, and books.
Samuelson	Yes, I agree.
Adele	And they'll start trying to kill us again, the envious assholes. They're doing it already. I'm sorry. It's become part of the ecology of the earth. (*Pause, recovers.*) Let's change the subject.

Samuelson	Okay.
Adele	It's planetary. Sorry.
Samuelson	Have you been auditioning?
Adele	No. Just talking to Norman.
Samuelson	Depressed?
Adele	Yes. So what? I was just thinking, Spinoza knew nothing of all this.
Samuelson	I disagree. He knew a lot. His work followed right after the Inquisition. It was still going on, in fact.
Adele	You're right. I'm sorry. God, I've got to stop doing that. Saying "sorry" all the time.
Samuelson	You will. It'll happen by itself.
Adele	Yeah. Like life. Like the world. Like the Universe. It's like everything is happening by itself. (*Laughs*) Bad line. Could be a line from Norman's nonexistent play.
Samuelson	What's happening with the "digital" play?
Adele	I don't know. Maybe there is no real play. He keeps asking me to write something or do something. It occurred to me recently—it could be about the money.
Samuelson	The money?
Adele	Yes. From my roommate, Jane. She's the elder of the group and they seem to know each other. I sound like I'm being paranoid.
Samuelson	Are they nice to you?
Adele	Most of the time. I did my rehab and they took me in. I should be grateful. And she does a great massage, Jane. (*Samuelson looks at his watch.*) Are we done?

Samuelson	Yes.
Adele	You think I can start coming once a week again?
Samuelson	No. Let's give it a little more time, as we're doing.
Adele	It's expensive.
Samuelson	I know. Think of it as an investment in your future.
	(*Pause.* ADELE *frowns. Lights* DIM OUT.)

20. (*Lights up as* ADELE *joins* NORMAN.)

Norman	You ever write about your ex?
Adele	My husband?
Norman	Yes.
Adele	Of course, I do. Not very edifying. Why?
Norman	Just curious.
Adele	Curiosity killed the cat. Do you have a play yet?
Norman	We do. We have an outline.
Adele	What do you mean, "an outline?"
Norman	I told you. We're going to improvise. Into the outline. From the outline.
Adele	No. You never told me.
Norman	I thought I told you.
Adele	You didn't. Not that I recall.
Norman	That's why I asked about your play.
Adele	Why?
Norman	Well, it's good material.
Adele	Isn't that stealing?
Norman	I mean, as an example. Of the kind of thing people can bring to the project. Not that we want the lines from your own play. Just so we know you can bring

	the right material to the project. That's what's attractive to us.
Adele	Bring material?
Norman	Yes. Perhaps something from your own work or life that can fit our theme. It's an experiment.
Adele	I don't know if I want to do that.
Norman	Well, that's understandable.
Adele	What's the outline?
Norman	I told you. I thought I told you.
Adele	I don't have a clue.
Norman	We want to talk about life as it might be organized by new digital processes, the new Physics, the Cybernet. Synthetic DNA. New ways of approaching the design of cities, sociology, government, politics. Another way of living. About saving life on earth. About the possiblity of another environment, one sustainable by humans, or some kind of humanity—
Adele	That's not an outline. It's an idea.
Norman	It's an important idea, though, don't you think?
Adele	I don't know if I can bring anything to it.
Norman	Yes, you can. You're all around it.
Adele	What does that mean?
Norman	You have experience. You have your own ideas. You have the chops.
Adele	Thanks, but where's the story? There has to be a story.
Norman	It's an experimental approach to a theatrical performance. A theme, with the dialogue filled in mostly with improvisation by the actors.
Adele	I can write lines. I can say lines.
Norman	We know that.

Adele	But they need to be about something meaningful for me.
Norman	Of course. Let me send you what we have. You can study it and see what you think. (*Pause*) Yes?
Adele	That might be good.
Norman	Great. I'll do that. What could be more meaningful than the survival of Life on Earth?
Adele	I give up. What? (NORMAN *doesn't reply.*) And the improvisation?
Norman	Yes?
Adele	Does it happen in performance?
Norman	No, once we have the language, we'll set it.
Adele	Because that's so important, don't you think? The rhythms, the diction, the characters, the dialogue—
Norman	Yes. We'll set all that. But we'll leave room for impromptu surprises. It's been done before. It can be something different and unique, because the actors have created their own characters and dialogue.
Adele	Where was this process done before?
Norman	In New York.
Adele	Did it work?
Norman	Some people think so.
Adele	Okay. Send me some stuff.
Norman	I'll do that. (*"Exits" happily.* DIM OUT *as* ADELE *rejoins* SAMUELSON.)

21. (*Lights up.*)

Adele	So then I was questioning my memory. Maybe he had said things I'd forgotten. And then I thought, "What

about my own survival? I don't give a damn about life on earth." On the other hand, I want to be on stage, I want to do something.

Samuelson You do have your own play.

Adele Yeah, but I don't have much of it. And it's a sad story. Nobody wants to hear about my crazy, sadistic mother and my junkie son, who died, and my own junkie life, and rehab, and re-converting, and so on. It's all a mess. And it isn't written yet.

Samuelson You don't like to talk about that, do you?

Adele No. I could jinx it.

Samuelson You don't feel like you deserve it.

Adele No.

Samuelson Why not?

Adele I don't know why. It's the way I grew up. Scorned by society. Life won't survive on earth, not this life, so it's all a gamble anyway. (*Pause*) It's an interesting idea. Improvising.

Samuelson Improvising?

Adele Yes, I've never done it. Except in class. But it's taking advantage of the actors. I don't know how I feel about that. And I know what you're going to say—that I don't feel the right to have feelings. I don't feel I have rights. And that would be true, too. Why is that?

Samuelson It's a cultural norm. Second-class citizens are considered to be servants. They are supposed to curtsy and be of service.

Adele I had some good teachers, thank God, or I would have ended up dead in somebody's bathroom, a needle stuck in my arm.

Samuelson	Probably so.
Adele	Or on the street with my throat cut. But I never remember.
Samuelson	You don't have to remember, we just have to keep talking.
Adele	No, I need to remember. It helps me to remember.
Samuelson	Takes time. It's an inside job. Takes time.
Adele	You always say that.
Samuelson	Because it's true.
Adele	Do I have to keep coming twice a week?
Samuelson	Yes, I think so—for now. Like I said, think of it as an investment in your future.
Adele	Okay. . . The future. . . (*DIM OUT.*)

22. (*Lights up. JANE and ADELE*)

Jane	But that's a part of any spiritual path—to bow and be of service.
Adele	I know, but I went too far in that direction. I was *davening* before everybody, in front of everybody. Overdoing it.
Jane	Were you?
Adele	Wanting to please. No hair out of place.
Jane	I never noticed. You sure about this guy?
Adele	Who? The casting director, Norman?
Jane	No. Your psychiatrist. Samuelson.
Adele	He's a psychologist.
Jane	Let's back up a minute.
Adele	Too much obedience.
Jane	We were talking about what's-his-name.
Adele	Samuelson.

Jane	Seems like he's going too far in the other direction.
Adele	The strangest thing is that I imagine myself one way, and in reality I'm the total opposite. Who has panic attacks.
Jane	Did you hear what I said?
Adele	Yes. The shrink. He's fine. Did you hear what I said?
Jane	You're not who you think you are. That's true of everybody.
Adele	I guess that's right. I think it's only me. (*Pause*)
Jane	How's your play going?
Adele	It's going, more or less.
Jane	Are we in it? Me and Grace and Eve?
Adele	There's no way to avoid that. A person writes about what's happening to them. But I think you have to be careful about putting real people in your play. People are sensitive. All writers do it. Speaking of the casting director, Norman? (*Pause*) Are you listening?
Jane	Yes. I'm listening. What about him?
Adele	I don't know if he's scamming me or not. He says he knows you.
Jane	You told me. I do know him, slightly. He came to a few meetings.
Adele	Would you give money to his project?
Jane	No. I don't think so.
Adele	Okay. Thanks. (*DIM OUT.*)

23. (*Lights up.* ADELE *and* SAMUELSON. *Pause as they settle into their seats.*)

Adele	I am feeling a little more libido, as they say.

Samuelson	You're coming back to life.
Adele	It's not that I wasn't looking around, I was looking at butts a little, looking at crotches, automatically. But I wasn't going to start anything, either. Just going to auditions and writing.
Samuelson	You're feeling more equal. More respect for yourself.
Adele	I think that's true. I hope that's true. I don't feel like getting into actual sex that much, but it's on my mind a little bit.
Samuelson	You had given up.
Adele	Yeah, I guess I did. I'm not sure what happened.
Samuelson	It's not so hard to understand. You were a junkie, you lost your son, your husband—who broke all your windows and left you stranded—you tried to begin a new life—eventually, you started having panic attacks.
Adele	What a mess.
Samuelson	You see what you just did? Unnecessary.
Adele	The panic attacks hit bottom. They say you have to hit bottom. I hit bottom right there. I just want to work. Which brings me to Norman and his far-out experimental project. True, there's a little libido there. He's a smart, good-looking guy. Young. But that's not it. I thought he had passed the test.
Samuelson	The test?
Adele	I thought he had passed the test—as someone I might like—but now I'm not so sure. He's not coming up with the material. And the other thing is. . . I'm not coming up with it, either. I'm not interested in any of that salami. That he's into. What does he expect is

Adele

247

going to happen? Digitally, no less. It's like a phony utopia. Never works, never. And dangerous, dangerous.

Samuelson You do that sometimes. Repeat. The second "dangerous" is apologetic.

Adele They got away with it. The Germans. Don't you think?

Samuelson I do. Yes. But what's to be done?

Adele I meant everything I said.

Samuelson I know you did. (*Pause. DIM OUT. "Exit" SAMUELSON. GRACE and EVE "enter."*)

24. (*Lights up. Pause.*)

Grace You could look for a job.

Adele I am looking for a job.

Eve I mean, you seem over your health problems.

Adele I'm not.

Grace What kind of job?

Adele I'm an actor.

Grace We know you're an actor.

Adele So?

Eve The panic attacks, the depression, that's all.

Adele I'm over the panic attacks.

Eve That's what I'm saying.

Adele I'm taking blood pressure meds.

Grace You used to teach.

Adele What does that have to do with anything?

Grace The auditioning isn't going anywhere, is it?

Adele Yes, it is.

Grace	Oh? Where?
Adele	I may have a part. In a play.
Grace	Oh. What's the part?
Adele	That's the thing. It doesn't exist yet.
Grace	Great.
Eve	Insane.
Adele	It's a very interesting premise.
Grace	Which is?
Adele	The digital salvation of the world.
Eve	Insane.
Grace	Where are the characters coming from?
Adele	Supposedly us. The actors. Through improvisation.
Eve	Can you do that?
Adele	I don't know. And I'm writing a play myself.
Eve	You can't make a living writing plays. And you have trouble writing.
Adele	I know that.
Grace	So that's why we're saying: get a job.
Eve	You used to teach.
Adele	You said that already.
Eve	You made a decent living.
Adele	The two plays could be connected. The stuff I'm writing or not writing could somehow contribute to this guy's idea. Norman's. I told you about him. He knows Jane. He used to be associated with the Spinoza Society.
Eve	Norman.
Grace	The guy's a flake.
Eve	The guy's a con.

Adele	You think he's a con?
Eve	Definitely.
Grace	He hung around and chatted people up, but he didn't do anything.
Adele	What was he supposed to do?
Grace	I don't know. Make coffee. Clean up. Contribute an idea once in a while. He's obviously bright.
Adele	Well, that's the thing.
Grace	What's the thing?
Adele	That he's bright.
Grace	Lots of people are bright.
Eve	Then what does he want?
Adele	I think it's Jane. I think he wants her money for his play. That's what I think.
Grace	Tell him to forget about it.
Adele	I just want to be on stage.
Eve	Good luck. (*Slow* DIM OUT. GRACE *leaves.* ADELE *and* EVE *stare at each other.*)
Adele	Remember you hit me.
Eve	I remember.
Adele	I'll get you back for that.
Eve	Try it. (*Exits. Dim out.*)

25. (*Enter* NORMAN. *Lights up.*)

Adele	Did you see *Night and Fog*?
Norman	Yes. Years ago.
Adele	What did you think?
Norman	I was sick to my stomach.
Adele	It's only thirty-one minutes long. I mean, the movie.

Norman	Long enough. And he got in there early. It had only been ten years. One camera. Plus the German footage. Black and white and color. That was a big deal in those days. I remember there was one shot, it showed a French policeman guarding some Jewish prisoners. The French government wanted it out of the film, or they wouldn't let it released. So Resnais had something painted over the man's hat so you wouldn't know he was a *gendarme*. Nobody noticed, and they released the film. (*ADELE bursts into tears. NORMAN takes her in his arms. ADELE subsides.*)
Norman	I've done some research.
Adele	Good for you.
Norman	There is Divine Reason. In the Tree of Life. The central column. I think Spinoza knew all about the Tree.
Adele	I'm sure he knew about the Tree of Life. But I don't think he ever converted.
Norman	The theme is Guardian Angels.
Adele	Yes. I read your outline.
Norman	Oh. Good.
Adele	Not so good.
Norman	Why not?
Adele	Not such a good outline.
Norman	Why not so good?
Adele	I do like the idea of Guardian Angels. Reminds me of the Anunnakki. You know who they are?
Norman	Not exactly.
Adele	They're like guardians. Originally, like I said, they were Sumerian gods—I think. Some people think they came from another planet. They came to help us. Some of them

merged with us. Some people think they'll come again to save us. It's like your idea of a digital revolution, a new species, with new kinds of thinking, new information, and so on. It's just like the Anunnakki. Perhaps they could work like a metaphor. The Anunnakki.

Norman	No. This is something I entirely believe in.
Adele	Suit yourself.
Norman	So you won't participate?
Adele	It's hubris, you know, to think human reason can fix things.
Norman	God—or nature—hasn't done too well with it, either. So we might as well give it a shot.
Adele	I'll do something. Something will happen, and I'll do it. (*Quick blackout.*)

26. (GRACE, EVE, *and* ADELE. *Pause.*)

Grace	You ever have sex?
Adele	No. Obviously.
Grace	Why not?
Adele	I'm not interested.
Eve	Maybe that's why.
Adele	Why what?
Eve	You have anxiety attacks.
Adele	I don't have anxiety attacks.
Eve	You did have anxiety attacks.
Adele	Not any more.
Eve	You're gay.
Adele	I'm not gay.
Eve	What are you?

Adele	I don't know what I am. I'm sexless. Androgynous.
Grace	You did have a child. Sorry to bring it up.
Adele	I was seventeen years old. I thought I should try.
Eve	So what are you?
Adele	Basically, I'm a junkie.
Eve	No. Besides that. Sexually.
Adele	An actress. Androgynous.
Eve	You play tough women.
Adele	It's easy. Even you could do it. Well, maybe not.
Eve	Thanks.
Adele	I have a feminine side. I just go there. Works good.
Eve	What about Norman?
Adele	He's barking up the wrong tree, as far as that goes.
Grace	You talk to your shrink about this stuff?
Adele	Of course.
Grace	You talk about it?
Adele	Yes. We have in the past.
Eve	I wouldn't be so high-fallutin' with Norman.
Adele	I'm not high-fallutin' and I don't need to get laid.
Eve	You think?
Adele	I'm not into that stuff.
Grace	Talk about it at least.
Adele	I just told you—never mind. (*Out*)

27. (*Pause. Lights up as* ADELE *rejoins* SAMUELSON.)

Adele	Grace and Eve think I should talk with you about sex.
Samuelson	What do you think?
Adele	I don't think so. (*Pause*) It's sort of been a hidden issue.
Samuelson	Yes.

Adele	Yeah. Cinderella, she gets her man in the end. Basically. I look in the mirror, and I see what you see.
Samuelson	Which is?
Adele	Neither here nor there. Tall. Skinny.
Samuelson	Attractive.
Adele	Come on.
Samuelson	Some people might think so.
Adele	Some. (*Pause*) I haven't had any anxiety attacks lately, so it must have been the blood pressure.
Samuelson	Anxiety attacks are caused by anxiety. But you're definitely getting better.
Adele	Oh. Thank you. (*Pause*) I do feel I have the ability and the smarts. I do feel competent.
Samuelson	There's a difference between confidence and ability.
Adele	Good point. Very good.
Samuelson	Thank you.
Adele	So what do I do about Norman? (*No answer*) I want to be on stage. (*Pause*) I don't feel much libido. (*Pause*) That's the thing about heroin. Sex is pretty much out of the picture. You're basically a dope processing machine. (*Pause*) I did talk to Jane. She more or less said "No," about Norman. She's not the type to support experimental theatre operations. (*Pause*) I do feel a little more libido, lately.
Samuelson	You're getting bettter.
Adele	You said that.
Samuelson	It's true.
Adele	Like Cinderella.
Samuelson	Yeah.

Adele	Thanks.
Samuelson	You're welcome. (*Quick* DIM OUT.)

28. (*Lights up. "Enter"* JANE. *Pause.*)

Adele	I'm having trouble sleeping.
Jane	It's anxiety.
Adele	Do you have anxiety?
Jane	Sometimes.
Adele	By the way. . . Why didn't you re-marry?
Jane	I didn't feel like it, as you know.
Adele	Made you anxious.
Jane	Definitely.
Adele	Did you have offers?
Jane	Of course. I had money.
Adele	You like being alone, don't you?
Jane	Must be that guy, Norman.
Adele	Not really, though he does make me think at night.
Jane	At least you know how to do things. Before Spinoza, I didn't know anything. Not how to cook or clean or make the bed or anything. Laundry. Shopping. Banking. Paying the bills. None of it. They put me to work in the Spinoza Society, and I learned. I learned how to paint there. How to be with others, to some extent, though I prefer solitude. About Norman. I think he's. . . un-moored. I don't know if that's a word, but what I mean is that he's not sure of his tools. You're one of his tools at the moment. Apparently. And you're not sure about being used.

Adele	No. I'm not.
Jane	Would you like a massage one day?
Adele	Of course, I'd love one!
Jane	You got it. Put it in my book. Maybe Friday?
Adele	Yes! (*Quick DIM OUT.*)

29. (*NORMAN "enters." Lights up. Pause.*)

Norman	One is sailing without a sail. One has to catch the wind some other way. And I don't think improvisation is a bad way to go. Rehearsed, ordered improvisation. Improvisation as a way of sailing. Of catching the wind. Once we get sailing, we'll have it. And it belongs to all of us.
Adele	I've heard that before.
Norman	We'll sign a legal agreement.
Adele	I've done that before, too. Didn't mean zilch. The story guy gets the credit. The idea is yours, actually. The outline.
Norman	Right. And the structure. And the connectors. Which will come from me. I'd call it a kind of poetry. Poetry of the future. Mathematical. Geometrical.
Adele	Very Spinoza.
Norman	Digital.
Adele	I don't believe in any of it.
Norman	That's okay.
Adele	Salvation—it's not happening. The trouble starts with holiers than those righteousness, and then they start killing people. You have a secular, scientific fantasy, Norman. I just believe in being on stage.

Norman	Right. What about the Anunnaki?
Adele	What about them?
Norman	They seem to fit the theme.
Adele	They're an entertaining idea. But if they're supposed to be looking out for the Jews, they haven't done a very good job of it. And I'm not sure about the connectors. What are the connectors?
Norman	They are bits. Key words, themes. Poems, numbers. Phrases. Organized to hold things together. The motif is the same: a new world, created consciously, by a new species of Man.
Adele	Excuse me for asking, but are you Jewish?
Norman	No.
Adele	That's a strike against you. Do you know why Jews are so important in the intellectual life of modern times? Relativity. We know that what we have today, including our lives, could be gone tomorrow. I stole that from Erik Erikson.
Norman	Put it in your text.
Adele	We'll see.
Norman	So, how are the Guardians treating you?
Adele	The Annunaki.
Norman	Sorry I asked.
Adele	Not too well. Sometimes they're there, sometimes not. Mostly, they're not. But I'm being helped in working on my play.
Norman	Say more.
Adele	I have a character. She even has a name—Marie. She's a surgeon, and she's mad. She rants and raves. She's very interested in modern technology, of course. But

mainly it's the human body, and sex. She is from Canada, Marie—Montreal, but she spent a lot of time in Paris. Bilingual. But unhinged. She can't stop talking.

Norman Sounds good.

Adele Will she fit into your plans?

Norman Yes. I think so. Definitely.

Adele Good. I'll work on it. (*Out*)

30. (*SAMUELSON and ADELE.*)

Adele So I go to a meeting last night. Jane has been nice to me, so I decide to go to a Spinoza Society meeting. So I go to the meeting. First of all, I'm late. Then I say this arrogant thing, which seemed familiar—the arrogance—then the meeting drags on, and instead of letting the secretary end the meeting, I ended the meeting. I ended the meeting kind of abruptly, which is kind of like breaking a protocol. I didn't feel guilty at first—I felt justified—and then it started: "You hurt their feelings, you broke a rule, you're arrogant, they hate you," and so on and so forth.

Samuelson You're tired of all that.

Adele Yes. That's why I quit. But it was arrogance, anyway.

Samuelson Well, you can't have a hair out of place.

Adele You keep saying that.

Samuelson Because it's true.

Adele It's a cliché already.

Samuelson	I'll try and put it another way.
Adele	Was it the arrogance?
Samuelson	I wasn't there.
Adele	What about conscience?
Samuelson	What about it?
Adele	Justifying arrogance—it's not right.
Samuelson	And you can't have a hair out of place.
Adele	No. I see what you're saying. (*Pause*) I do. (*Quick* DIM OUT.)

31. (*ADELE joins JANE. Lights back up. Pause.*)

Jane	I ran into Norman at the Society.
Adele	He ran into you on purpose.
Jane	So he did. Mentioned you in dulcet tones.
Adele	That's nice. Madmen and gangsters.
Jane	You mean Norman?
Adele	No, not Norman. I mean the rest of the world. I like Norman. He just wants to get his play on. You can't blame him for that. And his method is interesting. It can have an interesting effect on an audience. And I have a character for him. "Marie."
Jane	What is his method? I couldn't quite follow him.
Adele	Improvisation. Improvisation to find the material, the content, so a lot of it comes from the actors. That bothers me. But also, because of that, it ends up too topical and it can't last. It kind of reflects the culture of the times, which I guess is okay since he's talking about the end of this world and the beginning of another.

Jane	The End of Days.
Adele	Right. It's a new version of the Second Coming. But humans, as we know them, will be obsolete.
Jane	I wonder what Spinoza would think. He liked axioms and theorems.
Adele	He's turning over in his grave. (*Pause*) I was thinking of madmen and gangsters. Of neglect and abuse, and panic attacks and stomach pain, and blood pressure, and blood spattering on walls, and sewers blown up, and viruses and the Holocaust—and I think I might want to write my own play, not Norman's.
Jane	Massage tomorrow?
Adele	Right. Yes. Thanks. (*Quick DIM OUT.*)

32. (*ADELE rejoins SAMUELSON. Lights up. Pause.*)

Samuelson	So. You talked to Dr. Schine?
Adele	On the phone.
Samuelson	He could hear that you were better?
Adele	I think so. He filled my refill. I've known him since my junkie days. He always comes through. And I'll always be a junkie.
Samuelson	Why do you say that?
Adele	It was "getting off" then, in the argot of the streets. I always want to get off the train, the ride. Nowadays the first impulse to shoot up is still attractive—and then I think better of it.
Samuelson	What do you think then?

Adele	No way I'd go back to that terrible, humiliating life. I kicked methadone, you know, which nobody on earth is able to do.
Samuelson	You did it. Give yourself credit.
Adele	Took eighteen months. I wanted to join the Spinoza Society. Also, it neutralized my whole libido thing. Junk does that. And then came the panic attacks.
Samuelson	And now?
Adele	The libido is starting to come back a little. I'm a little attracted to Norman, sexually speaking. More than a little. But I'm not going to let it affect me, for the time being. (*Pause*) Another thing—now I've forgotten what I was going to say.
Samuelson	It'll come to you.
Adele	Something about my stepsisters. (*Pause*) It's the strangest phenomena. I feel like I'm talking about another person. Adele. A panic attack at the Spinoza society. It threw me into despair. I felt like a worthless worm. As Jane used to say.
Samuelson	Your confidence was destroyed.
Adele	Yes. I'm feeling better now. I feel okay. The contrast is amazing. (*Pause*) So I decided to get even with Eve.
Samuelson	For punching you?
Adele	Yes.
Samuelson	How did it go?
Adele	I took a swing at her.
Samuelson	And?
Adele	She grabbed me by the hair. And threw me on the bed.
Adele	Don't!

Eve	Now you'll get what you deserve, bitch!
Adele	No!
Adele	And then she started tearing off my clothes and kissing me and biting me. (*Sounds of a sexual struggle.*) At first I fought her off, and then I gave in. She grabbed me. I liked it and I didn't like it. I didn't like being forced. I liked it and I didn't like it. I'm definitely not better yet.
Adele	(*Aside*) In truth, I just made that up. Let's see if he can tell.
Samuelson	Adele?
Adele	Yes.
Samuelson	Did you just make that up?
Adele	Yes, a little projection, a little spice. For my play. Mainly, I was thinking of Norman.
Samuelson	Not your style.
Adele	No, but I might use it on stage. I had a certain feeling about Marie. And she reminded me of a terrific photographer I had read about in *The New Yorker,* also French. . . Her name might well have been Marie, as well. . . . . Sorry. Oh.
Grace	Adele doesn't come anymore to the Society.
Eve	People come and go, like Michelangelo.
Grace	That's not Eliot's line.
Eve	She's like a totally different person.
Grace	Yeah, and there's a glimmer appearing in her eye. I think it's her ego resurfacing.
Eve	She'd better watch it.
Adele	My ears are burning. (*She takes a theatrical posture "on stage," and becomes* MARIE:) "I was in the North

Woods up there in Canada and they had nothing
there and this man comes into the clinic with a lump
the size of a volleyball on his neck and nobody would
deal with it, and I was still an intern, but I had the
balls, I was the only one, and I volunteered, me, and
I got some local anesthetic and I cut the damn thing
off, blood was all over the floor, but I did it and got it
done and nobody else would do it, it was me, alone,
I wasn't married at that time, I was an intern, before
I went to France, and the guy lived, I think, we didn't
have digitals or cell phones even, it was unheard of, but
I had the balls, I was always heroic that way, I don't
know why that is, when I was only nine, or eight even,
my mother said you have God on you, or an angel,
you're going to do wonderful things, be a hero, and
I was, thank God, and I hope you believe in God,
because I do, I talk to Him, because there's no one else
to talk to, you know what I mean, there's no one else to
talk to on this earth, definitely not my husband, *c'est la
vie*, he can go fuck himself, but he died, now his whole
family is trying to disown me and take the house and
all the money, with lawyers and going to court every
fucking day, it's like going directly to hell, but I can
talk to God, thank God. (*Begin slow* DIM OUT, *as all
become an audience for* ADELE.) There was a kid came
in there, he had swallowed a penny and no one knew
how to get it out, or would even try, but me, me, I took
my scope and went down there and got that penny, or
the kid would certainly have choked to death, and

then, later on, in France, where I met my husband, and I thought he was a good guy, even normal, but he was mean, and dirty, and he didn't believe in God, and now his entire family is trying to kill me, with that fucking American court. . ." (*Blackout*)

33. (*Lights.* ADELE *and* SAMUELSON. *Pause.*)

Samuelson	It's the suffering one fears, usually. I think.
Adele	Still, why should we please? Why should we strive so hard to please?
Samuelson	It's human.
Adele	We're destroying the earth with poisons and plastic. As we speak. So, how can all that digital language turn itself into a play? And how is the play going to help? (*Pause*) None of what I said today may be true. None of it. (*Pause*) Where were we?
Samuelson	I'm not sure.
Adele	If I went out, I mean back to the street, I think I'd shoot up a big O. D. An overdose. The quick rush and out.
Samuelson	No more revenge?
Adele	You know, there was a Jewish brigade of the British Army in World War II. Legend has it that after the war, in '45, a bunch of them went on a revenge raid into Germany. It was a targeted raid, not random.
Samuelson	Was it true?
Adele	I don't know. Top secret. Nobody talked about it. But it makes me feel better. For a minute. (*Pause*)

Samuelson	Now?
Adele	I feel depressed now.
Samuelson	Why?
Adele	I was reading Saul Bellow the other day. An essay he wrote. Wonderful man, wonderful writer. Very intelligent. It was about what a novelist should do, which is to establish the measure of Man, the stature of Man, to raise his measure as a being. And we don't want to do that because we avoid the "edge of life," as he called it. There's a lot of resistance. The whole idea of Man as a worthy spiritual being. . . I'm sorry.
Samuelson	Good thing your acting teacher took hold of you when she did.
Adele	I wish I could remember her name. She got me my first shrink. Nice woman. She had the same name as me, only German-style, Feuerstein, Firestone. Nice woman. I didn't understand anything at the time. I'm not sure I do now. I'm sorry. Where was I? Oh, my mother taught me to read when I was small. I was four or five. Four. (*Pause*) I watched her disintegrate, you know. She wasn't always. . . She taught me to read and write. She walked me to the corner to go to school. DeKalb Avenue and Kosciuszko Street. There were only three kids in the family at the time. My father had a job for RKO, driving cans of film around. Then she started to crack. Attention. I don't remember much. No more attention. She was somewhere else. My friend, Norman—did I tell you about my friend, Norman?

Samuelson	Your friend?
Adele	Yes, Norman. Now I forget again what I was going to say. Oh, he was telling me how lucky I was, how I had a kind of Guardian Angel, because good things happened to me, like talent and intelligence, and finding a new home and the Spinoza Society, and so on. And sometimes Jane says things like that. And I noticed that I liked the idea. I liked the idea that I had a guide, a Guardian Angel, that it wasn't all up to me. No. Not me. An angel, watching over me, the way the Anunnaki watches over the Jews.
Samuelson	The who?
Adele	The Anunnaki. Never mind. Is it time?
Samuelson	Yes. (*Blackout*)

The End

Villon

Author's Note: Dialogue in **bold** is aimed directly or indirectly at the audience. Stage directions in ***italics and bold*** (as are many of Clotilde's and Isabeau's) are also spoken.

Characters

FRANÇOIS VILLON — *Great bandit/poet of fifteenth-century France. In his early thirties.*

CLOTILDE — *A woman in her forties, a hunchbacked, wizened old friend of Villon's, and a member of his gang.*

ISABEAU — *A beautiful young prostitute and a loyal member of Villon's "crew."*

BORGES — *An itinerant priest, also a member. Killed eventually by Villon.*

GUY TABARIE — *Twenties, formerly a soldier, of aristocratic origin, a sometime member of the gang.*

OLD GUILLAUME VILLON — *Foster father of Villon, an ecclesiastic at the University of Paris.*

PHILIPPE CHERMOYE — *An itinerant priest, murdered by Villon.*

THE LANDLORD — *A phony aristocrat working for the King.*

THE KING OF FRANCE

SCENE — *A forest hut in France in the fifteenth century. Minimalist. A stage, table and chairs. Stools. Seats along the sides are for the actors. There is no Offstage. No doors. Should easily transform into a rustic low-end tavern or a dingy Parisian bar.*

On the run in this play, the Villon group often
masqueraded as a troupe of actors and troubadours. Now
they enter and take seats alongside the stage, right and
left, while VILLON *remains upstage left in the semi-dark.*

Villon   Mesdames & Monsieurs, please sit down—fart as
much as you want—especially you old guys with
heart problems, like me—but now it's getting
dark, and, speaking from the grave and the
obscurity of the past, I must tell you what I think,
and not lie, which is not so easy, as you know,
though you may not be aware of the difference—
after all, it's the same old tragic/comic story of
jealousy and revenge, lust and rejection, youth
and age, beauty and ugliness, and so on—but we
must have night and day, darkness and light; we
must have these contraries, I don't know why, and
we must have darkness, above all, and I can't
explain that, either.

Clotilde   Please turn off your little cell phones and other
electronic devices. Anyone caught with one of
these things on during the performance of this play
will be removed by the French National Guard.

Villon   I celebrate you—Monsieur François Villon, a hero
in my youth, and a hero even in his own time
(the fifteenth century), who understood well the
power and ecstasy of language itself. They say you
invented the villanelle, and the ballade, true or not,
and concluded your career as a brawler, a thief and
a murderer. And you had no doubts about the

ambiguities and privileges and obligations of neither art, nor class, nor religion, which remained ambiguous, and who, like me (the Author), in my fantasy of myself, was a master of poetry and a class-jumper in my own youth, that is to say, to jump from poverty to scholar to thief and drug addict, to poet/playwright, and so on.

Clotilde   Or so he says. Maybe it's true and maybe it's not. At the moment, Villon is an actor hiding in the dark— you can see him there, just offstage. *Pause.* (LIGHTS UP) *Enter François Villon, about thirty, our Hero—he is short, not handsome, wears a dagger in a holster on his chest and carries a cane, which is actually a war club.* (*He crosses downstage in front of the audience.*)

Villon   Yes, as you can see, I travel well armed. The cudgel's handle represents the figure of Christ on the cross. It expresses an inner truth. I was trying to say to you, you and to all of your relatives, who believe like you, who are, in fact, believers like you, who would eat cows, and fight for gold, and worship a clay idol, maybe some fucker like me, dressed like a God—some carney or circus barker—excuse me? My apologies. You Americans are easily offended. Don't be offended, not by a poor little fucker like me, I could never be a God, or act like a God, especially one like my Master— it's out of the question, and I was as good a scholar as my namesake, my mentor, Guillaume Villon, with his beautiful hair and excellent advice!

(CLOTILDE *approaches him onstage.*)

Clotilde   (*A truly hunchbacked hag of indeterminate age*) What's with the beautiful hair and the excellent advice? That old man wore a wig and said little.

François   **This is Clotilde. She is a member of my company. No further explanation needed.**

Clotilde   **How do you do?** *(Curtsies)* **François Villon was adopted from the lower dregs of Parisian society and raised up to master the language of Latin and the niceties of the Church, whereupon he took on the name of his master, Villon, who was one of the foremost Catholic scholars of his day. Through him, François met the true nobility of the times, like Charles, the Duke of Orleans, who admired his poems.** Could they follow that, François?

François   I don't know. **The Duke was a self-appointed connoisseur of Poetry, that most excellent of Ancient Arts. Myself, I invented various new forms, like the villanelle, and the ballade, still in use today.**

Clotilde   **François was short and ugly, wore a dagger, carried a stick, and liked a good brawl. And he looks crooked at the moment, like me, wouldn't you say?**

François   Of course, Clotilde, it's a result of wounds inflicted by my dear mother.

Clotilde   Stop that, François!

François   Why? My mother liked to hit people!

Clotilde   You're attacking your mother!

François   Especially me!

Clotilde   You're doing it again!

François   What?

Clotilde   (*Of the audience*) You're alienating them.

François   No, I'm not. I'm telling the truth.

Clotilde   The truth be damned.

François   **No, wait, I apologize. This is a true story, full of romance, fighting, religion, murder, jokes, and even dancing. Here is a woodcut of the old fart** (*Show the woodcut of* VILLON.)**, and you see, yes, he has a weird stance. The dagger is prominent. He was of the poorest of the poor, but he became a well educated fellow, as the Lady said, having acquired a bachelor's degree and a master's at the University of Paris. He had a brilliant mind, as you can hear for yourself in his work, though he came to a bad end, despite all the help he got from the high born, in exile at various safe houses in France.**

Clotilde   **His fate is unknown. Some say he became an immortal vampire.**

François   **An old wive's tale, of course, as nobody knows, you see, following his last adventure, what happened to the poor fellow.**

Clotilde   **No doubt he's in an unmarked grave somewhere.**

François   So are you, Clotilde.

Clotilde   No doubt. Save for the magic of Theatre. Here I am. Voila.

François   Most people would be dead by now at your age, Clotilde.

Clotilde   Most people are, François.

François   *C'est vrai.*

Clotilde	I know. We'll boil each other in oil, François, and achieve immortality.
François	Good, Clotilde. Go ahead and boil. You'll need a fire and lots of water, so go ahead. Find the water.
Clotilde	**First he beats up his own mother, and then he insults me.**
François	They didn't see me beat up my mother yet, Clotilde.
Clotilde	Oh. Right.
François	They will soon. They're looking forward to it. **Now we must introduce the young maiden of our little Commedia—her name is Isabeau, so the old men in the audience can look at her without feeling that they have to make any moves, or do anything but sit back and admire and imagine.** (*ISABEAU steps onstage. A sigh from the audience.*)
Isabeau	How do you do, François?
François	Ah, Isabeau, so good to see you. Very well, thank you.
Isabeau	What are we about to perform?
Villon	We are about to show the story of my adoption. My parents fought like angry beasts, until my father died, covered with purple pustules all over his body. **So, now, this is the story of my adoption.** You two play my mother and my sister, and here comes my mentor, Old Villon. Since I'm only a kid at this point, I'll hide over here behind the fireplace. (*A knock on the "DOOR."*) That's him. Let him in.
Isabeau	Come in, Doctor. (*Enter the Elderly Doctor of Religion, OLD VILLON.*)
Old Villon	Good day.
Isabeau	Good day, Father.

Old Villon	You don't need to call me "Father." (*Sniffs*) What do you people eat? Worms and trash?
Isabeau	Yes, Father.
Old Villon	It stinks in here.
Isabeau	It sure does, though I can't smell it anymore.
Old Villon	You know, I'm a church chaplain and a famous scholar of Ecclesiastical Law.
Isabeau	Yes, Father.
Clotilde	What's that?
Old Villon	What?
Clotilde	"Ecclesiastical."
Old Villon	It's the church, dear. Where is the master of the house?
Clotilde	Dead, sir, these many years.
Villon	(*Off*) You knew all that already, sir.
Old Villon	Someone is behind the fireplace.
Isabeau	It's my brother. He's hiding.
Old Villon	From me?
Isabeau	I believe so.
Old Villon	Come on out of there, Son.
Villon	(*Reappearing*) Here I am, sir.
Old Villon	No point in hiding. We all know what's going to happen, and your father's dead.
Clotilde	Yes, but you never know where they go, the dead, do you, sir?
Villon	We were just talking about that, sir. Hopefully they're not eating each other, sir.
Old Villon	(*Startled*) Hopefully not, boy. No point in that, is there?
Villon	They go back into the ground, Father, from whence they came?
Old Villon	Yes. How did he die, may I ask?

Clotilde	He boiled over, sir.
Isabeau	He erupted in sores, turned blue, and gave up the ghost, sir.
Clotilde	He was a common laborer, sir.
Old Villon	And how old is your brother?
Isabeau	He is eleven, sir.
Old Villon	I heard your brother was smart for his age, though short, and built a little crooked.
Isabeau	He is, sir. Just look at him.
Old Villon	Can you offer tea?
Clotilde	No.
Villon	Yes! (*A basket of tea flies from behind the "fireplace."*)
Old Villon	Oh, I see you have supernatural aid. That's nice.
Isabeau	He stole it, sir.
Old Villon	Oh. Water?
Clotilde	No water.
Old Villon	So this is useless.
Isabeau	I'm afraid so, Father.
Old Villon	It's absurd, tea without water.
Isabeau	He stole the tea off a cart in the village.
Old Villon	You may as well admit it, boy.
Isabeau	It's not his fault.
Villon	They won't let us access to the spring, Father.
Old Villon	Who is "they?"
Isabeau	The townspeople, sir.
Old Villon	Why not?
Villon	They say we are degenerate animals.
Clotilde	Shut up.
Old Villon	What do you do, Mother, beat your children every day? Discipline?

Clotilde	(*As* VILLON'S *mother*) Yes.
Old Villon	That's nice. I mean, that's good. And your boy, too?
Clotilde	Yes. That's what I was taught by my own mother, sir, beat the crap out of the kids.
Old Villon	Where? In the poorhouse?
Clotilde	No, sir, I lived in this shithole of a hut in Paris all my life.
Isabeau	Who did you say your name was, sir?
Old Villon	My name is Villon. Guillaume Villon.
Isabeau	And she hits my brother over the head, once in a while, with a pot, Monsieur Villon.
Old Villon	How unfortunate.
Isabeau	But true, sir. That's why he's a little crooked.
Villon	From getting hit over the head.
Isabeau	And I think he's growing a sore head, like his mother.
Villon	From being hit over the head with a pot, like I said.
Old Villon	Is that why you were hiding behind the fireplace?
Villon	Yes, sir.
Clotilde	Liar.
Villon	No, sir. I have no wish to be a student, or a doctor, and learn useless things.
Isabeau	He only wants to beg and steal and kick the shit out of the younger kids.
Old Villon	**Wonderful country, France, civilized centuries ago by the Romans.**
Clotilde	The poor live like pigs, sir.
Isabeau	The poor live *with* pigs, sir.
Old Villon	What if I took him off your hands?
Clotilde	Why should you?
Old Villon	I've heard he's very bright, and that he can read.

Clotilde	He can read posters.
Isabeau	He can read the bible.
Clotilde	He memorizes songs and figures.
Isabeau	He has a welt on his back.
Old Villon	From being beaten and humiliated, I suppose.
Clotilde	He needs discipline. He needs control.
Old Villon	But I've been told that the boy's a genius.
Clotilde	Maybe he is. As long as he helps his mother.
Old Villon	What does he do to help?
Clotilde	Mainly, he collects garbage.
Isabeau	And he fights. He's good with knives.
Clotilde	They should know.
Old Villon	Who should know?
Clotilde	The people of the town of Paris.
Old Villon	What do you mean?
Isabeau	He carries a dagger and a club. Take a look.
Old Villon	Can he hunt?
Isabeau	He's a city boy, sir. He hunts other boys.
Old Villon	I'll take him on if he can cook.
Isabeau	He can't cook. And he writes poetry, nasty poetry.
Old Villon	What do you mean?
Clotilde	He attacks the nobility, he attacks the church. He can be in a sour mood and do sinful things.
Old Villon	He does, eh? We'll cure him of that.
Clotilde	That's what you think.
Old Villon	Then you'll be glad to have him off your hands.
Clotilde	It'll cost you, sir.
Old Villon	What, pray?
Clotilde	Gold, pray.
Old Villon	We Churchmen live by our wits.

Clotilde	Money, sir.
Old Villon	I don't have any money or gold, just a good job at the University. And no divine interference that will give me any money. Once in a while, I'll write a treatise on something. In Latin. I'll feed him and give him a place to sleep, and teach him Latin and French grammar, and how to think.
Clotilde	In exchange for what, sir?
Old Villon	I need someone to guard my presence and meager possessions, build fires, cook and clean, and lead my mule if I go on a trip.
Villon	I can't cook.
Isabeau	He loathes cooking.
Old Villon	He'll learn.
Clotilde	Three gold pieces should do it.
Old Villon	Make it one. (*Pause*) And I'll give him a small salary.
Villon	(*Alerted*) How much?
Old Villon	I don't know. A percentage.
Villon	What percentage?
Old Villon	The university will decide.
Clotilde	You have enough of an income?
Old Villon	Yes and no.
Clotilde	Very clever.
Old Villon	Some do and some don't.
Clotilde	Very clever.
Old Villon	Do we have a deal?
Villon	It's a deal.
Isabeau	I don't believe him.
Villon	Shut up. I'm going.
Isabeau	We'll call the police, sir, the gendarmes!

Old Villon	They have gendarmes around here?
Villon	No problem, sir. They never come this way. (*Sweetly*) Ah, dear Mother?
Clotilde	Yes?
Villon	You are my sweet mother, who swaddled me and suckled me and protected me and looked after my every need?
Clotilde	No. Actually, I starved you and beat the hell out of you and, soon as you were old enough, I sent you out to steal. And then you slept on that bed of rocks over there that stunk of cat piss and dog shit.
Villon	How sweet. Guess what I have for you now, dearest Mom?
Clotilde	I could never guess, dear boy. (*Old Villon looks on as François and the others—miming—administer a vicious, thorough beating to his "mother," Clotilde. It should be complete and elaborate. They finally finish. A long pause with heavy breathing, physical collapses, phony blood, etc.*)
Villon	There! *Now you've seen it, Clotilde—the beating of my mother.*
Clotilde	So that's how you treat me, your own mother, you little bastard!
Villon	That's all you deserve, *maman*.
Clotilde	Very good, Son. I'll get you back for that.
Villon	Fuck you and all the rest of the company.
Isabeau	Not me, you little shit. I'll cut your balls off. **And she's not our real mother, remember, she's an actress/whore from the Champs-Élysées, impersonating our mother.**
Villon	**And Isabeau is a prostitute from the North, not my real sister, who can also act her ass off.**

280

Clotilde	**And who is the Old Man? Is it the Old Man himself, or some itinerant pretending to be him for a coin or two? Is he a ghost? An actor? A vampire? A zombie?** François, I don't think they can follow that.
Villon	All right, Clotilde, just stop talking to the audience. We have to make a living. Proceed. That was your last beating, Mother, for this performance anyway. Say thanks to this old man.
Clotilde	No thanks, Old Man.
Old Villon	May I speak with him privately?
Clotilde	Ask him yourself.
Old Villon	Boy? (*Taking* VILLON *aside*) Do you believe in God?
Villon	I don't know. I don't think so.
Old Villon	Do you wish to, Son?
Villon	I don't know. I'm only a kid.
Old Villon	You will learn. As payment in return, you will be my secretary, one of my servants, and my apprentice. You'll enjoy a better moral life.
Villon	I doubt I will ever be of your kind, and never a good servant. Why? Because all I know is the sewer and the streets and fighting for my life. My anger is pure. And not only that, you will never understand a man of my intelligence. My intelligence is beyond your capacity. I am far more intelligent than you, almost as though I were another kind of being. All you can do is pretend to be superior. And when I follow, I carry a garrote and a dagger and a club and will kill without mercy if I have to. Agreed?
Old Villon	If that is my lot, Boy. But I think, under my influence, that you will change for the better.

Villon	Actually, you are a phony academic Christian prick, but I'll go along with it, because I want to get out of the hell I'm in now, and I have no other options at the moment. But don't think you will ever be able to predict my behavior, not ever, because I can cut your throat in a minute, or in two. Or his or hers. And I might. Or, I might not. *D'accord?*
Old Villon	*(After a pause) Ouis.* Come and see me at the university, and we will provide.
Villon	I will, sir. Expect me at the next full moon.
Old Villon	*Au revoir.*
Isabeau	**The scene, through the magic of lighting, and a few props, is now transformed into a dingy Paris bar.**
Clotilde	Say, "Time passes."
Isabeau	Time passes. **I should add that François got his bachelor's degree at the church of St. Benoit Le Bentourne and his master's at the University of Paris, living as a roustabout student of his day. He had dropped his parents' names and took the name of his benefactor, François Villon. I had met François in the Rue St. Jacques. On his way here—you can see him approaching now—is a Breton, Guy Tabarie, formerly a soldier, now a bona fide Master of Arts, and a crook, and this other creature entering stage left is the vagabond priest, Phillipe Chermoye. Along with Chermoye is another itinerant priest whose name is Borges. Clotilde is now waiting on tables for all of us.**
Clotilde	Put your daggers away before someone gets hurt.

Philippe	Listen to her. She's as drunk as we are. (*GUY TABARIE steps onstage.*)
Villon	And who is this? Ah, Monsieur Tabarie.
Clotilde	**This is Guy Tabarie, formerly a soldier, as Isabeau has just told you.**
Villon	How are you, Guy?
Guy	Very well, thank you.
Villon	I know you can fight.
Guy	I can.
Villon	But can you act? We are now actors.
Guy	I think so.
Villon	Well, I can act very well. And I'm also a poet, as you know.
Guy	I do know.
Villon	I've even invented my own forms, believe it or not. Excellent ones, I might add. I've learned from my masters.
Guy	Yes, the great Poet from the gutters of Paris.
Clotilde	And the University of Paris.
Guy	I doubt I can act as well as you write.
Clotilde	No doubt about it.
Guy	Members of the nobility are my specialty.
Clotilde	Just be yourself. Nothing to it.
Guy	Did your master teach you to fight, too?
Villon	No, he is a true Scholastic. We have Borges, the priest, for that. He does our fighting. Eh, Borges?
Borges	Yes. Me and you, François.
Guy	And me.
Borges	Of course.

Villon	I learned in the street, before I was twelve. We knock some heads around, and then the priest prays. But we do our own careful planning and depend on secrecy and trust.
Borges	Are you up for that, Tabarie?
Guy	I believe I am. What are you planning?
Villon	Later, Borges.
Borges	Of course.
Guy	So. Let's hear a poem. (OF ISABEAU) And who is this beauty?
Clotilde	Her name is Isabeau.
Villon	She's from the North.
Clotilde	Hands off.
Guy	I see. Can she write, too?
Villon	She can. She is my best student.
Guy	Really? Say a poem.
Isabeau	No.
Guy	Why not?
Isabeau	I am not a performing bear, sir.
Philippe	No, a bitch is more like it.
Villon	Don't insult the girl in front of my face, Philippe, if you don't mind.
Isabeau	Thank you, François.
Philippe	(*Sarcastic*) My hero. Student, indeed.
Villon	Be careful how you speak, sir.
Philippe	I speak excellent French, sir, say my prayers in Latin, and was a novice before she was born.
Isabeau	You are a common bandit, Philippe, in monk's clothing.
Villon	Never mind, Isabeau.
Guy	Isabeau. A lovely name for a lovely wench.

Isabeau	Keep your compliments to yourself, sir, if you please.
Villon	Why don't you say a poem, Guy? You're a Master of Arts, after all. Say something from Virgil.
Guy	That wasn't one of the arts, as you know François. I learned sermonizing and law.
Villon	Give us a sermon, then.
Guy	Why not the priest? Philippe?
Philippe	*Merde.*
Clotilde	He's drunk.
Philippe	I'll give you a poem.
Guy	Go on, then.
Philippe	I'll fart. (*Farts*) There's your poem.
Clotilde	Bravo, maestro. **We're back in the Commedia.**
Philippe	I won't give good poetry out to street urchins and whores.
Villon	I asked you politely. Watch what you say, you phony child-fucker.
Philippe	One doesn't merely watch, you snotnose, one listens to one's betters.
Villon	How would you like a small dagger up your windpipe, you blowhard?
Clotilde	François.
Philippe	You wouldn't dare.
Clotilde	He would, Chermoye.
Philippe	My sword is a large one, Villon, made by Vikings. It could kill you with one blow.
Villon	I have a smaller one at my thigh, Chermoye. I never go unarmed. It kills well, too. Quick as a fly.
Philippe	You may try, you little piece of shit. Make a move.

Villon	I'd kill a priest a day, if I could. You live off the fat of the land and the English.
Guy	The fat English! Ha! That's a good one!
Philippe	People like you have no business pretending to be men of learning.
Villon	People like who?
Philippe	Street dogs and thieves.
Clotilde	CHERMOYE!

(*A silence*)

Villon	Say, "Time passes slowly."
Isabeau	Time passes slowly (*Staged as described*) **During the slow time, everyone sits silently, tensely, then Philippe suddenly attacks Villon's throat with his large sword. Villon gets out the small dagger at his thigh. A general brawl breaks out. It shouldn't take too long. The battle is unequal, when suddenly Villon finds a rock and hits Philippe over the head with it, and the priest falls to the floor. Villon thrusts his dagger. A silence as Villon pulls out the dagger, and then hits the priest again hard on the head with the rock. Another silence.**
Clotilde	François!
Villon	What, Clotilde?
Clotilde	Look what you've done!
Guy	We must go to the Duke.
Villon	He attacked me first. You all saw it.
Isabeau	Look—he's still alive!

Philippe	I forgive you, François. It was my fault and the wine. Let it be known to all that I forgive him. (*Dies*)
Guy	We'll let it be known, Philippe. (PHILIPPE *rises and leaves the stage*.)
Clotilde	Say, "time passes."
Isabeau	Time passes. **Lights change and we are in the safe house again, around the fire. It doesn't take long.**
Guy	François.
Villon	What, Tabarie?
Guy	Conjugate the Latin, "to be afraid."
Villon	No.
Guy	Why not?
Villon	I don't feel like it.
Guy	Moody, aren't you?
Villon	You would be too, if you understood the shithole we're in now. Starving, surrounded by the English.
Guy	I do understand it.
Villon	Then why do you keep smiling?
Guy	It's the wine we stole from what's-his-name. The priest. Chermoye. Are you afraid?
Villon	No. I'm not afraid. I'm not afraid of the English. I'm not afraid of men and I'm not afraid of women. And I'm not afraid of dead priests. And I'm not afraid of the king.
Clotilde	Bravo, François!
Villon	People think all kinds of shit about other people and they're wrong ninety-nine percent of the time. There's no need to be afraid.
Guy	I will say that you priests have a good thing going.
Borges	How so?

Guy	You can live like a criminal and be a savior at the same time.
Borges	There's no more room in the churches. There they need novices and a few scribes and farmers. The rest of us need to defend ourselves and make a living.
Guy	You can knock someone's brains out and say a Hail Mary and ride off into the sunset on the poor fool's horse.
Borges	Alas and alack. It's either him or me. And we can give the last rites, after all.
Guy	After all.
Borges	Someone has to do it.
Villon	There's too many gangs in these woods and each one of them has a resident priest.
Guy	I agree. It can be boring, hiding and fighting all the time. That's why we took you on.
Borges	Why? Because I can use a cudgel?
Guy	Yes, and we like your mind for the prayers. You have a gift, apparently. But the cudgel comes in handy, too.
Villon	I met a Spanish Jew. He was surprised I could speak his language.
Borges	Hebrew?
Villon	No, Ladino. It's part Hebrew, part Spanish.
Borges	They won't last in Spain.
Villon	Why not?
Borges	Because of the church's Inquisition. But why do you bring it up?
Villon	A matter of doctrine: He said God does not have children.
Borges	He'll be among the first, then, to be expelled. Expect it sooner rather than later.
Guy	Can he?

Villon	Who?
Guy	God. Have children?
Borges	God?
Villon	Why should he bother?
Borges	To save us all from perdition.
Villon	So he impregnates a teenager, and *voila*, we're all saved?
Borges	I can see that you don't believe it.
Villon	No. But I can write very fine verses for churches and priests.
Guy	When you are not knocking they're heads off.
Villon	It's then I write them, because of remorse. **I don't know if that's true: I feel a certain energy, and I write.** I feel bad, and then writing makes me feel better. **I don't know if that's true, either.** In any case, I'm writing one now.
Guy	The king has set you free.
Villon	Into exile. Villon, the murderer. I wrote this song. Shall we hear it?

Le Testament Ballade A S'amye

False beauty that costs me so dear,
Rough indeed, a hypocrite sweetness,
Amor, like iron on the teeth and harder,
Named only to achieve my sure distress,
Charm that's murderous, poor heart's death,
O covert pride that sends men to ruin,
Implacable eyes, won't true redress
Comfort a poor man, without crushing?

Much better elsewhere to search for
Aid: It would have been more to my honor,
Retreat I must, and fly with dishonor,
Though none else then would have cast a lure.
Help me, help me, you greater and lesser!
End then? With not even one blow landing?
Or will Pity, in line with all I ask here,
Comfort a poor man, without crushing?

That time will come that will surely wither
Your bright flower, it will wilt and yellow,
Then if I can grin, I'll call on laughter,
But, yet, that would be foolish though
You'll be pale and ugly and I'll be old,
Drink deep then, while the stream's still flowing:
And don't bring trouble on all men so,
Comfort a poor man, without crushing.

Amorous Prince, the greatest lover,
I want no evil that's of your doing,
But, by God, all noble hearts must offer
To comfort a poor man, without crushing.

(During the recital, ISABEAU repeats the final stanza
couplets in French. VILLON ends with a flourish.
"Bravos" expressed.)

Borges   It sounds perfectly natural, like confession. Good for the soul.

Villon   Thank you, Borges. Just a love poem.

Borges	The main thing is not to take it all literally. After all, we are born incarnate, all of us.
Villon	Like horses and sheep.
Borges	Very like. Can you make a fire and keep watch?
Villon	Yes, Borges.
Borges	I'll sleep for a few hours, and then take my turn. But first I'll say my prayers. "Dear God, we had to take this poet in because if we didn't he'd end up in a poor house, or a mad house, or in prison, as he's very bright. Ordinary life has no future for him. This way, he has a future. What, we don't know. Hard to predict. We apologize for his earlier behavior—as well as *our* own early behavior—and hope to be forgiven." Amen.
Villon	Amen.
Borges	**His foster father adopted him, presto! And now he is Villon. I am called Old Borges. I was a priest when priests were still priests and sat around with pen and paper writing up the bible.**
Guy	You can't write, Borges.
Borges	Never mind.
Guy	Where are you going?
Borges	I have to take a leak. Goodbye and good luck. (*"Door" slams*)
Guy	I'll go, also.
Villon	Where to?
Guy	To the Duke. To plead your cause. (*Exits*)
Villon	*Merci. Au revoir.*
Clotilde	The nerve of that fellow. "To the Duke." Tabarie's not got long to live, I'll warrant. (*Exits with a bread basket.*)

Villon	I agree with you there, Clotilde. *Bueno.* Let's check outside. Isabeau?
Isabeau	(*Appearing*) Yes? What's the matter?
Villon	Where is Clotilde? She was here a moment ago!
Isabeau	To the village, for bread.
Villon	*Bon.* You go around the house and then come back to the door on some kind of pretext. Take a lantern.
Isabeau	What about Borges?
Villon	He may not come back. He may run away. He may trip and fall. He could hang himself, for all I know.
Isabeau	What else?
Villon	He could go mad.
Isabeau	So why should I go out there?
Villon	Use a pretext.
Isabeau	Yes? What pretext?
Villon	This is absurd. That old man Borges is in his dotage. You'd better go with him. Keep an eye on him. And watch for Clotilde. (*BORGES steps back on.*) Oh, Borges, you're back.
Borges	Have you told them that I have no faith, Villon?
Isabeau	Say again?
Borges	You've told them that I have no faith?
Villon	No, Borges, though you haven't any that I can see.
Isabeau	Yes. Good. (*Stomps her foot and spins.*) There, François, I went around the house, and now I'm back. Borges, you have no faith.
Villon	But you haven't moved, Isabeau.
Isabeau	I say, I have moved.
Villon	I say you have not.
Borges	You followed me?

Isabeau	I was supposed to go with you, but you didn't go anywhere.
Villon	True, but never mind, we'll start over.
Isabeau	No.
Villon	Why?
Isabeau	I'm afraid of wolves.
Villon	Take Borges.
Borges	No.
Villon	All right, I'll go myself.
Borges	Good. I've come to tell you that the toilet is blocked, and therefore there is no water.
Isabeau	Can you say that again?
Borges	The toilet is blocked and there is no water.
Isabeau	Thank you.
Borges	You're welcome.
Isabeau	**Excuse me, but they didn't have toilets in those days. They had outhouses. Or they shat in the woods. Can you imagine, the stench?**
Villon	Never mind.
Isabeau	Excuse me, François.
Villon	What now?
Isabeau	I have to go to the bathroom to pee. So what shall I do?
Villon	Go outside and pee.
Isabeau	What did you say? (CLOTILDE *enters with a basket of bread.*)
Villon	I meant to say, go outside and take a leak.
Clotilde	I just came from outside.
Villon	Not you.
Isabeau	It's unseemly for a girl to go outside by herself and take a leak.

Villon	People do it all the time. Clotilde?
Clotilde	Not me, François.
Isabeau	Not me.
Villon	What then?
Isabeau	Perhaps a pot? Do you have a pot?
Villon	Perhaps a chamber pot?
Isabeau	Yes, a chamber pot. I'll need to look around. I know I had one, or I used to have one.
Villon	Look around, please.
Isabeau	Thank you, very much. I'm looking.
Clotilde	(*Staged*) ***A pantomime of looking for a chamber pot. It can't last too long. Voila!***
Villon	All right, I've found one.
Isabeau	Very good.
Villon	Thank you.
Isabeau	Turn around, please.
Villon	(*Hesitating*) All right.
Isabeau	Turn around.
Villon	Go outside, why don't you?
Isabeau	No, thanks.
Villon	Why not?
Isabeau	Then, the whole thing is pointless, because the forest is full of wolves. Will you make that clear, Clotilde?
Clotilde	The whole thing is pointless, because the forest is full of wolves.
Isabeau	Thank you.
Villon	Okay, then go ahead and piss, why don't you?
Isabeau	Turn around, asshole. You too, François.
Villon	Okay. (*He turns around but peeks.*)
Isabeau	Thank you. You too, Borges.

Borges	(*Reluctantly*) All right.
Isabeau	Thank you, very much.
Villon	So, go ahead already. (*She pisses, augmented by the* SOUND *of pissing.*)
Isabeau	(*Finishing*) Thank you, very much.
Villon	Gladly. Very enjoyable. (*To* CLOTILDE) You can empty the pot outside, if you feel like it.
Clotilde	What do you mean, "If I feel like it?"
Villon	Never mind. Do what you want.
Clotilde	Open the door.
Villon	Open the door, Isabeau. (*ISABEAU opens the "door"—a pause, darkness outside—and throws out the piss. Pause. A* SCREAM. *Pause.*)
Villon	I hope nobody was standing there.
Borges	I'll retrieve my cudgel.
Villon	Do. Retrieve your cudgel.
Isabeau	So will I.
Clotilde	So will I.
Borges	Women shouldn't carry cudgels.
Clotilde	We are bandits, Borges, not maids.
Villon	Let's hope nobody was out there.
Clotilde	But apparently, there was.
Villon	Not a wolf or a two-legged, I hope. Let's wait. (*A silence as they wait.*)
Clotilde	***A scary silence as we wait.***
Isabeau	Seems all right, then, *n'est-ce pas?*
Villon	Let's hope for the best.
Clotilde	Let's hope for the best.
Villon	Whatever the fuck that means.
Isabeau	It means hoping for the best, as opposed to the worst.

Villon	Of course, darling.
Clotilde	"Darling?"
Villon	May I have the pot?
Isabeau	No, I think I'll hang on to it.
Villon	Very good. Hang on to it. Perhaps we should keep the pause?
Clotilde	**We'll keep the pause.** (*Pause*)
Villon	Good. Do you suppose we should rinse the pot now?
Clotilde	There is no water.
Villon	Sorry. I forgot.
Isabeau	Do you have a towel?
Villon	Here.
Isabeau	It's dirty.
Villon	Put it in the laundry.
Clotilde	**Now we observe how Clotilde wipes the pot and throws the towel away into the laundry. It doesn't take too long.**
Villon	And now?
Isabeau	Perhaps we should start over now?
Villon	No doubt about it.
Isabeau	Okay, start over.
Clotilde	Are you in one of your moods?
Isabeau	**What does she mean by that?**
Clotilde	We can't start over!
Villon	The toilet is blocked and there is no water.
Isabeau	Go fuck yourself, why don't you?
Villon	Thank you. What did I do to deserve that remark?
Isabeau	I didn't mean to say that.
Villon	Then why did you say it?
Isabeau	I don't know.

Villon	And I called her darling, *n'est-ce pas?* (*Taking in the scene*) **Very interesting. A beautiful private part, the taking of a piss, observation by a bunch of voyeurs. All in the same scene. Extraordinary.**
Isabeau	Excuse me?
Villon	I said, a beautiful moss-patch, and a group of voyeurs, who paid, the taking of an actual piss, and the accompanying sound of water flowing, to boot.
Isabeau	Oh. Of course.
Clotilde	A beautiful what?
Villon	Moss patch. I never said that before. Onstage. Let's keep that.
Isabeau	It's not that we hardly know each other.
Villon	I know. I had quite noticed you, which you noticed, and then you got clever and more beautiful, and now you took an excellent leak.
Isabeau	I'm Hungarian.
Villon	**I see. That explains everything.**
Isabeau	Say again?
Villon	You're Hungarian, and an anti-Semite. (*Pause*) I can tell by your accent. (*Pause*) Did I notice you first, or you me?
Isabeau	Go fuck yourself.
Villon	There. You said it again. And then to come here and play the harlot, play the fool, and take a piss, and so on, in front of a paying audience.
Isabeau	You poetic idiot. You changed my life.
Villon	Thank you, very much.
Isabeau	I meant it. But I am underpaid. And I'd not have done it—
Villon	If you weren't so vain.

Isabeau	Correct. **All European history dissolves into this moment.** (*Pause*) You're an alchemist. Let the imagery dissolve.
Villon	I'm not an alchemist. I'm a poet.
Isabeau	Let it dissolve.
Clotilde	(*Projections*) *A sequence, or montage, of dissolving historical images, featuring classical imagery of beautiful women, along with the sound of water flowing—a waterfall, or rain, or a stream, etc. We observe and listen to the sequence. It shouldn't take too long, but long enough.*
Isabeau	As you can see and hear. It's the good old human condition.
Villon	Murder and rape, mainly rape, and excrement, and bones, I think, and the base instinct for power and glory, is all we know of the past, present, and future.
Clotilde	I can't believe he just said that. The Poet.
Villon	Never mind. I heard it somewhere. Don't quote me.
Isabeau	Why not?
Villon	I'm not exactly sure why. Sit down.
Isabeau	Why?
Villon	I don't know why.
Isabeau	It's so you can feel taller and bigger than me, that's why.
Villon	No, Isabeau. My dagger makes us equal.
Isabeau	Because it'll never happen, dagger or no.
Villon	Why not, pray?
Isabeau	You're too short, pray, and too old. That's why.
Villon	I see. But I couldn't care less, darling.
Isabeau	And don't say "pray." You don't know anything about it. And don't say "darling," because you don't mean it.
Villon	No. Mainly, I'm wondering why the door is still open.

Borges	Indeed.
Isabeau	So what's the big deal? I'll shut the door. (BORGES *steps into the "doorway."*)
Borges	It's the protocol of the thing. I'm trying to seduce you, I think.
Isabeau	You're too old, Borges, and weird. Step away from the door.
Villon	Good. Take a hike, Borges.
Isabeau	Bye, bye.
Borges	Wait. Hear me out. I missed my chance, no doubt about it—I missed it without knowing how I missed it. How could that happen? An intelligent, sensitive, thieverish man like me, with a masculine mind and wise, and all that, and I missed that I was missing my chance while I missed it.
Clotilde	That was incomprehensible.
Villon	What he meant is, he missed it, then, in the so-called Past. He missed it now, in the present, and then he missed it again. (*Pause*) Something is wrong with all of us. Why?
Isabeau	Why?
Borges	Don't ask. There's no answer.
Villon	Nature didn't finish with us, apparently.
Clotilde	I know why.
Isabeau	Why?
Clotilde	We don't pay attention to what's happening. We're too busy paying attention to other things.
Villon	Shut the door.
Clotilde	I'll shut the door. (*Shuts the "door" with a* BANG)
Villon	We don't know true happiness. And we can't understand why.

Isabeau	Speak for yourself.
Borges	I mean, how we always miss our chances.
Isabeau	Are you making up shit now? Are you bullshitting me now? Because, to tell you the truth, Clotilde, we women miss nothing.
Villon	Well, I was noticing the fine shape of your butt just now. I mean, again. I mean, for the thousandth time. Again.
Isabeau	Forget it, François.
Villon	You never know.
Isabeau	Never know what?
Villon	What stirs the heart, gives life and meaning, existentially speaking.
Isabeau	You mean like pissing? You mean like sex?
Villon	Sex of course, but something more, something totally inexplicable, like a new theory of the universe, where there are dimensions of vibration, which cause things to be as they are, like now.
Isabeau	You're a whoremaster and a hard-on, whose days are passing. It's sad, but true.
Villon	Alas.
Isabeau	I like you, Villon, don't get me wrong, but we women don't miss things. We let them go by. We're as sensitive as ripe apples, or pears.
Villon	I like that imagery.
Borges	So do I.
Isabeau	And nothing goes by, not a breath, not a whisper, that we miss. Not a tinge.
Villon	What a shame. You're all whores, after all, *n'est-ce pas?*
Isabeau	Life goes on that way. Where would you be without us?
Clotilde	Unborn.

Villon	Rushing into the dark, the infinite dark, the dark that has no end.
Isabeau	You can put it like that.
Villon	That's how it ends, rushing into the dark, perhaps mindlessly, endlessly.
Isabeau	You should have been a priest, François.
Villon	I have a master's degree in religion.
Isabeau	Then he is a priest, technically, I suppose.
Villon	I'm no priest. I'm missing a part.
Isabeau	Which one?
Villon	I lack a certain fundamental. Humility. I'm like the French whoremongers of old. And I have a bad temper.
Clotilde	**Especially when he drinks, which is often.**
Villon	That's me. François Villon. I was adopted. I could have been a somebody, a Doctor of Philosophy. I got my master's degree, but I ended up a poet who ran with thieves.
Isabeau	So you identify with him?
Villon	I AM him.
Isabeau	How is that possible?
Villon	You never know. I could have transmigrated or reincarnated.
Isabeau	I see.
Clotilde	That's helpful.
Villon	Mainly, it's acting. You're not looking, Isabeau. You're not even looking in my direction.
Isabeau	I hear you, François. One thing?
Villon	Yes?
Isabeau	What or who is a "somebody?"

Villon	You know, regular. Someone who knows things. Normal. He shows up to dig his ditch, he goes home to his kids, he obeys his superiors, goes to church, dies in his dreams, is mourned by his relatives—and then he is put back into the soil, where he serves the underground creatures of the earth, while the priest says some Latin mumbo-jumbo at his grave. Mainly, he is born and dies without a question.
Clotilde	What's the question?
Villon	What's going on with all this living and dying?
Isabeau	Say, "Go back a minute."
Clotilde	**Go back a minute.**
Isabeau	Serves as what, monsieur?
Villon	As food.
Isabeau	And your poetics, sir? How will they taste to the tongue?
Villon	Like fine wine, my dear. Like the finest of French wine.
Isabeau	A good response, François.
Villon	(*Bowing*) Your servant, my dearest Isabeau.
Isabeau	Clotilde!
Clotilde	*Oui, madame?*
Isabeau	Say "amen" again.
Clotilde	**Amen.**
Borges	To bed, to sleep, something Shakespearean. . .
Isabeau	He wasn't born yet. Say, "The night passes and we hear the singing of birds."
Clotilde	***The night passes and we hear the singing of birds.***
Isabeau	It's a beautiful morning.
Clotilde	It's all right.
Isabeau	Just say, "it's a beautiful morning."
Clotilde	***It's a beautiful morning. The sun rises and birds sing.***
Villon	Now we'll have to meet up with my associates.

Isabeau	Who are they?
Villon	Thieves, murderers, whores, priests, teenagers, and the like. They are our audience.
Isabeau	Where are they?
Villon	They'll be appearing anon, out of the woods. Soon as they get a good look at you my beauty.
Isabeau	Oh.
Villon	Clotilde, say, "time and space change magically."
Clotilde	**Time and space change magically.**
Villon	Time and space change magically and we're in the woods.
Clotilde	***Time and space change magically and we're in the woods. A moment of paranoia. Eyes and ears in the greenery of France.*** (*Pause*)
Isabeau	**Hello, out there. This is Isabeau, and you will never get to make it with me, though I may give you the impression that you have a chance (a woman's craft, that), and if you buy me a drink, at the right time—timing is everything—I might scratch your balls. That is to say, I might, but, actually, I won't. I'm a dyed-in-the-wool female on the make, totally unlike the one you think of constantly, in your dreams.**
Villon	Well said, that.
Isabeau	Thank you very much. (TABARIE *steps back on.*)
Clotilde	And you remember Monsieur Guy Tabarie.
Villon	Certainly, I do. Off to see the Duke.
Guy	All is well, François.
Villon	Still, are his men out there?
Guy	In the woods, sir. I have my rapier.

Villon	Ah, a dandy—I am a dagger man myself.
Guy	Typical for a thief.
Villon	And can you fight with that thing, too?
Guy	Try me.
Villon	I believe I will, but not for the moment. How about a cudgel?
Guy	A cudgel, a sword, a dagger, whatever you like.
Villon	How about your mind? Can you fight with your mind, sir? As with a *bon mot*, or a rhyme?
Guy	Do you mean to insult me, sir?
Villon	I am not of the nobility, Guy, I am of the sewer, but I promise you, one day I will smash your face in shit.
Isabeau	Not now, François.
Villon	Never mind, we have things to do now.
Guy	What are you doing?
Villon	We are preparing to perform. We are itinerant actors for the moment.
Guy	For whom?
Villon	For them! (*Sweeping gesture*)
Guy	I don't see anyone out there.
Villon	Not yet.
Isabeau	It takes time.
Borges	Give it a minute.
Clotilde	**Eyes and ears in the forest of France.**
Villon	After all, it's only morning. Coffee, anyone? **Did they have coffee in those days? Well, no matter.**
All	Yes, please!
Villon	**The coffee's made and we can all have a cup!** (*They mime the drinking of coffee, along with sighs of satisfaction, burps, etc.*)

304

Villon	Well, very good, and I think our audience has fully arrived. (*Silence. Then a* RUSTLING SOUND *from the woods*)
Guy	Where are they?
Villon	(*Pointing*) There! Clotilde? (*They all look out at the audience.*)
Villon	Glad to see you again. And who are they, pray?
Isabeau	Don't say, "pray," it's an illusion, taught to you by priests, and you don't believe it anymore than I do—that is your woodsy audience, François. And over here is that French whore you're so crazy about, whose name I forget. And over there is the beautiful and innocent and vanity-oppressed little teenaged blonde—we used to call them birds—I mean, broads, totally in love with themselves.
Villon	Like you, Isabeau.
Isabeau	Actually, I meant her.
Clotilde	We haven't been properly introduced.
Isabeau	So what?
Clotilde	How old is she, nine? Too young for you, François.
Villon	I'm thirty-one now, and a Master of Arts.
Isabeau	He's a child.
Villon	I'm not.
Clotilde	I meant the girl actually.
Isabeau	Mainly, in fact, he's sort of a Genius. Why, I don't know. He was born that way, I suppose. **You remember Clotilde and Borges?**
Clotilde	**Borges is a prematurely old man who can't get it up anymore.**
Borges	Let's move on with it, shall we?
Clotilde	And the young maiden shall remain nameless.

Villon	She understands, I'm sure. (*Winks at the "blonde" in the audience.*)
Clotilde	Okay, so we already have a bunch of ambiguities here, and I'm not positive that the audience has the intelligence to handle it. They are forest creatures, after all.
Villon	Give them a chance, why don't you?
Isabeau	I'm sorry, I have already made a series of judgments, probably false, and I don't have the time to apologize, we're in a theatrical presentation—for your benefit, François, after all.
Villon	Mine?
Clotilde	Very well, I'll give them a chance. (OLD VILLON *steps onstage.*)
Old Villon	Hold on a minute—give me a chance as well, why don't you?
Isabeau	Clotilde?
Clotilde	No.
Old Villon	Why? Is it because I'm a horny, ugly, addled old man?
Clotilde	Yes.
Old Villon	Not true. I am a gentleman from Paris, the University of Paris, with various aliases—but, I assure you, I am an intelligent person, a talented intellectual, an ordained priest, as they say—but it's true, it's true, I'm an actor, as well, and I'm playing a dead person at the moment, long dead, relatively speaking. In any event, to be honest, I don't have the old force, after all. Who could blame you or her, if you reject me on no basis but that? That's enough—lack of youth, lack of force. I suppose we'll come back to this—this is very important, it's just not what I'm trying to say right now, at least, not what I meant to say—not what I thought I was saying—I was

trying to say something more important, to earn your love and respect. Mainly, I'm not him, whoever I was, I'm—Old Villon, now. Guillaume Villon, the Elder.

Isabeau We see you, old man, but the play in the woods is about to start.

Guy How naive.

Clotilde He is not the fool he appears to be, sir.

Guy Yes, he is.

Borges I think so, too.

Isabeau Shut up, Borges. You're ugly and fat and as senile as he is and you'll die in a minute or two.

Borges Who, me?

Isabeau Yes, you. Be quiet.

Clotilde Unless you drink some of our blood first. (*Cackles*)

Isabeau What did she say?

Villon Oh, that's all lies and you know it. Made up centuries from now. We are not vampires.

Old Villon Just a minute or two. Give me a minute or two. **How could this be happening to me?** I'm just trying to point out the general idiotic hypocrisy of human life. I think that's what I was doing.

Clotilde When was this?

Old Villon A moment ago.

Isabeau His time's up, François.

Villon He was trying to tell the truth. Isn't that right? Isn't that enough? Isn't that honorable?

Clotilde **Petulance appears.**

Isabeau I don't care if it's right or wrong, or enough, or honorable, so long as it's true. **I don't know why I said that.**

Clotilde Me, neither.

Old Villon	Isn't that true? What I say? Isn't it true? All right, you don't know the first or second thing about it. You don't know anything about it, actually.
Isabeau	About what?
Old Villon	**The story of my life. My life and your life.** (*Pause*) So that's what it's all come to, this whole introduction, as if something important is happening, something important and moral and entertaining, and wise.
Isabeau	Wise?
Old Villon	I think I'll kill myself. Find me a rope.
Isabeau	I don't find ropes for people who want to kill themselves.
Old Villon	Who do you find them for?
Isabeau	Those who want to kill others.
Old Villon	My goodness! You're a cruel thing, aren't you?
Isabeau	Yes. And you're a dead man walking.
Old Villon	Holy shit, and I thought you liked me.
Isabeau	Yes, but that's besides the point, because death is sitting on your left shoulder, and taking a shit. Right now, as we speak. (*An outcry*)
Villon	Whoa!
Clotilde	That was hard.
Villon	That was hard.
Guy	That was hard.
Old Villon	You don't give a rat's ass, do you?
Isabeau	I do, when your balls are up and the rest of you is down.
Old Villon	Why?
Isabeau	Why? You ask me, why?
Old Villon	No. I didn't ask you.
Isabeau	You did, old man, but, go ahead and ask me again.

Old Villon	Why?
Isabeau	You think I'm a barnyard cow? You think I'm a turkey or a pig?
Old Villon	No more, no less. Yes.
Isabeau	Well, you're honest. That's why I do like you. I do. But you are a slave to what they call Nature. The nature of killing and the nature of desire, which are the same.
Old Villon	You just made that up.
Isabeau	I don't think so. Why would you say that?
Old Villon	I'm a classical actor, that's why. (*A sensual pause*)
Isabeau	**He's an old clown, and he will never fuck me.** Don't give up, darling. Miracles do happen, *n'est-ce pas?*
Clotilde	How awkwardly coquettish!
Old Villon	I have all kinds of fantasies at the moment.
Isabeau	You want to tell me a few? Or maybe just one?
Old Villon	No. I mean, Yes. As an old man, I like neither men nor women. One is biology and the other is perversion. But you, I adore.
Isabeau	I love you too, darling.
Old Villon	**Rarely has such an opportunity been presented in the great halls of literature! Even in the Far East!**
Isabeau	Oh, go on. Shut up about literature, and make your move.
Old Villon	Fine. Take your clothes off, and let me play with you.
Isabeau	On stage?
Old Villon	Why not?
Isabeau	And then what?
Old Villon	We'll drink some wine.
Isabeau	It won't do you any good, old man.
Old Villon	I'll think of something.
Isabeau	Let's just say we did it and go from there.

Old Villon	I know—let's pretend another day goes by, so I have a little time to think it over. Clotilde?
Clotilde	Sir?
Old Villon	Say, "A day goes by."
Clotilde	No. Do I look like a parrot to you?
Villon	Say it, Clotilde.
Clotilde	**A day goes by.**
Old Villon	Thank you. (*Pause*)
Guy	So?
Clotilde	Yes?
Villon	A day has passed. Have you found your solution, sir?
Old Villon	No, I have not. Clotilde?
Clotilde	Sir?
Old Villon	Say, "Another day has passed."
Clotilde	**Another day is past.**
Old Villon	Thank you. Did she take off her clothes?
All	Yes!
Isabeau	You missed it, old man.
Old Villon	Oh no!
Clotilde	One misses things. (*Pause*) It's a shame.
Guy	Well? (OLD VILLON *mumbles.*) Did you say something? (*Silence*)
Old Villon	I think I'll leave the stage now.
Guy	Good choice.
Villon	Watch your mouth, Tabarie. This accomplished scholar of the Law is my benefactor. Leave it to me. Go, take a rest, old man. (OLD VILLON *steps off.*) Yes, Tabarie, I've figured it out.
Guy	Pray tell.
Villon	Villon. Meaning myself. He's immortal.

Guy	Yes?
Villon	He lives forever, because of his poetry, not because he's a vampire.
Isabeau	Was that an answer to a question that was asked?
Villon	A puzzle, dear, a riddle. And yet he has to hang around the earth and play different parts, depending on the circumstances.
Isabeau	*Mon dieu*, is that opaque, or what?
Villon	Why?
Clotilde	There are teenagers in the audience, and they don't know what opaque means.
Isabeau	Obscure, then. They don't know what "obscure" is either.
Clotilde	It means he has to hang around, like a ghost, in the wings, as it were, and wait for his cue, and play different roles.
Isabeau	That explains it. He's an actor.
Guy	Sounds like perdition to me.
Villon	(*Of* TABARIE) And why must we deal with this excuse for the life of a man?
Guy	I beg your pardon?
Villon	I mean you, sir.
Clotilde	Contain yourself, François. He has connections.
Villon	Where, in jail?
Clotilde	Shut up. In the church. In the nobility.
Villon	I see. My lips are sealed. **Unlike his.** Now, why did this misfortune—being lost on stage—happen to my poor fellow, Old Man Villon, my benefactor? Come on out, old man. (OLD VILLON *steps back onstage.*)
Old Villon	Because it is you, my adopted son, who is immortal. It is you who are the master, the Poet, François Villon.

	Myself, I was merely a Doctor of Philosophy, and I have a missing part, too.
Isabeau	He has a missing part, too?
Old Villon	You have all these broken men, like I was saying—
Clotilde	You never said anything about broken men—
Old Villon	—but if you look inside me, you'll see there's a part missing and that's why the Doctor of Philosophy doesn't function very well, and that's why he won't be able to rise up to heaven.
Villon	What's the missing part?
Old Villon	Well, some say it's the memory, but I say it's the soul. You look inside the person, and there's a part missing, and it turns out to be the soul. And you can't put a new one in.
Villon	Why not? Why not through suffering? Why not redemption? Why not confession? And so on?
Old Villon	It has to be there in its youth.
Guy	**This metaphor is not working.**
Old Villon	All right, I'll put it another way.
Isabeau	No. Let me try. Please.
Clotilde	After all, Isabeau—
Isabeau	I know, there are teenagers in the audience. All right, here's my two cents worth. A soul is a device in a person that gives him Confidence, Self-esteem, Self-respect. It has to be put in there almost right away, so it can be nurtured by his parents, especially Mom. And if it's missing, well, there's nothing you can do. Take a pill, maybe, only they haven't invented the pill yet. The Self-respect pill. And they don't know how to operate and put a spleen in or something, not that they know what a spleen is. But I don't think it's the soul. They'd kill the guy. So, you take Old Villon, who has a missing

part, like me, who is himself missing, and he goes missing, and there you have the whole story of a missing part. (*Pause*) **I'm sorry.** (*Steps back in confusion.*)

Clotilde   I couldn't make heads nor tails of that.

Villon   And it stays missing?

Old Villon   Right. I'm going back offstage now. Excuse me. (*Exits to his place.*)

Guy   Strange fellow. (*A knock on the "DOOR."*)

Villon   Saved.

Isabeau   Who can that be?

Guy   The police?

Borges   The fire inspector?

Isabeau   Who could it be?

Villon   Say again?

Isabeau   I say, there's someone at the door. (*Another knock*)

Villon   Come in?

Isabeau   We got distracted, someone came to the door.

Villon   When?

Isabeau   While I was speaking, sir.

Villon   I see. Who's there?

Landlord   It's me, sir—the Landlord.

Isabeau   It's one of the king's men. I'm sure of it.

Villon   Come in, come in. (*Enter the* LANDLORD, *dressed like an aristocrat, perhaps with an eye-patch.*) Shut the door. Someone shut the door.

Clotilde   (*Shutting the "DOOR"*) And who are you, sir?

Landlord   I am the Sheriff of Anger. (*Pronounced AN-JAY*)

Villon   I am François Villon.

Clotilde   I am Clotilde.

Landlord   Which one is Villon?

Villon   I am the only François Villon.

Isabeau	**Of the great François Villon, nobody knows what happened to him. He disappeared. He could have been gibbeted or preserved in ice, for all we know. Killed by wayfarers. Strung up by the sheriff's posse. Eaten by mammoths. Strangled by his girlfriend. Garroted by goons. Or become a vampire. Nobody knows. And presumably he had a missing part, too, like a bull without a dick, and a bad temper when he was drunk.**
Clotilde	We must all think of the mystery of that.
Guy	A vagabond. Vanquished by history.
Isabeau	Could have been an earthquake or a volcano that killed him. A meteorite or a tsunami.
Guy	So what could the sheriff want with us now?
Landlord	The rent.
Guy	That's what we have to deal with, Hatred of the Old, Hatred of the Weak, a Lack of Self-respect, and the Unknown.
Clotilde	And the rent.
Landlord	*Ouis.*
Villon	And they all have their judgments and criticisms, these landlords, and whores, on top of the ones that were already there, waiting their turn, like bubbles in a beaker.
Isabeau	I liked that.
Clotilde	I'm not sure I followed that.
Landlord	I'm not sure, either.
Isabeau	Definitely, you didn't follow it at all.
Clotilde	What was there to follow, eh?
Villon	The history of religion and morality. On earth.

Landlord	*Très bon.* Do you have it or not?
Villon	What?
Landlord	The rent.
Villon	Probably not.
Landlord	Then I'll have to evict you, out into the dark and dangerous night. (Sound *of wolves howling*) Where there are wolves.
Clotilde	There are no wolves outside.
Isabeau	How do you know?
Clotilde	It's a sound cue in a performance.
Guy	Yes, and, after all, so were the sacrifices in Mexico. Where they tore your hearts out and threw them down the stairs. For an audience. So the sun would move across the sky. Isn't that so, Sheriff?
Landlord	Quite so, Monsieur Tabarie.
Villon	Great. Very intelligent. What does the rent have to do with it?
Clotilde	**Seems idiotic, doesn't it? Killing people on the basis of a belief that has nothing to do with reality?**
Guy	Yes. So, what are we to do with that, that stupid version of reality, that the gods are sailing across the sky fueled by human blood, that stupid demeaning reality, that stupid motherfucking fact that no one wants to believe?
Clotilde	Are you outraged, Tabarie?
Guy	I am outraged. Even now, people believe all kinds of lies. Like a golden calf will be born to the Jews, and the temple rebuilt and so on. And the war between Gog and Magog. And then the evangelicans will go up to heaven hanging on to Jesus's foot.
Villon	Is that how it goes?

Guy	Well, I'm not sure, exactly. We had a Crusade, not long ago. Killed off half the population.
Villon	I am myself outraged.
Isabeau	But, more than that, I'm worried and fearful and I don't know what's going to happen next.
Clotilde	About the rent?
Isabeau	About anything. Actually, to tell the truth, about myself.
Villon	Say on, Isabeau.
Isabeau	It's because I'm so disappointed.
Clotilde	Shall I tell you why?
Isabeau	I have a feeling you're going to do exactly that—tell me why.
Landlord	She threw piss on me as I was waiting!
Villon	Say again?
Landlord	She threw piss on me as I was waiting. There I was, preparing to knock on the door, when suddenly it opens and piss flies out.
Borges	Are you wet?
Landlord	Yes. I am wet.
Villon	Holy shit, and fuck it all, that's all I'm going to say.
Guy	Let's pull ourselves together.
Villon	Pull yourself together, asshole.
Guy	Okay.
Clotilde	Let's find some dry clothes. (*Staged*) **They pantomime finding dry clothes. It doesn't take too long.**
Isabeau	Here, put these on.
Clotilde	Excuse me. **He quickly puts on something dry.**
Landlord	Thank you.
Guy	Now, what were we talking about?
Clotilde	The most important thing of all.

Landlord	Which is the rent, eh?
Clotilde	Of course, it's the rent. But not only the rent. Think about it, Tabarie. And don't take all day.
Guy	I've thought about it.
Villon	So what did you come up with?
Guy	It's about humiliation, and the disintegration of the bodily functions, and bad luck.
Clotilde	Okay. That's three things. Let's take those one at a time.
Guy	Humiliation. (*Long silence*)
Clotilde	Yes?
Guy	Bodily functions and bad luck. That's what it's about.
Villon	Could you give one fucking example?
Guy	Not having the rent. Okay? The rent is due because the month is up and you don't have the money. You don't have it because you've been arrested.
Villon	I was betrayed.
Guy	Because you've been betrayed and you have no confidence.
Villon	Say, "A year ago, before a year has passed."
Clotilde	That means the same thing.
Villon	**A year ago.**
Isabeau	**We planned a perfect crime.**
Villon	**We got away with a lot of money.**
Guy	**Five hundred crowns.**
Clotilde	**Around Christmas.**
Villon	**At the College de Navarre.**
Guy	(*To Isabeau*) You have no confidence because your mother didn't love you when you were an infant so you'll probably never have it, and your king or duke or whatever he is, is not someone who wants someone

around with a missing part. Okay? And the other thing is bad luck, because you could have found a duke or a duchess who doesn't mind having someone around with a missing part, because he has a missing part himself, or he's too preoccupied with himself to notice, or you could have lost a bet on a horse or something.

Villon	I see. Anything else?
Guy	I can't think of anything else at the moment.
Clotilde	He can't think of anything else at the moment.
Isabeau	Thank you.
Villon	It's all a lie. I had a brilliant plan, breaking into the chapel, and so on, everything as it was, nothing amiss, not a lock unturned, not a speck out of place, and we disappeared with five hundred golden crowns.
Clotilde	And no one knew until now, three months later.
Isabeau	What about bad luck?
Guy	I told about the horse. I told about the chapel.
Villon	Tell them what happened, Clotilde.
Clotilde	**Once the robbery at Navarre was discovered, a year later, our master, François Villon, left Paris and lit out for the forests of France. But Guy Tabarie knew the hiding places, for he had been in on the job.**
Tabarie	**"I know where the little shithead is," said he, to the sheriff or whatever they had as lawmen in those days, "and for a few pieces of gold, I'll take you to him."**
Clotilde	Some broken down tavern in the woods.
Tabarie	I recall when the sonofabitch got me up against the wall with his cudgel and nearly strangled me with it.

Villon	I don't trust you, Tabarie. You're too much the fancy man. Me, I am Paris low-life, but if anything happens to us, I will get you. Do you believe me?
Tabarie	I do, François.
Villon	Then be warned.
Tabarie	**But I betrayed him anyway. There was money for me, and no hope for Villon.**
Villon	*We're in the present now.*
Isabeau	**He mentioned the horse. He mentioned the brilliant robbery, the betrayal.**
Guy	**There's more to it than that. Some people feel good about themselves no matter what happens. They lose on a horse, they still feel good. They do something like rob a church and get caught and go to jail and they still feel good. They feel good about themselves, no matter what happens. That's luck.**
Isabeau	**Is that good?**
Clotilde	**Is that normal?**
Villon	Actually, it's stupid. What we have here is betrayal, pure and simple.
Landlord	Let's have the rent and I'll clear it all up for you. (*Pause*)
Villon	I'm not sure where the money is.
Borges	We have the rent, but we're not sure where the money is. Give us a moment of looking for the money.
Clotilde	(*Staged*) ***They pantomime looking for the money. It doesn't take too long. They find the money.***
Guy	Aha! We've found it!
Landlord	Bravo! Hand it over.
Clotilde	Here it is. (*A pause*)
Landlord	There's nothing in there but a piece of paper.

Villon	It's in the bank.
Clotilde	The money is in the bank.
Landlord	What's this?
Clotilde	This is a check.
Isabeau	That's a check.
Landlord	I can't take checks.
Villon	Why not?
Clotilde	Why not, pray?
Guy	Don't say, "pray." The check is a worthless piece of shit. Why? Because we don't believe in banks anymore. Banks have no meaning and are worthless. In fact, banks have not been invented yet.
Clotilde	I'm sure they had banks. There must have been banks.
Guy	There were no banks, and there were no checks. There was barter, and IOUs. The Jews had money, but they kept it in the family. Let's say you have a ship full of wine, which you wanted to exchange in the Levant for a ship full of spices?
Isabeau	And?
Guy	I put up for the wine and I take an IOU from my cousin in the Levant. The ship makes it, everybody gets paid, and then they might loan money to the king so he could outfit his cavalry. And that's how we got these big financial houses, but there were no banks, per say.
Borges	I don't know if I believe this guy.
Villon	I don't either.
Borges	Banks have no meaning and are worthless?
Landlord	That's what I said. Let's have the cash.
Villon	We've decided to tell the truth.
Landlord	At last.

Villon	We have to go somewhere and dig up the money. Say "A day is passed and we'll dig up the money."
Clotilde	**A day is passed and we'll dig up the money.**
Villon	No. Just say "A day is passed." We'll go to our secret spot and dig up the money.
Clotilde	**A day is passed. They've dug up the money. You missed it.**
Villon	Okay, here's the money.
Landlord	Thanks very much. (*To* ISABEAU) You can stay another week.
Clotilde	You were going to say?
Isabeau	What was I going to say?
Clotilde	We don't know. About luck?
Isabeau	Right. I never had that. No matter what happens, I feel bad about myself. I win the lottery and I feel bad. He winks at me and I feel bad. I find a hundred pieces of gold on the street and I still feel bad. That's the missing part I was telling you about, and I think me and Villon, or me, Villon, was or is—missing the part.
Villon	I make up for it, Isabeau, with a vicious temper and a taste for brawling. And a little talent.
Clotilde	And drink.
Villon	And now I'll tell you something else. Ask me "What?"
Guy	What?
Villon	Entrances and exits. Now I'm going to prepare the plan so that we can refurbish our finances. So, Mister Guy and the Landlord—take a hike.
Guy	Why me?

Villon	I'll spare you for now, you treacherous fop. And you, Landlord, return us our money or I'll kill you where you stand. (*Pulls his dagger.*)
Guy	Do as he says.
Borges	Why not kill them both?
Villon	Not a bad idea, but I made a deal with the king. We're on the king's hunting lands actually, not this asshole's. It is a genuine IOU. The money, Landlord. Clotilde?
Clotilde	Sir?
Villon	Say, "A moment passes."
Clotilde	**A moment passes.**
Villon	"The phony Landlord returns money."
Clotilde	**The phony landlord returns the money.**
Villon	"And he and Tabarie head for the door."
Clotilde	**And he and Tabarie head for the door.**
Isabeau	You're not afraid of the wolves?
Villon	There are no wolves. Only the king's men. Go! (*TABARIE and the LANDLORD scamper off.*) I'll see you again before long!
Clotilde	Goodbye!
Isabeau	What does that mean, Goodbye?
Borges	It means, Go with God, originally, I think.
Isabeau	Look at all those happy teenagers. All they want to do is have a fruit cup, down at the stand, and wait in line, and pay up, and have their icy fruit cup, and they are happy.
Villon	The plan is this. In the Chapel of Anger, there are three hundred gold crowns…
Clotilde	I'm so glad I dropped in. Let's make sure no one's around.
Isabeau	I'll go. (*ISABEAU heads for the "door" and trips, slapstick style.*)
Isabeau	Hello.

Clotilde	How are you?
Isabeau	Not so good.
Villon	What happened?
Isabeau	I slipped, obviously, and nearly broke my ass.
Villon	Sorry.
Isabeau	Fuck that, let's get on with it.
Borges	Holy shit.
Isabeau	Why do you keep saying that, priest?
Borges	I don't know.
Villon	My fellow robbers—
Isabeau	I know, the teenagers enjoyed that part.
Clotilde	(*To ISABEAU*) I thought it was pretty funny, actually.
Isabeau	Not funny, Clotilde.
Villon	Borges, go outside and listen. (*The priest goes downstage and all take an attitude of listening. A moment passes. The priest returns.*)
Borges	Only the audience, actually. Yes, there are teenagers.
Isabeau	Let's do the play then, in the meantime, before we do our planning.
Borges	What's the play?
Villon	All right, this priest, Borges, wants to impregnate Isabeau, she doesn't agree, and, in the meanwhile, the Universe fails.
Isabeau	That's so optimistic, I don't know if I can stand it. How can the Universe fail?
Clotilde	It flies off into nothingness, and meanwhile, we suffer like worms.
Villon	A comedy.
Isabeau	A tragedy.

Borges	Let's do the adoption of Villon, by the Doctor, Old Villon. And then do the murder of the priest, Chermoye, by our own Villon.
Clotilde	We did the adoption already.
Borges	Oh, right.
Clotilde	We did the murder of the priest already, and François was forgiven and released.
Isabeau	Then we need to do our planning.
Villon	No. Let's wait a while and do the scene first. Say it's one week later or something, Clotilde.
Clotilde	**It's one week later or something.**
Villon	I want to have a drink. Out there, or on my horse. Don't come with me. Excuse me. I think I'll drink right here. Then I'll tell you about the plan.
Clotilde	Can I have a sip?
Villon	Yes.
Clotilde	So what do you need with the booze?
Villon	It's a love scene. Borges here will play the lover.
Borges	Me?
Villon	I see the way you look at her.
Borges	Give me a drink to begin.
Isabeau	Me, too.
Clotilde	(*Staged*) ***They drink. They drink again. A moment passes.***
Villon	Begin. I'll start. "I can see why he likes you."
Isabeau	"Oh?"
Villon	"Do you want to know why?"
Isabeau	"I do know why."
Villon	"Why?"

Isabeau	"The smoothness and youth of my skin, my shapely breasts, my long legs and perfect thighs, my almost breathing mossy bush, which serves paradise."
Villon	Well said, dear Isabeau.
Borges	My compliments in return, observations from the living actor.
Clotilde	Well, it's only a play.
Borges	So let's go back.
Clotilde	Why?
Borges	I enjoyed it, as did they. Let's go back. I'm at the door about the toilet.
Villon	*¿Otra vez?*
Borges	*Ouis!* (*Knocking at the "DOOR"*)
Clotilde	Come in!
Borges	"She pissed on me, you idiot."
Clotilde	"No she didn't. She pissed in a bowl and threw the piss out the door, where, unfortunately, you were standing there, spying."
Borges	"I was not spying."
Clotilde	"Then what were you doing?"
Borges	"I was waiting for my entrance."
Villon	Very good.
Borges	"Without a cue. Or a clue."
Villon	Very clever.
Borges	And you will pay, sir.
Villon	No doubt about that.
Borges	If not with your life, then your soul, which you have spent your life cultivating.
Villon	You are not God.

Borges	Never mind. Now we change places. You, sir, stand at the door.
Villon	I don't think so.
Borges	You don't?
Villon	No.
Borges	You won't stand by the door?
Villon	No.
Borges	And wait?
Villon	No.
Borges	Even if it opens and the heavenly light pours in?
Villon	No. Piss pours out, you idiot. You think I'm some stupid, wayward youth?
Borges	No.
Villon	You think I'm a complete shake-in-the boots, afraid of his grandmother?
Borges	I think the second part is true. In other words, you're not a complete idiot, but you are afraid of your grandmother.
Villon	Go out and shut the door. (*BORGES goes out and slams the "DOOR." SOUND of door slamming.*)
Borges	(*Outside*) NOW WHAT?
Villon	Nothing to it. Give it a pause. (*Pause*) Wait. (*SOUND of a knock at the "DOOR."*)
Isabeau	Come in?
Borges	(*Outside*) NO TRICKS!
Isabeau	(*Giggling*) Okay.
Borges	No shit or piss coming out the door!
Clotilde	***A silence.*** (*A silence*)
Isabeau	I'll open the door.
Villon	Open the door.

Clotilde	**The "door" swings open. Nobody is there.** (SOUND *of door opening.*)
Isabeau	Who's there?
Borges	(*Outside*) Nebuchadnezzer!
Isabeau	Who?
Borges	It's God himself, you fucking idiot!
Isabeau	There's nothing coming out the door.
Borges	Nothing?
Villon	Absolutely nothing.
Borges	All right, then.
Villon	All right, what? Are you leaving?
Borges	I might.
Villon	Bye-bye.
Borges	But I do like your woman in there.
Isabeau	Too bad. Bye!
Borges	No. I'll make you a trade.
Villon	What for what?
Borges	I'll say a prayer for a poem.
Villon	All right, then, if you think that'll save you. Come back in and listen up.

(BORGES *re-enters and kneels before* VILLON. *Pictures of hanged men appear on the upstage screens.*)

Villon	Men my brothers who after us live,
	have your hearts against us not hardened.
	For—if of poor us you take pity,
	God of you sooner will show mercy.
	You see us here, attached.
	As for the flesh we too well have fed,

long since it's been devoured or has rotted.
And we the bones are becoming ash and dust.

Of our pain let nobody laugh,
but pray God
    would us all absolve.

If you my brothers I call, do not
scoff at us in disdain, though killed
we were by justice. Yet you know
all men are not of good sound sense.
Plead our behalf since we are dead naked,
with the Son of Mary the Virgin,
that His grace be not for us dried up,
preserving us from hell's fulminations.

We're dead after all. Let no soul revile us,

but pray God
    would us all absolve.

Rain has washed us, laundered us,
and the sun has dried us black.
Worse—ravens plucked our eyes hollow
and picked our beards and brows.
Never ever have we sat down, but
this way, and that way, at the wind's
good pleasure ceaselessly we swing 'n' swivel,
more nibbled at than sewing thimbles.

Therefore, think not of joining our guild,
but pray God
> would us all absolve.

Prince Jesus, who over all has lordship,
care that hell not gain of us dominion.
With it we have no business, fast or loose.

People, here be no mocking,
but pray God
> would us all absolve.

Villon   (*Continued*) There. From *Ballade of the Hanged Men.*
One of my most famous and important poems. What do
you think?

Clotilde   Terrible translation. That's what I think.

Borges   I'll say my prayer now.

Clotilde   Make it short. Don't alienate them.

Borges   Never mind. His poem was also a prayer. May God save
François Villon, Clotilde and Isabeau, and poor old
Borges.

Clotilde   *Bon.* Let's get on to the *denouement,* and then we'll be
done. We can relax and have an ice and go home. Tell
them what happened to your life, François.

Villon   As happens always in the history of Man, I went astray
for whatever reason. Mainly, in my case, because I no
longer believed.

Borges   This is a sin, François.

Villon   A street thug, I had been adopted by a priest, who taught
me religion. He taught me to stay awake, pay attention,

and pray eighteen times a day. In Latin. The man was a doctor of religion and his name was Villon. I took his name for myself out of respect and admiration. Many a meeting I went to, and many a service, and many a cloister, and then I got tired of the whole thing and started drinking and whoring and stealing. Christianity seemed a poor choice, as opposed to banditry, and so I became a bandit, and I did my best on that score, but you know what happens, a wrong trail, an arrow in the back, a knife in the chest, a man or woman's betrayal, pretty soon I was as dead as a door nail.

Isabeau   And the poems?

Villon   Evidence of real talent, and intelligence that only comes once or twice a century. But of course, no one knows, and you don't, either. We fade into the ground and are gone eventually, like the rain. I'll tell you what happened. **Since nobody knows, I can make up anything.** I was riding like the wind, exhilarated by the speed and the fresh air, feeling companionable with my companions, equal with my equals, afraid of nothing— and I looked back and laughed with joy, and when I looked forward again, bam! Right into a tree limb. Just about knocked my head off. I was dead before I hit the ground.

Clotilde   **In truth, he was pardoned by the ascension of King Louis XI, spent some time in a cloister, got into a street fight, was sentenced to be hanged, spared by the Parliament, and then banished.**

Villon   The robbery happened after all that happened.

Clotilde   I hope they can follow this, François.

330

Villon	So do I, or it's the dungeon for us, or worse. So, I'll say what I think, while I can, about mankind and priests and all their crap, like the study of Arts and Sciences, and the Romans and the Greeks—a history of slaughter justified by lies. Religion causes hatred and murder. Interesting to look at these lies. They are lies of the vanity of men, endless in their inventory. So, a thousand years from now, let's say five thousand years from now, guess what? They'll be doing the same thing—lying and justifying as they kill and be killed. It's a hell of a situation. The only differences will be in who's to blame, who should die, *en masse*, for the errors of crazy people? Well, no one knows, and the religions have no solution, and neither does philosophy or scholarship. The continuing massacre continues.
Isabeau	So, it is hopeless.
Villon	Yes, it's hopeless.
Isabeau	But you mentioned a community.
Villon	I meant a community to bury the dead. That's all I meant. A community to bury the dead. That's all we have to hope for.
Borges	And immortality?
Villon	Everything is immortal.
Borges	Everything?
Villon	Everything. Who knows, Borges? Why not? You don't know and I don't know. And if nothing dies, who cares?
Borges	I don't understand you.
Villon	You're a priest, a believer. You think it has meaning? Objects flying through the blackness? For no apparent reason?
Borges	You think it's meaningless?

Villon	I think it's meaningless. I do feel badly about the whole deal. But it has nothing to do with anything personal— I could kill you now, and feel nothing but the urge to flee—and I resent all those stupid and lying ideas about me in the first place, and I don't mind for an instant that you will pay for all that.
Borges	How will I pay?
Villon	I think I'll kill you now.
Clotilde	Wait a minute. Let's play cards.
Villon	This Borges owes me money, this priest who goes around with murderers and thieves and makes a living off of whores. And I don't like the way he stares at Isabeau.
Isabeau	I don't either.
Borges	I want to fuck that good-looking whore, Isabeau.
Villon	You can't afford her.
Borges	Why not?
Villon	You don't have enough money.
Borges	Give me two hours and I'll have enough for two Isabeaus.
Villon	No chance.
Borges	I know this bitch. She's put out for me before.
Isabeau	What a lie!
Borges	I beg your pardon?
Isabeau	I'm not in your class, not even in your dreams.
Villon	Telling stories about Villon in the forest, attacking women and children, living in caves, etc. Here is Villon and he is well-armed. (*A pause. Then* VILLON *leaps across the table and plunges a dagger deep into the priest's chest.*)
Clotilde	Villon!

Villon	Don't worry about it. I've been hoping to do that for years.
Clotilde	And now what?
Villon	I'll cross a border. I'll get a job in a church. I'll write poems. I know some so-called nobility that owe me favors. People I've pummeled for them, people I've poisoned for them. Don't worry about me.
Clotilde	You'll need a horse.
Villon	I'll take yours. Do you mind?
Clotilde	No. Of course not.
Villon	Thank you very much, and Good-bye!
Clotilde	Wait a minute, we're not done. (*VILLON stays*) Wake up, Borges. (*BORGES stands, starts off right*) Not that way, Borges. (*BORGES exits left*)
Villon	Say something now about medieval France, Clotilde.
Clotilde	Right. **So now we're in a tavern in medieval France, some kind of weird Paradise, where minstrels sang and played flutes and tambourines, somewhere, let's say between Saint Remy and Avignon, and our hero, Villon, is one of them.**

(*MUSIC*)

Clotilde	**The French forest is not what you think it is, or what I think it is. For one thing, it resounds with insects. The whole of Southern France clamors for attention, as if there was a God up there, bending down, astonished and discomforted, and impatient**

**with the idiots below. The God coughs and blows
his nose. Villon sings:**

BALLADE OF DEAD LADIES

Tell me now in what hidden is
  Lady Flora, the lovely Roman?
Where is Hipparchi, and where is Thais,
  Neither of them the fairer woman?
Where is Echo, beheld of no man,
  Only heard on revier and mere—
She whose beauty was more than human?
  But where are the snows of yesteryear?

Where's Heloise, the learned nun,
  For whose sake Abelard, I ween,
Lost manhood and put priesthood on?
  (From Love such dule and teen!)
And where, I pray you, is the queen
  Who willed that Buridan should steer
Sewed in a sack's mouth down the Seine?. . .
  But where are the snows of yesteryear?

White Queen Blanche, like a queen of lilies,
  With a voice like any mermaiden—
Bertha Broadfoot, Beatrice, Alice,
  And Ermengarde the lady of Maine—
And the good Joan, whom Englishmen
  At Rouen doomed and burned her there—
Mother of God, where are they then?. . .

But where are the snows of yesteryear?

Nay, never ask this week, fair lord,
  Where they are gone, nor yet this year,
Except with this for an overword—
  But where are the snows of yesteryear?

Clotilde	Very nice, François.
Villon	Thank you. It's a poem everybody knows. One of my best.
Clotilde	François?
Villon	Yes, I know, there may be teenagers in the audience. But they ought to know, *n'est-ce pas*, where they're headed, what their beauty means, what their vanity means, what their heartbreaking means, these ball-shearers and whores.
Clotilde	You sound bitter.
Villon	I am bitter. But I feel all right because I've managed to fend for myself and survive. So far. With my dagger and my dick intact, and with some good planning. **After the robbery in the chapel, which made us temporarily rich, my master and foster father, Villon, my mentor and chaplain and professor, had died, naturally, but I had taken his name, in reverence.** (*Just at that moment, the* LANDLORD *walks into the tavern and approaches* VILLON.)
Landlord	And then you proceeded to get your degrees and hang around with whores and thieves.
Villon	You rhymed, sir.
Landlord	I am a cultivated gentleman.
Villon	But your guts still stink, sir.

Landlord	No doubt of it, François.
Villon	I might add, my mentor never judged me sir, one way or the other, and shared my questions about religion.
Landlord	What is religion?
Villon	Being right all the time.
Landlord	Your mentor knew his man.
Villon	He did, sir.
Landlord	Are you prepared to die?
Villon	Of course not, sir.
Landlord	Prepare.
Villon	On the other hand, I don't know what death is, though I've seen a lot of it. And you?
Landlord	Yes, I am helped by the comforts of religion.
Villon	Yes, sir. Big help there, sir.
Landlord	Say your prayers, at least.
Villon	I have no prayers, sir.
Landlord	Say them anyway.
Villon	God help me.
Landlord	The Church will want its money, and the king will want a poem or two.
Villon	I want Tabarie.
Landlord	He is a swordsman of some repute, Villon.
Villon	I'll knock him on the head with my club, sir.
Landlord	And the money?
Villon	Gone.
Landlord	Poems for the gentry?
Villon	I'm retired, sir.
Landlord	Even for the king?
Villon	I'll talk with the king.
Landlord	All right, we'll keep you locked up here for a while, Villon, until all is decided.

336

Villon	Honored, sir.
Landlord	There's a woman here, to see you. Actually, I don't know if she's a man or a woman.
Villon	Hunchbacked?
Landlord	Yes. I've seen her before.
Villon	Clotilde. Bring her to me, if you don't mind.
Landlord	Here she is. (*Exits.* CLOTILDE *steps onstage.*)
Villon	*Bon, bon.* I'm glad to see you. You're actually a hunchbacked devil, *n'est-ce pas?*
Clotilde	Yes. And an old friend of yours who has come to help you.
Villon	Thanks a lot.
Clotilde	Don't kill any more people.
Villon	I have one person in mind, and then, it's into the woods.
Clotilde	Why?
Villon	Because people are savages and not to be trusted. One minute he is your priest and your friend, and the next he betrays you. Why? He has his own ego to protect. His own ego he cannot see, but he can see yours, which is attached to your weakness, your sulking and your pride. But I have no inhibition because of it. In other words, if you insult me, I might mourn, or I might kill you.
Clotilde	Which do you prefer?
Villon	You know which, Clotilde.
Clotilde	To kill.
Villon	*Vraiment.* And to think I could have been a scholar, supported by the state.
Clotilde	I have remained your friend.
Villon	True.

Clotilde	What is your great doubt, Villon?
Villon	I am a genius of poetry. But I don't believe that God exists. Do you?
Clotilde	Why not? Call it what you want. Something endless, eternal, something indescribable, as the Muslims say, or the Jews.
Villon	A poet must be more precise. Something exists, never too big to describe. And then again, some things can't be spoken of.
Clotilde	(*Tapping her hunch*) I'm here now, apparently.
Villon	Yes, and I was lying a moment ago. Mainly, I want to be free of myself, and without being seen by the others. Clear and blameless, without the pangs of conscience.
Clotilde	I agree with that. That would be good.
Villon	Yes, maybe for a minute or two. That's what I like about the forest. One roams, one takes one's life in his own hands.
Clotilde	We might live on a farm somewhere, you and I, and raise goats.
Villon	For one thing, I am wanted by the authorities. For another, I am a genius, which implies intelligence, which comes from the unknown, which the high-born admire. For another, I can't get over my anger, on the one hand, and I don't mind killing. Then I feel bad about it and write a poem. Sometimes. But my anger knows no bounds.
Clotilde	Anger is a failing of the Teaching.
Villon	How so, Clotilde?
Clotilde	We are unprepared for the savagery of life, and yet expected to live as though we were. (SOUND *of horses arriving*, OFF)

Villon	Sounds like the king himself, or somebody else really important.
Clotilde	Shall I let him in?
Villon	Why not? (*Enter the* KING) My liege.
King	Villon. (*Of* CLOTILDE) What is that?
Villon	My fiancée, Clotilde.
King	Does she have to be here?
Villon	Wait outside, Darling.
Clotilde	Of course, my dearest. (*Exits*)
King	I've come with your last chance, Villon.
Villon	I've had many of those.
King	That you have. But this is truly the last one.
Villon	And what might that be, sir?
King	Banishment. You must disappear. Go to some village cloister in the provinces and meditate and write. Perhaps you will learn then who you really are.
Villon	I knew who I was before I was Villon.
King	Oh? And who was that?
Villon	The lowest of the low, the dregs on the bottom.
King	You should have risen by now, had you chosen to do so.
Villon	I know. I did try. I even asked God to help me. And the Old Man Villon did, too.
King	And? Why did you fail?
Villon	I preferred life among my peers, people of my own kind. And I have not failed. I am the best poet of my time.
King	Life among bandits, among thieves?
Villon	I had a knack for it, sir.
King	You are a poet, with one of the finest educations one can have in France, and yet you brawled and murdered your way through life. Why?

Villon	I've told you. I preferred the life. And I do have a temper. I did ask for help from that weakness.
King	From whom?
Villon	From the old Master, from you, even from God.
King	To no avail.
Villon	Maybe he's still thinking about it. God, I mean. Maybe he gave me talent instead, and a bit of brains. And the courage to charge first with my stick and strike first with my dagger.
King	It's a shame, Villon.
Villon	That it is, my Lord. May I ask one more dispensation from you?
King	Ask.
Villon	Let me stay in Paris. I'll change my name and reform. I can become a tutor or an educated servant or a janitor in a church.
King	No. Listen to my words. I can't protect you anymore. You need to go somewhere far and live quietly, or we'll have to hang you. Go to a monastery or become the village drunk somewhere and live in a hut. We can't see you or hear of you anymore.
Villon	And then we'll go a-riding over hill and dale.
King	No more sarcasm from you, Villon.
Villon	My apologies, your Lordship.
King	Yes, no more brawling in taverns and beating up aristocrats and killing priests. And no more robbing of churches. Didn't your Master teach you anything about a virtuous life?
Villon	No. We were just talking about that.
King	Who was?

Villon	My fiancée and I.
King	Indeed. What have you decided?
Villon	Perhaps a monastery.
King	Excellent. And you can write your poems, which are oddly devotional at times.
Villon	And other things, too. Heretical, too.
King	You'll be able to concentrate on your religion.
Villon	Actually, I think I'll head for the countryside. We understand each other, the peasants and I. We know that even Kings have to take a crap every day, for example, though he has others to wash his ass.
King	I can also kill you now with a flip of my wrist or a word to my men.
Villon	I'd be careful if I were you.
King	Quite right. You charge first, and hit with your stick.
Villon	Always.
King	All right, enough. We've agreed. Once you've settled, send me your poems now and then. I'll try and preserve them for the future.
Villon	I am in your debt.
King	That you are.
Villon	Thank you, sir.
King	You're welcome. *Au revoir.* Oh, summon your creature. She has something for you. A parting gift. (*Exits*)
Villon	Clotilde!
Clotilde	(*Off*) I'm coming, François!
Villon	Then hurry up! (*Enter* CLOTILDE *with* TABARIE)
Clotilde	Look what I've brought you, François.
Villon	Wonderful! A fat white worm from the pigsty, with a hat!

Guy	Watch your mouth, Villon.
Villon	Why should I? The King and his men are gone. And you, sir, are no threat.
Guy	What do you want?
Villon	Conjugate the Latin for "to die," Tabarie.
Guy	I will not, sir.
Villon	I'll warrant you are here to pay for your sins, Tabarie.
Guy	Not what I was told, Villon.
Villon	Oh, you're thinking that the king expects you to kill me?
Tabarie	Yes.
Villon	In front of my fiancée?
Clotilde	Fat chance.
Villon	What could he have been dreaming?
Clotilde	To get rid of you both, most likely.
Guy	You are no swordsman, Villon.
Villon	Never learned, street rat that I am, but I can use a dagger.
Clotilde	And he's excellent with clubs. I saw him almost knock a man's head off once. Then he had to use his dagger at the throat. Blood started running down the gutter.
Guy	I've seen that horror for myself.
Villon	He's been around, our Tabarie.
Clotilde	I know.
Guy	I'll skewer you, Villon, like a swine. Poets have no immunity from swords.
Villon	Quite right, or the treachery of friends. The king has given me leave to go to the country. You will die here or spend the rest of your life in a dungeon.
Guy	And you?

Villon	Me, I'm heading for the woods with my paramour, like I said. (CLOTILDE *laughs*) You thought you'd get away with betraying our robbery of the church at Navarre. Now it's time to repent.
Guy	You are no priest, Villon, you're a killer of priests.
Villon	Repent, or I'll kill you myself.
Guy	No. You repent.
Villon	I have too much for which to repent. It would take all day. I don't have the time.
Guy	Nor I.
Villon	Oh? Going somewhere?
Guy	Back to Paris.
Villon	Good for you. What will you do there, join a gang and then betray them? Hell of a way to make a living.
Guy	Look what you've got, Villon.
Clotilde	He's got me. (GUY *scoffs*)
Villon	And my club and dagger and a little talent.
Guy	Go ahead, then, and use them if you can.
Villon	Do you know what it's like, sir? To live on your wits day to day and beg and steal and run from your mother and want and not to be satisfied, ever? To be hungry and dirty and beaten and in rags?
Clotilde	And so on?
Guy	I do not.
Villon	You do not.
Guy	That is correct.
Villon	Very well, then. Now you will have a chance to learn something. Clotilde?
Clotilde	Yes?

Villon	Get a message to Isabeau in the city. Tell her this two-face is coming and warn our friends. You will learn, Tabarie.
Clotilde	Yes, François.
Villon	Do not think of us poor as animals without minds, Tabarie.
Guy	They would enslave me and then have me killed, monsieur.
Villon	Do not think we are incapable of vengeance, Tabarie.
Guy	So be it. (*No one moves,* SOUNDS *off, of* DOGS)
Clotilde	We'd better go.
Villon	Say time stops, Clotilde.
Clotilde	**Time stops.** (VILLON *pulls his dagger.*)
Guy	Wait!
Villon	Down on your knees, Tabarie. (GUY *falls to his knees.*) Death is the reward for the treachery of friends.
Guy	Spare me, sir, and I'll serve you well.
Clotilde	Time does not stop, François.
Villon	It stops for this traitor now. (SOUND *of the* DOGS, *closer.*)
Clotilde	There's no time, François.
Villon	Time to cut his throat, Clotilde.
Clotilde	Time to ride, François. (SOUND *of* DOGS *ferociously barking.*) We'll take him with us.
Villon	All right. A pleasure to look forward to, eh? Monsieur Tabarie will come with us. Let's go.
Guy	Where are we going?
Villon	Over hill and dale, Tabarie.
Clotilde	He only kills priests.
Villon	**Well, off we went, on horses stolen from the King's manor. I took care of Tabarie eventually, around an evening fire, when he annoyed me with his**

braggadocio and about his phony nobility, the treacherous idiot. I knocked him on the head with my stick and daggered him. We are not so far from cavemen after all. I myself have seen pictures on cave walls superior to all the portraits of the Saints you see nowadays. No humans, only tigers and deer. Speaking of pictures, once, as we rode, just for a hundredth of a second, I saw a picture in my own mind of some young women, in the forest, ordinary, beautiful young women, not actresses or whores, just ordinary women, but beauties, living their lives, their culture, morally, beautifully, with children, with families. They were some sort of religious group, before they were cut down by the King's men, they had been upholding the honor of a Moral Life, under God, under the guidance of their priests—and I thought, these murderers, the King's men, that they should go to hell, and then I thought, there is no hell for these killers, because there is no Christian hell, no hell for them to go to, to suffer the anguish of murderers, nothing but darkness and silence, and they had escaped, they had escaped the Terror of History. And then I thought, I will take my revenge, myself, and then I saw, there was no "I" strong enough, there was no revenge in me or in Nature, as in the story of Job, there was no recompense, no balance, no punishment of Evil, only accident and vicious blaming for the weaknesses of Man, the blaming of Others, and then I saw leaves blowing in the wind, leaves blowing in the wind, a wind which will itself die into nothingness and Silence. At that point, I was ready to die also, in solidarity with my kind, and I died. I thought.

Clotilde Just one moment more, darlings.

Villon *(Cont'd)* What am I? I have realized myself. That is to say, I am a worm like you, and it's even possible I am like a vessel, or a retort, or a jar, in which salts are mixing, and I arise from their mixture like a chemical God, a spiritual being, an immortal, though I sometimes doubt it, given my weaknesses and fears, and shames and so on and so on and so on, afraid of this and that, misunderstood by everyone and loved by no one—perhaps Clotilde, alas—and yet I run free now in the forest of Time, with my cohorts, my criminal friends and outcasts—free as the wind, no, more free than the wind, which is constrained by the turning of earth—until they catch me and hang me, or stab me, and tell lies about me, and so on and so forth, because now I disappear except for my words, and you will never catch me dead, because my words are living, and they live as long as you live, you liar, they live as long as you live.

The End